536 PUZZLES

&

CURIOUS PROBLEMS

536 PUZZLES &
CURIOUS PROBLEMS

BY

Henry Ernest Dudeney

EDITED BY MARTIN GARDNER, EDITOR OF
THE MATHEMATICAL GAMES DEPARTMENT,
Scientific American

Charles Scribner's Sons · New York

Charles Scribner's Sons
Macmillan Publishing Company
866 Third Avenue, New York, NY 10022
Collier Macmillan Canada, Inc.

ISBN 684-71755-7
Library of Congress Catalog Card
Number 67-15488

Macmillan books are available at special
discounts for bulk purchases for sales pro-
motions, premiums, fund-raising, or edu-
cational use. For details, contact:

Special Sales Director
Macmillan Publishing Company
866 Third Avenue
New York, NY 10022

20, 19, 18, 17, 16, 15, 14

Printed in the United States of America

Contents

Introduction

Henry Ernest Dudeney (the last name is pronounced with a long "u" and a strong accent on the first syllable, as in "scrutiny") was England's greatest maker of puzzles. With respect to mathematical puzzles, especially problems of more than trivial mathematical interest, the quantity and quality of his output surpassed that of any other puzzlist before or since, in or out of England.

Dudeney was born at Mayfield, in Sussex, on April 10, 1857, the son of a local schoolmaster. His father's father, John Dudeney, was well known in Sussex as a shepherd who had taught himself mathematics and astronomy while tending sheep on the downs above Lewes, a town fifty miles south of London. Later he became a schoolmaster in Lewes. Henry Dudeney, himself a self-taught mathematician who never went to college, was understandably proud to be the grandson of this famous shepherd-mathematician.

Dudeney began his puzzle career by contributing short problems to newspapers and magazines. His earliest work, published under the pseudonym of "Sphinx," seems to have been in cooperation with the American puzzlist, Sam Loyd. For a year and a half, in the late 1890's, the two men collaborated on a series of articles in *Tit-Bits,* an English penny weekly. Later, using his own name, Dudeney contributed to a variety of publications including *The Weekly Dispatch, The Queen, Blighty,* and *Cassell's Magazine.* For twenty years his puzzle page, "Perplexities," which he illustrated, ran in *The Strand Magazine.* This was a popular monthly founded and edited by George Newnes, an enthusiastic chess player who had also started and formerly edited *Tit-Bits.*

The Canterbury Puzzles, Dudeney's first book, was published in 1907. It was followed by *Amusements in Mathematics* (1917), *The World's Best Word Puzzles* (1925), and *Modern Puzzles* (1926). Two posthumous collections appeared: *Puzzles and Curious Problems* (1931) and *A Puzzle-Mine* (undated). The last book is a mixture of mathematical and word puzzles that Dudeney had contributed to *Blighty*. With few exceptions, it repeats puzzles contained in his earlier books. *The World's Best Word Puzzles,* published by the London *Daily News,* contains nothing of mathematical interest.

Dudeney's first two books have, since 1958, been available to American and British readers as paperback reprints. *Modern Puzzles* and *Puzzles and Curious Problems,* in many ways more interesting than the first two books because they contain less familiar puzzles, have long been out of print and are extremely hard to obtain. The present volume includes almost the entire contents of those two books.

Readers familiar with the work of Sam Loyd will notice that many of the same puzzles appear, in different story forms, in the books of Loyd and Dudeney. Although the two men never met in person, they were in frequent correspondence, and they had, Dudeney once said in an interview, an informal agreement to exchange ideas. Who borrowed the most? This cannot be answered with finality until someone makes a careful study of the newspaper and magazine contributions of both men, but it is my guess that most of the borrowing was done by Loyd. Dudeney never hesitated to give credits. He often gives the name or initials of someone who supplied him with a new idea, and there are even occasional references to Loyd himself. But Loyd almost never mentioned anyone. Mrs. Margery Fulleylove, Dudeney's only child, recalls many occasions on which her father fussed and fumed about the extent to which his ideas were being adapted by Loyd and presented in America as the other puzzlist's own. Loyd was a clever and prolific creator of puzzles, especially in his ability to dramatize them as advertising novelties, but when it came to problems of a more mathematically advanced nature, Dudeney was clearly his superior. There are even occasions on record when Loyd turned to Dudeney for help on difficult problems.

Geometrical dissections—cutting a polygon into the smallest number of pieces that can be refitted to make a different type of polygon—was a field in which Dudeney was unusually skillful; the present volume contains many surprising, elegant dissections that Dudeney was the first to obtain. He was also an expert on magic squares and other problems of a combinatorial nature, being the first to explore a variety of unorthodox types of magic squares, such as prime-number squares and squares magic with respect to operations other than addition. (There is an excellent article by Dudeney, on magic squares, in the fourteenth edition of the *Encyclopaedia Britannica*.) In recreational number theory he was the first to apply "digital roots"—the term was probably coined by him—to numerous problems in which their application had not been previously recognized as relevant. (For a typical example of how digital roots furnish a short cut to an answer otherwise difficult to obtain, see the answer to Problem 131 in this volume.)

Dudeney was tall and handsome, with brown hair and brown eyes, a slightly aquiline nose, and, in his later years, a gray mustache and short chin whiskers. As one would expect, he was a man of many hobbies. "He was naturally fond of, and skilled at games," his wife Alice wrote in a preface to *Puzzles and Curious Problems,* "although he cared comparatively little for cards. He was a good chess player, and a better problemist. As a young man he was fond of billiards, and also played croquet well." In his elderly days he enjoyed bowling every evening on the old bowling green within the Castle Precincts, an area surrounding the ruins of an old castle in Lewes. The Dudeneys owned a two hundred-year-old house in this area, where they were living at the time of Dudeney's death on April 24, 1930. (In Alice Dudeney's preface this date erroneously appears as 1931.)

Mrs. Fulleylove recalls, in a private communication, that her father's croquet lawn, "no matter how it was rolled and fussed over, was always full of natural hazards. Father applied his mathematical and logical skill to the game, with special reference to the surface of our lawn. He would infuriate some of our visitors, who were not familiar with the terrain, by striking a ball in what appeared to be the wrong direction. The ball would go up, down, around the hills and through valleys, then roll gaily through the hoop . . . ."

Alice Dudeney speaks of her husband as a "brilliant pianist and organist," adding that, at different times, he was honorary organist of more than one church. He was deeply interested in ancient church music, especially plain song, which he studied intensively and taught to a choir at Woodham Church, Surrey. Mrs. Fulleylove tells me that her father, as a small boy, played the organ every Sunday at a fashionable church in Taunton, Somerset. He was a faithful Anglican throughout his life, attending High Church services, keenly interested in theology, and occasionally writing vigorous tracts in defense of this or that position of the Anglican church.

As a little girl, Mrs. Fulleylove sometimes accompanied her father to his London club for dinner. She remembers one occasion on which she felt very proud and grown-up, hoping the waiter and other guests would notice her sophistication and good manners. To her horror, her father, preoccupied with some geometrical puzzle, began penciling diagrams on the fine damask tablecloth.

In his later life, Mrs. Fulleylove writes, her father lost interest in all composers except Richard Wagner. "He had complete transpositions for the piano of all Wagner's works, and played them unceasingly—to the great grief of my mother and myself, who preferred the gentler chamber music.

"The house at Littlewick, in Surrey," Mrs. Fulleylove continues, "where we lived from 1899 to 1911, was always filled with weekend guests, mostly publishers, writers, editors, artists, mathematicians, musicians, and freethinkers." One of Dudeney's friends was Cyril Arthur Pearson, founder of the *Daily Press* and of C. Arthur Pearson, Ltd., a publishing house that brought out Dudeney's *Modern Puzzles*. Other friends included Newnes and Alfred Harmsworth (later Lord Northcliffe), another prominent newspaper publisher.

"Father provided me, by degrees, with a marvelous collection of puzzle toys, mostly Chinese, in ebony, ivory, and wood . . . ," Mrs. Fulleylove recalls. "He was a huge success at children's parties, entertaining them with feats of legerdemain, charades, and other party games and stunts . . . .

"We had a mongrel terrier that I adored. His name, for some obscure reason, was Chance. One day father fell over the dog's leash and broke his arm. His comment, made without anger, was a quotation: 'Chance is but direction which thou canst not see.' "

In an interview in *The Strand* (April, 1926) Dudeney tells an amusing story about a code message that had appeared in the "agony column" of a London newspaper. A man was asking a girl to meet him but not to let her parents know about it. Dudeney cracked the code, then placed in the column a message to the girl, written in the same cipher, that said: "Do not trust him. He means no good. Well Wisher." This was soon followed by a code message from the girl to "Well Wisher," thanking him for his good advice.

Alice Dudeney, it should be added, was much better known in her time than her husband. She was the author of more than thirty popular, romantic novels. A good photograph of her provides the frontispiece of her 1909 book, *A Sense of Scarlet and Other Stories,* and her biographical sketch will be found in the British *Who Was Who.* "A Sussex Novelist at Home," an interview with her that appeared in *The Sussex County Magazine* (Vol. 1, No. 1, December 1926, pp. 6–9), includes her picture and photographs of the "quaint and curious" Castle Precincts House where she and her husband then lived.

Dudeney himself tried his hand on at least one short story, "Dr. Bernard's Patient," (*The Strand,* Vol. 13, 1897, pp. 50–55). Aside from his puzzle features, he also wrote occasional nonfiction pieces, of which I shall mention only two: "The Antiquity of Modern Inventions" (*The Strand,* Vol. 45, 1913,

p. 389 f) and "The Psychology of Puzzle Crazes" (*The Nineteenth Century,* a New York periodical, Vol. 100, December 1926, p. 868 f).

I have rearranged and reclassified the puzzles that appear in this collection, but only minimally edited the text. British words such as "petrol" have been changed to their American equivalents; long paragraphs have been broken into shorter ones to make for easier reading; and in problems about money American currency has been substituted for British. Some of Dudeney's money problems, so dependent on the relationships between British coins that they cannot be formulated with American currency, have been omitted. In the few cases where duplicate problems, with only trivially different story lines, appeared in the two books I have chosen the version I considered best and left out the other. Titles for problems remain unaltered so that those who may wish to check back to the former appearance of a puzzle can do so easily. The illustrations reproduce the original drawings (some of them done by Mrs. Fulleylove when she was a young girl), enlarged and occasionally retouched to make them clearer.

I have added several footnotes to the puzzles and in the answer section appended a number of comments that are bracketed and initialed. Some of these additions correct errors or point out how an answer has been improved or a problem extended by later puzzle enthusiasts. I hope no one will suppose that these comments reflect in any way on Dudeney's genius. The greatest of mathematicians build on the work of predecessors, and their work in turn is the foundation for the work of later experts. The mathematical-puzzle field is no exception. Dudeney was one of its greatest pioneers, perhaps the greatest, and it is a tribute to him that he was able to invent problems of such depth that decades would pass before others would find ways of improving his answers.

It is Mrs. Fulleylove who is mainly responsible for the book now in the reader's hands. We were in touch first by correspondence; then in 1966, when she took up residence in a New York City suburb, she informed me that she had obtained world reprint rights for *Modern Puzzles* and *Puzzles and Curious Problems*. Would I be interested, she asked, in editing them into a single book? I replied that I would indeed. Enthusiasts of recreational mathematics will rejoice in the appearance of this long inaccessible material, the cream of Dudeney's later years. They will find the book a rich source of unusual problems, many of them leading into fascinating regions that have yet to be fully explored.

For much of the information in my notes I am indebted to Victor Meally, Dublin County, Ireland. Although he is mentioned often in the notes, there are many places where I followed his excellent and generously given advice without referring to him. I also wish to thank Harry Lindgren, Canberra, Australia; Thomas H. O'Beirne, Glasgow; and C. C. Verbeek, the Hague, for other valuable suggestions.

Martin Gardner

HASTINGS-ON-HUDSON, N.Y.

"Amusement is one of the fields of applied mathematics."

W. F. WHITE

A SCRAP BOOK OF ELEMENTARY MATHEMATICS.

Arithmetic
&
Algebraic Problems

Arithmetic & Algebraic Problems

1. CONCERNING A CHECK

A man went into a bank to cash a check. In handing over the money the cashier, by mistake, gave him dollars for cents and cents for dollars. He pocketed the money without examining it, and spent a nickel on his way home. He then found that he possessed exactly twice the amount of the check. He had no money in his pocket before going to the bank. What was the exact amount of that check?

2. DOLLARS AND CENTS

A man entered a store and spent one-half of the money that was in his pocket. When he came out he found that he had just as many cents as he had dollars when he went in and half as many dollars as he had cents when he went in. How much money did he have on him when he entered?

3. LOOSE CASH

What is the largest sum of money—all in current coins and no silver dollars—that I could have in my pocket without being able to give change for a dollar, half dollar, quarter, dime, or nickel?

4. GENEROUS GIFTS

A generous man set aside a certain sum of money for equal distribution weekly to the needy of his acquaintance. One day he remarked, "If there are five fewer applicants next week, you will each receive two dollars more." Unfortunately, instead of there being fewer there were actually four more persons applying for the gift.

"This means," he pointed out, "that you will each receive one dollar less." How much did each person receive at that last distribution?

5. BUYING BUNS

Buns were being sold at three prices: one for a penny, two for a penny, and three for a penny. Some children (there were as many boys as girls) were given seven pennies to spend on these buns, each child to receive exactly the same value in buns. Assuming that all buns remained whole, how many buns, and of what types, did each child receive?

6. UNREWARDED LABOR

A man persuaded Weary Willie, with some difficulty, to try to work on a job for thirty days at eight dollars a day, on the condition that he would forfeit ten dollars a day for every day that he idled. At the end of the month neither owed the other anything, which entirely convinced Willie of the folly of labor. Can you tell just how many days' work he put in and on how many days he idled?

7. THE PERPLEXED BANKER

A man went into a bank with a thousand dollars, all in dollar bills, and ten bags. He said, "Place this money, please, in the bags in such a way that if I call and ask for a certain number of dollars you can hand me over one or more bags, giving me the exact amount called for without opening any of the bags."

How was it to be done? We are, of course, only concerned with a single application, but he may ask for any exact number of dollars from one to one thousand.

8. A WEIRD GAME

Seven men engaged in play. Whenever a player won a game he doubled the money of each of the other players. That is, he gave each player just as much money as each had in his pocket. They played seven games and, strange to say, each won a game in turn in the order of their names, which began with the letters A, B, C, D, E, F, and G.

When they had finished it was found that each man had exactly $1.28 in his pocket. How much had each man in his pocket before play?

9. DIGGING A DITCH

Here is a curious question that is more perplexing than it looks at first sight. Abraham, an infirm old man, undertook to dig a ditch for two dollars. He engaged Benjamin, an able-bodied fellow, to assist him and share the money fairly according to their capacities. Abraham could dig as fast as Benjamin could shovel out the dirt, and Benjamin could dig four times as fast as Abraham could do the shoveling.

How should they divide the money? Of course, we must assume their relative abilities for work to be the same in digging or shoveling.

10. NAME THEIR WIVES

A man left a legacy of $1,000.00 to three relatives and their wives. The wives received together $396.00. Jane received $10.00 more than Catherine, and Mary received $10.00 more than Jane. John Smith was given just as much as his wife, Henry Snooks got half as much again as his wife, and Tom Crowe received twice as much as his wife. What was the Christian name of each man's wife?

11. MARKET TRANSACTIONS

A farmer goes to market and buys a hundred animals at a total cost of $1,000.00. The price of cows being $50.00 each, sheep $10.00 each, and rabbits 50¢ each, how many of each kind does he buy? Most people will solve this, if they succeed at all, by more or less laborious trial, but there are several direct ways of getting the solution.

12. THE SEVEN APPLEWOMEN

Here is an old puzzle that people are frequently writing to me about. Seven applewomen, possessing respectively 20, 40, 60, 80, 100, 120, and 140 apples, went to market and sold all their apples at the same price, and each received the same sum of money. What was the price?

13. A LEGACY PUZZLE

A man left legacies to his three sons and to a hospital, amounting in all to $1,320.00. If he had left the hospital legacy also to his first son, that son would have received as much as the other two sons together. If he had left it to his second son, he would have received twice as much as the other two sons together. If he had left the hospital legacy to his third son, he would have received then thrice as much as the first son and second son together. Find the amount of each legacy.

14. PUZZLING LEGACIES

A man bequeathed a sum of money, a little less than $1,500.00, to be divided as follows: The five children and the lawyer received such sums that the square root of the eldest son's share, the second son's share divided by two, the third son's share minus $2.00, the fourth son's share plus $2.00, the daughter's share multiplied by two, and the square of the lawyer's fee all worked out at exactly the same sum of money. No dollars were divided, and no money was left over after the division. What was the total amount bequeathed?

15. DIVIDING THE LEGACY

A man left $100.00 to be divided between his two sons Alfred and Benjamin. If one-third of Alfred's legacy be taken from one-fourth of Benjamin's, the remainder would be $11.00. What was the amount of each legacy?

16. A NEW PARTNER

Two partners named Smugg and Williamson have decided to take a Mr. Rogers into partnership. Smugg has 1½ times as much capital invested in the business as Williamson, and Rogers has to pay down $2,500.00, which sum shall be divided between Smugg and Williamson, so that the three partners shall have an equal interest in the business. How shall the sum be divided?

17. POCKET MONEY

"When I got to the station this morning," said Harold Tompkins, at his club, "I found I was short of cash. I spent just one-half of what I had on my railway ticket, and then bought a nickel's worth of candy. When I got to the terminus I spent half of what I had left and ten cents for a newspaper. Then I spent half of the remainder on a bus and gave fifteen cents to that old beggar outside the club. Consequently I arrive here with this single nickel. How much did I start out with?"

18. DISTRIBUTION

Nine persons in a party, A, B, C, D, E, F, G, H, K, did as follows: First A gave each of the others as much money as he (the receiver) already held; then B did the same; then C; and so on to the last, K giving to each of the other eight persons the amount the receiver then held. Then it was found that each of the nine persons held the same amount.

Can you find the smallest amount in cents that each person could have originally held?

19. REDUCTIONS IN PRICE

"I have often been mystified," said Colonel Crackham, "at the startling reductions some people make in their prices, and wondered on what principle they went to work. For example, a man offered me a motorcycle two years ago for $1,024.00; a year later his price was $640.00; a little while after he asked a level $400.00; and last week he was willing to sell for $250.00. The next time he reduces I shall buy. At what price shall I purchase if he makes a consistent reduction?"

20. HORSES AND BULLOCKS

A dealer bought a number of horses at $344.00 each, and a number of bullocks at $265.00 each. He then discovered that the horses had cost him in all $33.00 more than the bullocks. Now, what is the smallest number of each that he must have bought?

21. BUYING TURKEYS

A man bought a number of turkeys at a cost of $60.00, and after reserving fifteen of the birds he sold the remainder for $54.00, thus gaining 10¢ a head by these. How many turkeys did he buy?

22. THE THRIFTY GROCER

A grocer in a small business had managed to put aside (apart from his legitimate profits) a little sum in dollar bills, half dollars, and quarters, which he kept in eight bags, there being the same number of dollar bills and of each kind of coin in every bag. One night he decided to put the money into only seven bags, again with the same number of each kind of currency in every bag. And the following night he further reduced the number of bags to six, again putting the same number of each kind of currency in every bag.

The next night the poor demented miser tried to do the same with five bags, but after hours of trial he utterly failed, had a fit, and died, greatly respected by his neighbors. What is the smallest possible amount of money he had put aside?

23. THE MISSING PENNY

Here is an ancient puzzle that has always perplexed some people. Two market women were selling their apples, one at three for a penny and the other at two for a penny. One day they were both called away when each had thirty apples unsold: these they handed to a friend to sell at five for 2¢. It will be seen that if they had sold their apples separately they would have fetched 25¢, but when they were sold together they fetched only 24¢.

"Now," people ask, "what in the world has become of that missing penny?" because, it is said, three for 1¢ and two for 1¢ is surely exactly the same as five for 2¢.

Can you explain the little mystery?

24. THE RED DEATH LEAGUE

The police, when making a raid on the headquarters of a secret society, secured a scrap of paper similar to the one pictured.

"That piece of paper," said the detective, throwing it on the table, "has worried me for two or three days. You see it gives the total of the subscriptions for the present year as $3,007.37, but the number of members (I know it is under 500) and the amount of the subscription have been obliterated. How many members were there in the Red Death League, and

what was the uniform subscription?"

Of course, no fraction of a cent is permitted.

25. A POULTRY POSER

Three chickens and one duck sold for as much as two geese; one chicken, two ducks, and three geese were sold together for $25.00. What was the price of each bird in an exact number of dollars?

26. BOYS AND GIRLS

Nine boys and three girls agreed to share equally their pocket money. Every boy gave an equal sum to every girl, and every girl gave another equal sum to every boy. Every child then possessed exactly the same amount. What was the smallest possible amount that each then possessed?

27. THE COST OF A SUIT

"Hello, old chap," cried Russell as Henry Melville came into the club arrayed in a startling new tweed suit, "have you been successful in the cardroom lately? No? Then why these fine feathers?"

"Oh, I just dropped into my tailor's the other day," he explained, "and this cloth took my fancy. Here is a little puzzle for you. The coat cost as much as the trousers and vest. The coat and two pairs of trousers would cost $175.00. The trousers and two vests would cost $100.00. Can you tell me the cost of the suit?"

28. A QUEER SETTLING UP

Professor Rackbrane told his family at the breakfast table that he had heard the following conversation in a railway carriage the night before.

One passenger said to another, "Here is my purse: give me just as much money, Richard, as you find in it."

Richard counted the money, added an equal value from his own pocket, and replied, "Now, John, if you give me as much as I have left of my own we shall be square."

John did so, and then stated that his own purse contained $3.50, while Richard said that he now had $3.00. How much did each man possess at first?

29. APPLE TRANSACTIONS

A man was asked what price per 100 he paid for some apples, and his reply was as follows: "If they had been 4¢ more per 100 I should have got five less for $1.20." Can you say what was the price per 100?

30. PROSPEROUS BUSINESS

A man started business with a capital of $2,000.00, and increased his wealth by 50 per cent every three years. How much did he possess at the expiration of eighteen years?

31. THE BANKER AND THE COUNTERFEIT BILL

A banker in a country town was walking down the street when he saw a five-dollar bill on the curb. He picked it up, noted the number, and went to his home for luncheon. His wife said that the butcher had sent in his bill for five dollars, and, as the only money he had was the bill he had found, he gave it to her, and she paid the butcher. The butcher paid it to a farmer in buying a calf, the farmer paid it to a merchant who in turn paid it to a laundry woman, and she, remembering that she owed the bank five dollars, went there and paid the debt.

The banker recognized the bill as the one he had found, and by that time it had paid twenty-five dollars worth of debts. On careful examination he discovered that the bill was counterfeit. What was lost in the whole transaction, and by whom?

32. THEIR AGES

If you add the square of Tom's age to the age of Mary, the sum is 62; but if you add the square of Mary's age to the age of Tom, the result is 176. Can you say what are the ages of Tom and Mary?

33. MRS. WILSON'S FAMILY

Mrs. Wilson had three children: Edgar, James, and John. Their combined ages were half of hers. Five years later, during which time Ethel was born, Mrs. Wilson's age equalled the total of all her children's ages. Ten years more have now passed, Daisy appearing during that interval. At the latter event Edgar was as old as John and Ethel together. The combined ages of all the children are now double Mrs. Wilson's age, which is, in fact, only equal to that of Edgar and James together. Edgar's age also equals that of the two daughters.

Can you find all their ages?

34. DE MORGAN AND ANOTHER

Augustus De Morgan, the mathematician, who died in 1871, used to boast that he was x years old in the year x^2. Jasper Jenkins, wishing to improve on this, told me in 1925 that he was $a^2 + b^2$ in $a^4 + b^4$; that he was $2m$ in the year $2m^2$; and that he was $3n$ years old in the year $3n^4$. Can you give the years in which De Morgan and Jenkins were respectively born?

35. "SIMPLE" ARITHMETIC

When visiting an insane asylum, I asked two inmates to give me their ages. They did so, and then, to test their arithmetical powers, I asked them to add the two ages together. One gave me 44 as the answer, and the other gave 1,280. I immediately saw that the first had subtracted one age from the other, while the second person had multiplied them together. What were their ages?

36. ANCIENT PROBLEM

Here is an example of the sort of "Breakfast Problem" propounded by Metrodorus in 310 A.D.

Demochares has lived one-fourth of his life as a boy, one-fifth as a youth, one-third as a man, and has spent thirteen years in his dotage. How old is the gentleman?

37. FAMILY AGES

A man and his wife had three children, John, Ben, and Mary, and the difference between their parents' ages was the same as between John and Ben and between Ben and Mary. The ages of John and Ben, multiplied together, equalled the age of the father, and the ages of Ben and Mary multiplied together equalled the age of the mother. The combined ages of the family amounted to ninety years. What was the age of each person?

38. MIKE'S AGE

"Pat O'Connor," said Colonel Crackham, "is now just one and one-third times as old as he was when he built the pig sty under his drawing-room window. Little Mike, who was forty months old when Pat built the sty, is now two years more than half as old as Pat's wife, Biddy, was when Pat built the sty, so that when little Mike is as old as Pat was when he built the sty, their three ages combined will amount to just one hundred years. How old is little Mike?"

39. THEIR AGES

Rackbrane said the other morning that a man on being asked the ages of his two sons stated that eighteen more than the sum of their ages is double the age of the elder, and six less than the difference of their ages is the age of the younger. What are their ages?

40. BROTHER AND SISTER

A boy on being asked the age of himself and of his sister replied:

"Three years ago I was seven times as old as my sister; two years ago I was four times as old; last year I was three times as old; and this year I am two and one-half times as old."

What are their ages?

41. A SQUARE FAMILY

A man had nine children, all born at regular intervals, and the sum of the squares of their ages was equal to the square of his own. What was the age of each? Every age was an exact number of years.

42. IN THE YEAR 1900

A correspondent, in 1930, proposed the following question. The reader may think, at first sight, that there is insufficient data for an answer, but he will be wrong:

A man's age at death was one twenty-ninth of the year of his birth. How old was he in the year 1900?

43. FINDING A BIRTHDAY

A correspondent informs us that on Armistice Day (November 11, 1928) he had lived as long in the twentieth century as he had lived in the nineteenth. This tempted us to work out the day of his birth. Perhaps the reader may like to do the same. We will assume he was born at midday.

44. THE BIRTH OF BOADICEA

A correspondent (R. D.) proposes the following little puzzle:

Boadicea died one hundred and twenty-nine years after Cleopatra was born. Their united ages (that is, the combined years of their complete lives) were one hundred years. Cleopatra died 30 B.C. When was Boadicea born?

45. ROBINSON'S AGE

"How old are you, Robinson?" asked Colonel Crackham one morning.

"Well, I forget exactly," was the reply; "but my brother is two years older than I; my sister is four years older than he; my mother was twenty when I was born; and I was told yesterday that the average age of the four of us is thirty-nine years."

What was Robinson's age?

46. A DREAMLAND CLOCK

In a dream, I was travelling in a country where they had strange ways of doing things. One little incident was fresh in my memory when I awakened. I saw a clock and announced the time as it appeared to be indicated, but my guide corrected me.

He said, "You are apparently not aware that the minute hand always moves in the opposite direction to the hour hand. Except for this improvement, our clocks are precisely the same as those you have been accustomed to."

Since the hands were exactly together between the hours of four and five oclock, and they started together at noon, what was the real time?

47. WHAT IS THE TIME?

At what time are the two hands of a clock so situated that, reckoning as minute points past XII, one is exactly the square of the distance of the other?

48. THE AMBIGUOUS CLOCK

A man had a clock with an hour hand and minute hand of the same length and indistinguishable. If it was set going at noon, what would be the first time that it would be impossible, by reason of the similarity of the hands, to be sure of the correct time?

Readers will remember that with these clock puzzles there is the convention that we may assume it possible to indicate fractions of seconds. On this assumption an exact answer can be given.

49. THE BROKEN CLOCK FACE

Colonel Crackham asked his family at the breakfast table if, without having a dial before them, they could correctly draw in Roman numerals the hours round a clock face. George fell into the trap that catches so many people, of writing the fourth hour as IV, instead of IIII.

Colonel Crackham then asked them to show how a dial may be broken into four parts so that the numerals on each part shall in every case sum to 20. As an example he gave our illustration, where it will be found that the separated numerals on two parts sum to 20, but on the other parts they add up to 19 and 21 respectively, so it fails.

50. WHEN DID THE DANCING BEGIN?

"The guests at that ball the other night," said Dora at the breakfast table, "thought that the clock had stopped, because the hands appeared in exactly the same position as when the dancing began. But it was found that they had really only changed places. As you know, the dancing commenced between ten and eleven oclock. What was the exact time of the start?"

51. MISTAKING THE HANDS

"Between two and three oclock yesterday," said Colonel Crackham, "I looked at the clock and mistook the minute hand for the hour hand, and consequently the time appeared to be fifty-five minutes earlier than it actually was. What was the correct time?"

52. EQUAL DISTANCES

A few mornings ago the following clock puzzle was sprung on his pupils by Professor Rackbrane. At what time between three and four oclock is the minute hand the same distance from VIII as the hour hand is from XII?

53. RIGHT AND LEFT

At what time between three and four oclock will the minute hand be as far from twelve on the left side of the dial plate as the hour hand is from twelve on the right side of the dial plate?

54. AT RIGHT ANGLES

Rackbrane asked his young friends at the breakfast table one morning this little question:

"How soon between the hours of five and six will the hour and minute hands of a clock be exactly at right angles?"

55. WESTMINSTER CLOCK

A man crossed over Westminster Bridge one morning between eight and nine oclock by the tower clock (often mistakenly called Big Ben, which is the name of the large bell only, but this by the way). On his return between four and five oclock he noticed that the hands were exactly reversed. What were the exact times that he made the two crossings?

56. HILL CLIMBING

Weary Willie went up a certain hill at the rate of one and a half miles per hour and came down at the rate of four and a half miles per hour, so that it took him just six hours to make the double journey. How far was it to the top of the hill?

57. TIMING THE CAR

"I was walking along the road at three and a half miles an hour," said Mr. Pipkins, "when the car dashed past me and only missed me by a few inches."

"Do you know at what speed it was going?" asked his friend.

"Well, from the moment it passed me to its disappearance round a corner I took twenty-seven steps and walking on reached that corner with one hundred and thirty-five steps more."

"Then, assuming that you walked, and the car ran, each at a uniform rate, we can easily work out the speed."

58. THE STAIRCASE RACE

This is a rough sketch of the finish of a race up a staircase in which three men took part. Ackworth, who is leading, went up three steps at a time, as arranged; Barnden, the second man, went four steps at a time, and Croft, who

is last, went five at a time. Undoubtedly Ackworth wins. But the point is, how many steps are there in the stairs, counting the top landing as a step?

I have only shown the top of the stairs. There may be scores, or hundreds, of steps below the line. It was not necessary to draw them, as I only wanted to show the finish. But it is possible to tell from the evidence the fewest possible steps in that staircase. Can you do it?

59. A WALKING PUZZLE

A man set out at noon to walk from Appleminster to Boneyham, and a friend of his started at two P.M. on the same day to walk from Boneyham to Appleminster. They met on the road at five minutes past four oclock, and each man reached his destination at exactly the same time. Can you say at what time they both arrived?

60. RIDING IN THE WIND

A man on a bicycle rode a mile in three minutes with the wind at his back, but it took him four minutes to return against the wind. How long would it take him to ride a mile if there was no wind? Some will say that the average of three and four is three and one-half, and it would take him three and one-half minutes. That answer is entirely wrong.

61. A ROWING PUZZLE

A crew can row a certain course upstream in eight and four-sevenths minutes, and, if there were no stream, they could row it in seven minutes less than it takes them to drift down the stream. How long would it take to row down with the stream?

62. THE ESCALATOR

On one of the escalators on the London subway I find that if I walk down twenty-six steps I require thirty seconds to get to the bottom, but if I make thirty-four steps I require only eighteen seconds to reach the bottom. What is the height of the stairway in steps? The time is measured from the moment the top step begins to descend to the time I step off the last step at the bottom onto the level platform.

63. SHARING A BICYCLE

Two brothers had to go on a journey and arrive at the same time. They had only a single bicycle, which they rode in turns, each rider leaving it in the hedge when he dismounted for the one walking behind to pick up, and walking ahead himself, to be again overtaken. What was their best way of arranging their distances? As their walking and riding speeds were the same, it is extremely easy. Simply divide the route into any *even* number of equal stages and drop the bicycle at every stage, using the cyclometer. Each man would then walk half way and ride half way.

But here is a case that will require a little more thought. Anderson and Brown have to go twenty miles and arrive at exactly the same time. They have only one bicycle. Anderson can only walk four miles an hour, while Brown can walk five miles an hour, but Anderson can ride ten miles an hour to Brown's eight miles an hour.

How are they to arrange the journey? Each man always either walks or rides at the speeds mentioned, without any rests.

64. MORE BICYCLING

Referring to the last puzzle, let us now consider the case where a third rider has to share the same bicycle. As a matter of fact, I understand that Anderson and Brown have taken a man named Carter into partnership, and the position today is this: Anderson, Brown, and Carter walk respectively four, five, and three miles per hour, and ride respectively ten, eight, and twelve miles per hour. How are they to use that single bicycle so that all shall complete the twenty miles' journey at the same time?

65. A SIDECAR PROBLEM

Atkins, Baldwin, and Clarke had to go on a journey of fifty-two miles across country. Atkins had a motorcycle with a sidecar for one passenger. How was he to take one of his companions a certain distance, drop him on the road to walk the remainder of the way, and return to pick up the second friend, who, starting at the same time, was already walking on the road, so that they should all arrive at their destination at exactly the same time?

The motorcycle could do twenty miles an hour, Baldwin could walk five miles an hour, and Clarke could walk four miles an hour. Of course, each went at his proper speed throughout and there was no waiting.

I might have complicated the problem by giving more passengers, but I have purposely made it easy, and all the distances are an exact number of miles—without fractions.

66. THE DISPATCH RIDER

If an army forty miles long advances forty miles while a dispatch rider gallops from the rear to the front, delivers a dispatch to the commanding general, and returns to the rear, how far has he to travel?

67. THE TWO TRAINS

Two railway trains, one four hundred feet long and the other two hundred feet long, ran on parallel rails. It was found that when they went in opposite directions they passed each other in five seconds, but when they ran in the same direction the faster train would pass the other in fifteen seconds. A curious passenger worked out from these facts the rate per hour at which each train ran.

Can the reader discover the correct answer? Of course, each train ran with a uniform velocity.

68. PICKLEMINSTER TO QUICKVILLE

Two trains, A and B, leave Pickleminster for Quickville at the same time as two trains, C and D, leave Quickville for Pickleminster. A passes C 120 miles from Pickleminster and D 140 miles from Pickleminster. B passes C 126 miles from Quickville and D half way between Pickleminster and Quickville. Now, what is the distance from Pickleminster to Quickville? Every train runs uniformly at an ordinary rate.

69. THE DAMAGED ENGINE

We were going by train from Anglechester to Clinkerton, and an hour after starting an accident happened to the engine.

We had to continue the journey at three-fifths of the former speed. It made us two hours late at Clinkerton, and the driver said that if only the accident had happened fifty miles farther on the train would have arrived forty minutes sooner. Can you tell from that statement just how far it is from Anglechester to Clinkerton?

70. THE PUZZLE OF THE RUNNERS

Two men ran a race round a circular course, going in opposite directions. Brown was the best runner and gave Tompkins a start of one-eighth of the distance. But Brown, with a contempt for his opponent, took things too easily at the beginning, and when he had run one-sixth of his distance he met Tompkins, and saw that his chance of winning the race was very small.

How much faster than he went before must Brown now run in order to tie with his competitor? The puzzle is quite easy when once you have grasped its simple conditions.

71. THE TWO SHIPS

A correspondent asks the following question. Two ships sail from one port to another—two hundred nautical miles—and return. The *Mary Jane* travels outwards at twelve miles an hour and returns at eight miles an hour, thus taking forty-one and two-third hours for the double journey. The *Elizabeth Ann* travels both ways at ten miles an hour, taking forty hours on the double journey.

Seeing that both ships travel at the average speed of ten miles per hour, why does the *Mary Jane* take longer than the *Elizabeth Ann?* Perhaps the reader could explain this little paradox.

72. FIND THE DISTANCE

A man named Jones set out to walk from A————— to B—————, and on the road he met his friend Kenward, ten miles from A—————, who had left B————— at exactly the same time. Jones executed his commission at B————— and, without delay, set out on his return journey, while Kenward as promptly returned from A————— to B—————. They met twelve miles from B—————. Of course, each walked at a uniform rate throughout. How far is A————— from B—————?

I will show the reader a simple rule by which the distance may be found by anyone in a few seconds without the use of a pencil. In fact, it is quite absurdly easy—when you know how to do it.

73. THE MAN AND THE DOG

"Yes, when I take my dog for a walk," said a mathematical friend, "he frequently supplies me with some interesting puzzle to solve. One day, for example, he waited, as I left the door, to see which way I should go, and when I started he raced along to the end of the road, immediately returning to me; again racing to the end of the road and again returning. He did this four times in all, at a uniform speed, and then ran at my side the remaining distance, which according to my paces measured 27 yards. I afterwards measured the distance from my door to the end of the road and found it to be 625 feet. Now, if I walk 4 miles per hour, what is the speed of my dog when racing to and fro?"

74. BAXTER'S DOG

This is an interesting companion to the "Man and Dog" puzzle. Anderson set off from an hotel at San Remo at nine oclock and had been walking an hour when Baxter went after him along the same road. Baxter's dog started at the same time as his master and ran uniformly forwards and backwards between him and Anderson until the two men were together. Anderson's speed is two, Baxter's four, and the dog's ten miles an hour. How far had the dog run when Baxter overtook Anderson?

My correspondent in Italy who sends me this is an exact man, and he says, "Neglect length of dog and time spent in turning." I will merely add, neglect also the dog's name and the day of the month.

75. THE RUNNER'S REFRESHMENT

A man runs n times round a circular track whose radius is t miles. He drinks s quarts of beer for every mile that he runs. Prove that he will only need one quart!

76. EXPLORING THE DESERT

Nine travellers, each possessing a car, meet on the eastern edge of a desert. They wish to explore the interior, always going due west. Each car can travel forty miles on the contents of the engine tank, which holds a gallon of fuel, and each can carry nine extra gallon cans of fuel and no more. Unopened cans can alone be transferred from car to car. What is the greatest distance at which they can enter the desert without making any depots of fuel for the return journey?

77. EXPLORING MOUNT NEVEREST

Professor Walkingholme, one of the exploring party, was allotted the special task of making a complete circuit of the base of the mountain at a certain level. The circuit was exactly a hundred miles in length and he had to do it all alone on foot. He could walk twenty miles a day, but he could only carry rations for two days at a time, the rations for each day being packed in sealed boxes for convenience in dumping. He walked his full twenty miles every day and consumed one day's ration as he walked. What is the shortest time in which he could complete the circuit?

This simple question will be found to form one of the most fascinating puzzles that we have considered for some time. It made a considerable demand on Professor Walkingholme's well-known ingenuity. The idea was suggested to me by Mr. H. F. Heath.

78. THE BATH CHAIR

A correspondent informs us that a friend's house at A, where he was invited to lunch at 1 P.M., is a mile from his own house at B. He is an invalid, and at 12 noon started in his Bath chair from B towards C. His friend, who had arranged to join him and help push back, left A at 12:15 P.M., walking at five miles per hour towards C. He joined him, and with his help they went back at four miles per hour, and arrived at A at exactly 1 P.M. How far did our correspondent go towards C?

79. THE PEDESTRIAN PASSENGER

A train is travelling at the rate of sixty miles per hour. A passenger at the back of the train wishes to walk to the front along the corridor and in doing so walks at the rate of three miles per hour. At what rate is the man travelling over the permanent way? We will not involve ourselves here in quibbles and difficulties similar to Zeno's paradox of the arrow and Einstein's theory of relativity, but deal with the matter in the simple sense of motion in reference to the permanent way.

80. MEETING TRAINS

At Wurzletown Junction an old lady put her head out of the window and shouted:

"Guard! how long will the journey be from here to Mudville?"

"All the trains take five hours, ma'am, either way," replied the official.

"And how many trains shall I meet on the way?"

This absurd question tickled the guard, but he was ready with his reply:

"A train leaves Wurzletown for Mudville, and also one from Mudville to Wurzletown, at five minutes past every hour. Right away!"

The old lady induced one of her fellow passengers to work out the answer for her. What is the correct number of trains?

81. CARRYING BAGS

A gentleman had to walk to his railway station, four miles from his house, and was encumbered by two bags of equal weight, but too heavy for him to carry alone. His gardener and a boy both insisted on carrying the luggage; but the gardener is an old man and the boy not sufficiently strong, while the gentleman believes in a fair division of labor and wished to take his own share.

They started off with the gardener carrying one bag and the boy the other, while the gentleman worked out the best way of arranging that the three should share the burden equally among them. How would you have managed it?

82. THE ESCALATOR

"I counted fifty steps that I made in going down the escalator," said Walker.

"I counted seventy-five steps," said Trotman; "but I was walking down three times as quickly as you."

If the staircase were stopped, how many steps would be visible? It is assumed that each man travelled at a uniform rate, and the speed of the staircase was also constant.

83. THE FOUR CYCLISTS

The four circles represent cinder paths. The four cyclists started at noon. Each person rode round a different circle, one at the rate of six miles an hour, another at the rate of nine miles an hour, another at the rate of twelve miles an hour, and the fourth at the rate of fifteen miles an hour. They agreed to ride

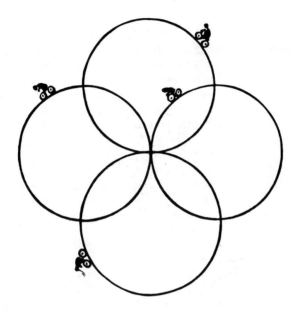

until all met at the center, from which they started, for the fourth time. The distance round each circle was exactly one-third of a mile. When did they finish their ride?

84. THE DONKEY CART

"Three men," said Crackham, "Atkins, Brown, and Cranby, had to go a journey of forty miles. Atkins could walk one mile an hour, Brown could walk two miles an hour, and Cranby could go in his donkey cart at eight miles an hour. Cranby drove Atkins a certain distance, and, dropping him to walk the remainder, drove back to meet Brown on the way and carried him to their destination, where they all arrived at the same time.

"How long did the journey take? Of course each went at a uniform rate throughout."

85. THE THREE CARS

Three cars travelling along a road in the same direction are, at a certain moment, in the following positions in relation to one another. Andrews is a certain distance behind Brooks, and Carter is twice that distance in front of Brooks. Each car travels at its own uniform rate of speed, with the result that Andrews passes Brooks in seven minutes, and passes Carter five minutes later. In how many minutes after Andrews would Brooks pass Carter?

86. THE FLY AND THE CARS

A road is 300 miles long. A car, A, starts at noon from one end and goes throughout at 50 miles an hour, and at the same time another car, B, going uniformly at 100 miles an hour, starts from the other end together with a fly travelling 150 miles an hour. When the fly meets car A, it immediately turns and flies towards B.

(1) When does the fly meet B?

The fly then turns towards A and continues flying backwards and forwards between A and B.

(2) When will the fly be crushed between the two cars if they collide and it does not get out of the way?

87. THE SUBWAY STAIRS

We ran up against Percy Longman, a young athlete, the other day when leaving Curley Street subway station. He stopped at the elevator, saying, "I always go up by the stairs. A bit of exercise, you know. But this is the longest stairway on the line—nearly a thousand steps. I will tell you a queer thing about it that only applies to one other smaller stairway on the line. If I go up two steps at a time, there is one step left for the last bound; if I go up three at a time, there are two steps left; if I go up four at a time, there are three steps left; five at a time, four are left; six at a time, five are left; and if I went up seven at a time there would be six steps left over for the last bound. Now, why is that?"

As he went flying up the stairs, three steps at a time, we laughed and said, "He little suspects that if he went up twenty steps at a time there would be nineteen steps for his last bound!" How many steps are there in the Curley Street subway stairway? The bottom floor does not count as a step, and the top landing does.

88. THE BUS RIDE

George treated his best girl to a bus ride, but on account of his limited resources it was necessary that they should walk back. Now, if the bus goes at the rate of nine miles an hour and they walk at the rate of three miles an hour, how far can they ride so that they may be back in eight hours?

89. A QUESTION OF TRANSPORT

Twelve soldiers had to get to a place twenty miles distant with the quickest possible dispatch, and all had to arrive at exactly the same time. They requisitioned the services of a man with a small car.

"I can do twenty miles an hour," he said, "but I cannot carry more than four men at a time. At what rate can you walk?"

"All of us can do a steady four miles an hour," they replied.

"Very well," exclaimed the driver, "then I will go ahead with four men, drop them somewhere on the road to walk, then return and pick up four more (who will be somewhere on the road), drop them also, and return for the last four. So all you have to do is to keep walking while you are on your feet, and I will do the rest."

They started at noon. What was the exact time that they all arrived together?

90. HOW FAR WAS IT?

"The steamer," remarked one of our officers home from the East, "was able to go twenty miles an hour downstream, but could only do fifteen miles an hour upstream. So, of course, she took five hours longer in coming up than in going down."

One could not resist working out mentally the distance from point to point. What was it?

91. OUT AND HOME

Colonel Crackham says that his friend, Mr. Wilkinson, walks from his country house into the neighboring town at the rate of five miles per hour, and, because he is a little tired, he makes the return journey at the rate of three miles per hour. The double journey takes him exactly seven hours. Can you tell the distance from his house to the town?

92. THE MEETING CARS

The Crackhams made their first stop at Bugleminster, where they were to spend the night at a friend's house. This friend was to leave home at the same time and ride to London to put up at the Crackhams' house. They took the same route, and each car went at its own uniform speed. They kept a look-out for one another, and met forty miles from Bugleminster. George that evening worked out the following little puzzle:

"I find that if, on our respective arrivals, we had each at once proceeded on the return journey at the same speeds we should meet at forty-eight miles from London."

If this were so, what is the distance from London to Bugleminster?

93. A BICYCLE RACE

Two cyclists race on a circular track. Brown can ride once round the track in six minutes, and Robinson in four minutes. In how many minutes will Robinson overtake Brown?

94. A LITTLE TRAIN PUZZLE

A nonstop express going sixty miles an hour starts from Bustletown for Ironchester, and another nonstop express going forty miles an hour starts at the same time from Ironchester for Bustletown. How far apart are they exactly an hour before they meet?

Because I have failed to find these cities on any map or in any gazetteer, I cannot state the distance between them, so we will just assume that it is more than 250 miles.

If this little puzzle gives the reader much trouble he will certainly smile when he sees the answer.

95. AN IRISH JAUNT

"It was necessary," said Colonel Crackham, "for me to go one day from Boghooley to Ballyfoyne, where I had to meet a friend. But the only conveyance obtainable was old Pat Doyle's rickety little cart, propelled by a mare whose working days, like her legs, were a bit over.

"It was soon evident that our rate of progress was both safe and steady, though unquestionably slow.

" 'I say, Pat,' I inquired after a few minutes' ride, 'has your engine got another speed?'

" 'Yes, begorra,' the driver replied, 'but it's not so fast.'

" 'Then we'll keep her on this gear,' said I.

"Pat assured me that she would keep going at one pace until she got to her journey's end. She wouldn't slow down and she wouldn't put on any spurts.

" 'We have been on the road twenty minutes,' I remarked, looking at my watch. 'How far have we come from Boghooley?'

" 'Just half as far as it is from here to Pigtown,' said Pat.

"After a rapid refreshment at Pigtown we went on another five miles, and then I asked Pat how far it was to Ballyfoyne. I got exactly the same reply. It was clear he could only think in terms of Pigtown.

" 'Just half as far as it is from here to Pigtown.'

"Another hour's ride and we were at the end of our journey."

What is the distance from Boghooley to Ballyfoyne?

96. A WALKING PROBLEM

A man taking a walk in the country on turning round saw a friend of his walking 400 yards behind in his direction. They each walked 200 yards in a direct line, with their faces towards each other, and you would suppose that they must have met. Yet they found after their 200 yards' walk that they were still 400 yards apart. Can you explain?

97. THE FALSE SCALES

A pudding, when put into one of the pans of these scales, appeared to weigh four ounces more than nine-elevenths of its true weight, but when put into the other pan it appeared to weigh three pounds more than in the first pan. What was its true weight?

98. WEIGHING THE GOODS

A tradesman whose morals had become corrupted during the war by a course of profiteering went to the length of introducing a pair of false scales. It will be seen from the illustration below that one arm is longer than the other, though they are purposely so drawn as to give no clue to the answer. As a consequence, it happened that in one of the cases exhibited eight of the little packets (it does not matter what they contain) exactly balanced three of the canisters, while in the other case one packet appeared to be of the same weight as six canisters.

The true weight of one canister was known to be exactly one ounce. What was the true weight of the eight packets?

99. WEIGHING THE BABY

"I saw a funny incident at the railway station last summer," said a friend. "There was a little family group in front of the automatic weighing machine, that registered up to 200 lb., and they were engaged in the apparently difficult task of weighing the baby. Whenever they attempted to put the baby alone on the machine she always yelled and rolled off, while the father was holding off the dog, who always insisted on being included in the operations. At last the man with the baby and Fido were on the machine together, and I took this snapshot of them with my camera."

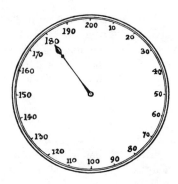

He produced a photograph, from which I have simply copied the dial, as that is all we need.

"Then the man turned to his wife and said, 'It seems to me, my dear, that baby and I together weigh 162 lb. more than the dog, while the dog weighs 70 per cent less than the baby. We must try to work it out at home.' I also amused myself by working it out from those figures. What do you suppose was the actual weight of that dear infant?"

100. FRESH FRUITS

Some fresh fruit was being weighed for some domestic purpose, when it was found that the apples, pears, and plums exactly balanced one another, as shown in the sketch. Can you say how many plums were equal in weight to one pear? The relative sizes of the fruits in the drawing must not be taken to be correct

(they are purposely not so), but we must assume that every fruit is exactly equal in weight to every other of its own kind.

It is clear that three apples and one pear are equal in weight to ten plums, and that one apple and six plums weigh the same as a single pear, but how many plums alone would balance that pear?

This appears to be an excellent method of introducing the elements of algebra to the untutored mind. When the novice starts working it out he will inevitably be adopting algebraical methods, without, perhaps, being conscious of the fact. The two weighings show nothing more than two simultaneous equations, with three unknowns.

101. WEIGHING THE TEA

A grocer proposed to put up 20 lbs. of China tea into 2-lb. packets, but his weights had been misplaced by somebody, and he could only find the 5-lb. and the 9-lb. weights. What is the quickest way for him to do the business? We will say at once that only nine weighings are really necessary.

102. AN EXCEPTIONAL NUMBER

A number is formed of five successive digits (not necessarily in regular order) so that the number formed by the first two multiplied by the central digit will produce the number expressed by the last two. Thus, if it were 1 2 8 9 6, then 12 multiplied by 8 produces 96. But, unfortunately, 1, 2, 6, 8, 9 are not successive numbers, so it will not do.

103. THE FIVE CARDS

I have five cards bearing the figures 1, 3, 5, 7, and 9. How can I arrange them in a row so that the number formed by the first pair multiplied by the number formed by the last pair, with the central number subtracted, will produce a number composed of repetitions of one figure? Thus, in the example I have shown, 31 multiplied by 79 and 5 subtracted will produce

2 4 4 4, which would have been all right if that 2 had happened to be another 4. Of course, there must be two solutions, for the pairs are clearly interchangeable.

104. SQUARES AND DIGITS

What is the smallest square number that terminates with the greatest possible number of similar digits? Thus the greatest possible number might be five and the smallest square number with five similar digits at the end might be 24677777. But this is certainly not a square number. Of course, 0 is not to be regarded as a digit.

105. THE TWO ADDITIONS

Can you arrange the following figures in two groups of four figures each so that each group shall add to the same sum?

$$1\ 2\ 3\ 4\ 5\ 7\ 8\ 9$$

If you were allowed to reverse the 9 so as to change it into the missing 6 it would be very easy. For example, 1, 2, 7, 8 and 3, 4, 5, 6 add up to 18 in both cases. But you are not allowed to make any such reversal.

106. THE REPEATED QUARTETTE

If we multiply 64253 by 365 we get the product 23452345, where the first four figures are repeated. What is the largest number that we can multiply by 365 in order to produce a similar product of eight figures with the first four figures repeated in the same order? There is no objection to a repetition of figures—that is, the four that are repeated need not be all different, as in the case shown.

107. EASY DIVISION

To divide the number 8,1 0 1,2 6 5,8 2 2,7 8 4 by 8, all we need do is to transfer the 8 from the beginning to the end! Can you find a number beginning with 7 that can be divided by 7 in the same simple manner?

108. A MISUNDERSTANDING

An American correspondent asks me to find a number composed of any number of digits that may be correctly divided by 2 by simply transferring the last figure to the beginning. He has apparently come across our last puzzle with the conditions wrongly stated. If you are to transfer the *first* figure to the *end* it is solved by 3 1 5 7 8 9 4 7 3 6 8 4 2 1 0 5 2 6, and a solution may easily be found from this with any given figure at the beginning. But if the figure is to be moved from the *end* to the *beginning*, there is no possible solution for the divisor 2. But there is a solution for the divisor 3. Can you find it?

109. THE TWO FOURS

I am perpetually receiving inquiries about the old "Four Fours" puzzle. I published it in 1899, but have since found that it first appeared in the first volume of *Knowledge* (1881). It has since been dealt with at some length by various writers. The point is to express all possible whole numbers with four fours (no more and no fewer), using the various arithmetical signs. Thus $4 \times 4 + \frac{4}{4}$ equals 17, and $44 + 4 + \sqrt{4}$ equals 50. All numbers up to 112 inclusive may be solved, using only the signs for addition, subtraction, multiplication, division, square root, decimal points, and the factorial sign 4! which means $1 \times 2 \times 3 \times 4$, or 24, but 113 is impossible.

It is necessary to discover which numbers can be formed with one four, with two fours, and with three fours, and to record these for combination as required. It is the failure to find some of these that leads to so much difficulty. For example, I think very few discover that 64 can be expressed with only two fours. Can the reader do it?

110. THE TWO DIGITS

Write down any two-figure number (different figures and no 0) and then express that number by writing the same figures in reverse order, with or without arithmetical signs. For example, $45 = 5 \times 9$ would be correct if only the 9 had happened to be a 4. Or $81 = (1 + 8)^2$ would do, except for the fact that it introduces a third figure—the 2.

111. DIGITAL COINCIDENCES

If I multiply, and also add, 9 and 9, I get 81 and 18, which contain the same figures. If I multiply and add 2 and 47, I get 94 and 49—the same figures. If I multiply and add 3 and 24, I get the same figures—72 and 27. Can you find two numbers that when multiplied and added will, in this simple manner, produce the same *three* figures? There are two cases.

112. PALINDROMIC SQUARE NUMBERS

This is a curious subject for investigation—the search for square numbers the figures of which read backwards and forwards alike. Some of them are very easily found. For example, the squares of 1, 11, 111, and 1111 are respectively 1, 121, 12321, and 1234321, all palindromes, and the rule applies for any number of 1's provided the number does not contain more than nine. But there are other cases that we may call irregular, such as the square of 264 = 69696 and the square of 2285 = 5221225.

Now, all the examples I have given contain an *odd* number of digits. Can the reader find a case where the square palindrome contains an *even* number of figures?

113. FACTORIZING

What are the factors (the numbers that will divide it without any remainder) of this number—1 0 0 0 0 0 0 0 0 0 0 0 1? This is easily done if you happen to know something about numbers of this peculiar form. In fact, it is just as easy for me to give two factors if you insert, say, one hundred and one noughts, instead of eleven, between the two ones.

There is a curious, easy, and beautiful rule for these cases. Can you find it?

114. FIND THE FACTORS

Find two whole numbers with the smallest possible difference between them which, when multiplied together, will produce 1234567890.

115. DIVIDING BY ELEVEN

If the nine digits are written at haphazard in any order, for example, 4 1 2 5 3 9 7 6 8, what are the chances that the number that happens to be produced will be divisible by 11 without remainder? The number I have written at random is not, I see, so divisible, but if I had happened to make the 1 and the 8 change places it would be.

116. DIVIDING BY 37

I want to know whether the number 49,129,308,213 is exactly divisible by 37, or, if not, what is the remainder when so divided. How may I do this quite easily without any process of actual division whatever? It can be done by inspection in a few seconds—if you know how.

117. ANOTHER 37 DIVISION

Here is an interesting extension of the last puzzle. If the nine digits are written at haphazard in any order, for example, 4 1 2 5 3 9 7 6 8, what are the chances that the number that happens to be produced will be divisible by 37 without remainder?

118. A DIGITAL DIFFICULTY

Arrange the ten digits, 1 2 3 4 5 6 7 8 9 0, in such order that they shall form a number that may be divided by every number from 2 to 18 without in any case a remainder. As an example, if I arrange them thus, 1 2 7 4 9 5 3 6 8 0, this number can be divided by 2, 3, 4, 5, and so on up to 16, without any remainder, but it breaks down at 17.

119. THREES AND SEVENS

What is the smallest number composed only of the digits 3 and 7 that may be divided by 3 and by 7, and also the sum of its digits by 3 and by 7, without any remainder? Thus, for example, 7 7 3 3 7 3 3 is divisible by 3 and by 7 without remainder, but the sum of its digits (33), while divisible by 3, is not divisible by 7 without remainder. Therefore it is not a solution.

120. ROOT EXTRACTION

In a conversation I had with Professor Simon Greathead, the eminent mathematician, now living in retirement at Colney Hatch,* I had occasion to refer to the extraction of the cube root.

"Ah," said the professor, "it is astounding what ignorance prevails on that elementary matter! The world seems to have made little advance in the process of the extraction of roots since the primitive method of employing spades, forks, and trowels for the purpose. For example, nobody but myself has ever discovered the simple fact that, to extract the cube root of a number, all you have to do is to add together the digits. Thus, ignoring the obvious case of the number 1, if we want the cube root of 512, add the digits—8, and there you are!"

I suggested that that was a special case.

*A large mental hospital in Middlesex, near London.—M. G.

"Not at all," he replied. "Take another number at random—4913—and the digits add to 17, the cube of which is 4913."

I did not presume to argue the point with the learned man, but I will just ask the reader to discover all the other numbers whose cube root is the same as the sum of their digits. They are so few that they can be counted on the fingers of one hand.

121. QUEER DIVISION

The following is a rather curious puzzle. Find the smallest number that, when divided successively by 45, 454, 4545 and 45454, leaves the remainders 4, 45, 454, and 4,545 respectively. This is perhaps not easy but it affords a good arithmetical exercise.

122. THREE DIFFERENT DIGITS

The professor, a few mornings ago, proposed that they should find all those numbers composed of three different digits such that each is divisible without remainder by the square of the sum of those digits. Thus, in the case of 112, the digits sum to 4, the square of which is 16, and 112 can be divided by 16 without remainder, but unfortunately 112 does not contain three *different* digits.

Can the reader find all the possible answers?

123. DIGITS AND CUBES

Professor Rackbrane recently asked his young friends to find all those five-figure squares such that the number formed by the first two figures added to that formed by the last two figures should equal a cube. Thus with the square of 141, which is 19,881, if we add 19 and 81 together we get 100, which is a square but unfortunately not a cube.

How many solutions are there altogether?

124. REVERSING THE DIGITS

What number composed of nine figures, if multiplied by 1, 2, 3, 4, 5, 6, 7, 8, 9, will give a product with 9, 8, 7, 6, 5, 4, 3, 2, 1 (in that order), in the last nine places to the right?

125. DIGITAL PROGRESSION

"If you arrange the nine digits," said Professor Rackbrane, "in three numbers thus, 147, 258, 369, they have a common difference of 111, and are, therefore, in arithmetical progression."

Can you find four ways of rearranging the nine digits so that in each case the three numbers shall have a common difference and the middle number be in every case the same?

126. FORMING WHOLE NUMBERS

Can the reader give the sum of all the whole numbers that can be formed with the four figures 1, 2, 3, 4? That is, the addition of all such numbers as 1,234, 1,423, 4,312, etc. You can, of course, write them all out and make the addition, but the interest lies in finding a very simple rule for the sum of all the numbers that can be made with four different digits selected in every possible way, but zero excluded.

127. SUMMING THE DIGITS

Professor Rackbrane wants to know what is the sum of all the numbers that can be formed with the complete nine digits (0 excluded), using each digit once, and once only, in every number?

128. SQUARING THE DIGITS

Take nine counters numbered 1 to 9, and place them in a row as shown. It is required in as few exchanges of pairs as possible to convert this into a square number. As an example in six pairs we give the following: 7 8 (exchanging 7 and 8), 8 4, 4 6, 6 9, 9 3, 3 2, which gives us the number 139,854,276, which is the square of 11,826. But it can be done in much fewer moves.

129. DIGITS AND SQUARES

One of Rackbrane's little Christmas puzzles was this: (1) What is the smallest square number, and (2) what is the largest square number that contains all the ten digits (1 to 9 and 0) once, and once only?

130. DIGITAL SQUARES

It will be found a very good puzzle to try to discover a number which, together with its square, shall contain all the nine digits once, and once only, the zero disallowed. Thus, if the square of 378 happened to be 152,694, it would be a perfect solution. But unfortunately the actual square is 142,884, which gives us those two repeated 4's and 8's, and omits the 6, 5, and 9.

There are only two possible cases, and these may be discovered in about a quarter of an hour if you proceed in the right way.

131. FINDING A SQUARE

Here are six numbers: 4,784,887, 2,494,651, 8,595,087, 1,385,287, 9,042,451, 9,406,087. It is known that three of these numbers added together will form a square. Which are they?

The reader will probably see no other course but rather laborious trial, and yet the answer may be found directly by very simple arithmetic and without any experimental extraction of a square root.

132. JUGGLING WITH DIGITS

Arrange the ten digits in three arithmetical sums, employing three of the four operations of addition, subtraction, multiplication, and division, and using no signs except the ordinary ones implying those operations. Here is an example to make it quite clear:

$$3 + 4 = 7; \quad 9 - 8 = 1; \quad 30 \div 6 = 5.$$

But this is not correct, because 2 is omitted, and 3 is repeated.

133. EQUAL FRACTIONS

Can you construct three ordinary vulgar fractions (say, ½, ⅓, or ¼, or anything up to ⅑ inclusive) all of the same value, using in every group all the nine digits once, and once only? The fractions may be formed in one of the following ways:

$$\frac{a}{b} = \frac{c}{d} = \frac{ef}{ghj}, \quad \text{or} \quad \frac{a}{b} = \frac{c}{de} = \frac{fg}{hj}.$$

We have only found five cases, but the fifth contains a simple little trick that may escape the reader.

134. DIGITS AND PRIMES

Using the nine digits once, and once only, can you find prime numbers (numbers that cannot be divided, without remainder, by any number except 1 and itself) that will add up to the smallest total possible? Here is an example. The four prime numbers contain all the nine digits once, and once only, and add up to 450, but this total can be considerably reduced. It is quite an easy puzzle.

$$
\begin{array}{r}
6\,1 \\
2\,8\,3 \\
4\,7 \\
5\,9 \\
\hline
4\,5\,0
\end{array}
$$

135. A SQUARE OF DIGITS

The nine digits may be arranged in a square in many ways, so that the numbers formed in the first row and second row will sum to the third row. We give three examples, and it will be found that the difference between the

2	1	8
4	3	9
6	5	7

2	7	3
5	4	6
8	1	9

3	2	7
6	5	4
9	8	1

first total, 657, and the second, 819, is the same as the difference between the second, 819, and the third, 981—that is, 162.

Can you form eight such squares, every one containing the nine digits, so that the common difference between the eight totals is throughout the same? Of course it will not be 162.

136. THE NINE DIGITS

It will be found that 32,547,891 multiplied by 6 (thus using all the nine digits once, and once only) gives the product 195,287,346 (also containing all the nine digits once, and once only). Can you find another number to be multiplied by 6 under the same conditions? Remember that the nine digits must appear once, and once only, in the numbers multiplied and in the product.

137. EXPRESSING TWENTY-FOUR

In a book published in America was the following: "Write 24 with three equal digits, none of which is 8. (There are two solutions to this problem.)"

The answers given are $22 + 2 = 24$, and $3^3 - 3 = 24$. Readers familiar with the old "Four Fours" puzzle, and others of the same class, will ask why there are supposed to be only these solutions. With which of the remaining digits is a solution equally possible?

138. THE NINE BARRELS

In how many different ways may these nine barrels be arranged in three tiers of three so that no barrel shall have a smaller number than its own below it or to the right of it? The first correct arrangement that will occur to you is 1 2 3 at the top, then 4 5 6 in the second row, and 7 8 9 at the bottom, and my sketch gives a second arrangement. How many are there altogether?

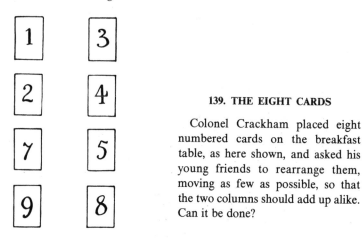

139. THE EIGHT CARDS

Colonel Crackham placed eight numbered cards on the breakfast table, as here shown, and asked his young friends to rearrange them, moving as few as possible, so that the two columns should add up alike. Can it be done?

140. FIND THE NUMBERS

Can you find two numbers composed only of ones which give the same result by addition and multiplication? Of course 1 and 11 are very near, but they will not quite do, because added they make 12, and multiplied they make only 11.

141. MULTIPLYING THE NINE DIGITS

They were discussing mental problems at the Crackhams' breakfast table when George suddenly asked his sister Dora to multiply as quickly as possible

$$1 \times 2 \times 3 \times 4 \times 5 \times 6 \times 7 \times 8 \times 9 \times 0.$$

How long would it have taken the reader?

142. CURIOUS MULTIPLICAND

Readers who remember the Ribbon Problem No. 83 in *The Canterbury Puzzles,* may be glad to have this slightly easier variation of it:

What number is it that can be multiplied by 1, 2, 3, 4, 5, or 6 and no new figures appear in the result?

143. ADDING THEIR CUBES

The numbers 407 and 370 have this peculiarity, that they exactly equal the sum of the cubes of their digits. Thus the cube of 4 is 64, the cube of 0 is 0, and the cube of 7 is 343. Add together 64, 0, and 343, and you get 407. Again, the cube of 3 (27), added to the cube of 7 (343), is 370. Can you find a number not containing a zero that will work in the same way? Of course, we bar the absurd case of 1.

144. THE SOLITARY SEVEN

```
* * * ) * * * * * * * * ( * 7 * * *
        * * * *
        ———
          * * *
          * * *
          ———
          * * * *
            * * *
            ———
            * * * *
            * * * *
            ———
```

Here is a puzzle, sent me by the Rev. E. F. O. It is the first example I have seen of one of these missing-figure puzzles in which only one figure is given, and there appears to be only one possible solution. And, curiously enough, it is not difficult to reconstruct the simple division sum. For example, as the divisor when multiplied by 7 produces only three figures we know the first figure in the divisor must be 1. We can then prove that the first figure in the dividend must be 1; that, in consequence of bringing down together the last two figures of the dividend, the last but one figure in the quotient must be 0, that the first and last figures in the quotient must be greater than 7, because they each produce four figures in the sum, and so on.

145. A COMPLETE SKELETON

This is an arrangement without any figure at all, constructed by Mr. A. Corrigan. Note the decimal dot in the quotient. The extension to four places of decimals makes it curiously easy to solve.

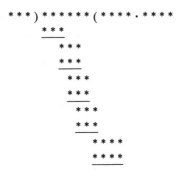

146. SIMPLE MULTIPLICATION

George Crackham produced this puzzle at the breakfast table one morning:

$$
\begin{array}{r}
* \, * \, * \, * \, * \, * \, * \, * \, * \\
2 \\
\hline
* \, * \, * \, * \, * \, * \, * \, * \, *
\end{array}
$$

He asked them to substitute for the stars all the ten digits in each row, so arranged as to form a correct little sum in multiplication. He said that the 0 was not to appear at the beginning or end of either number. Can the reader find an answer?

147. AN ABSOLUTE SKELETON

Here is a good skeleton puzzle. The only conditions are:

(1) No digit appears twice in any row of figures except in the dividend.

(2) If 2 be added to the last figure in the quotient it equals the last but one, and if 2 be added to the third figure from the end it gives the last figure but three in the quotient. That is to say, the quotient might end in, say, 9,742, or in 3,186.

We have only succeeded in finding a single solution.

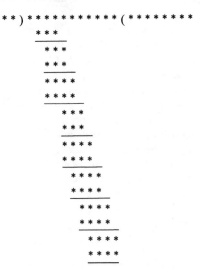

148. ODDS AND EVENS

```
* * * ) * * * * * * * * * * ( * * * * * * *
   O E *
   ‾‾‾‾‾‾‾
   * * * *
   O O * *
   ‾‾‾‾‾‾‾
     * * *
     E E *
     ‾‾‾‾‾
     * * *
     E O *
     ‾‾‾‾‾‾‾
     * * * *
     E E * *
     ‾‾‾‾‾‾‾
       * * *
       O O *
       ‾‾‾‾‾
```

The Rev. E. F. O. devised this skeleton problem in simple division. Every asterisk and letter represents a figure, and "O" stands for an odd figure (1, 3, 5, 7, or 9), while "E" represents an even figure (2, 4, 6, 8, or 0). Can you construct an arrangement complying with these conditions? There are six solutions. Can you find one, or all of them?

149. SIMPLE DIVISION

Can you restore this division problem by substituting a figure for every asterisk without altering or removing the sevens? If you start out with the assumption that all the sevens are given and that you must not use another, you will attempt an impossibility, though the proof is difficult; but when you are told that though no additional sevens may be used in divisor, dividend, or quotient, any number of extra sevens may be used in the working, it is comparatively easy.

```
* * * * 7 * ) * * 7 * * * * * * * ( * * 7 * *
          * * * * * *
          * * * * * 7 *
          * * * * * * *
            * 7 * * * *
            * 7 * * * *
            * * * * * * *
              * * * 7 * *
              * * * * * *
              * * * * * *
```

150. A COMPLETE SKELETON

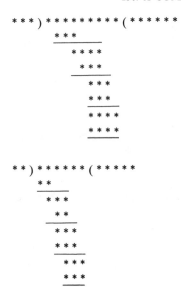

It will be remembered that a skeleton puzzle, where the figures are represented by stars, has not been constructed without at least one figure, or some added condition, being used. Perhaps the following (received from W. J. W.) comes a little nearer the ideal, though there are two division sums and not one, and they are related by the fact that the six-figure quotient of the first happens to be the dividend of the second. There appears to be only one solution.

151. ALPHABETICAL SUMS

There is a family resemblance between puzzles where an arithmetical working has to be reconstructed from a few figures and a number of asterisks, and those in which every digit is represented by a letter, but they are really quite different. The resemblance lies in the similarity of the process of solving. Here is a little example of the latter class. It can hardly be called difficult.

```
P R ) M T V V R ( R S R
      M V R
      ─────
        K K V
        K M D
        ─────
          M V R
          M V R
```

Can you reconstruct this simple division sum? Every digit is represented by a different letter.

152. ALPHABETICAL ARITHMETIC

Here is a subtraction puzzle that will keep the reader agreeably employed for several minutes.

Let AB multiplied by C = DE. When DE is taken from FG, the result is HI:

$$
\begin{array}{r}
-\ F\,G \\
D\,E \\
\hline
H\,I
\end{array}
$$

Each letter stands for a different figure (1, 2, 3, 4, 5, 6, 7, 8, or 9) and 0 is not allowed.

153. FIGURES FOR LETTERS

Professor Rackbrane the other morning gave his young friends this rather difficult problem. He wrote down the letters of the alphabet in this order:

$$A\,B\,C\,D \times E\,F\,G\,H\,I = A\,C\,G\,E\,F\,H\,I\,B\,D$$

Every letter, he said, stood for a different digit, 1 to 9 (0 excluded). The number represented by the first four digits, when multiplied by the number containing five digits, equals the number containing all the nine digits in the order shown. Can you substitute digits for letters so that it works?

154. THE SHOPKEEPER'S PUZZLE

A shopkeeper, for private marking, selects a word of ten letters (all different) such as NIGHTMARES, where each letter stands for one of the figures 1, 2, 3, 4, 5, 6, 7, 8, 9, 0, in their order. So NI stands for $12.00, and $34.00 would be GH. Assuming this little addition sum is in such a private code, can you find the man's key word? It is not difficult.

$$
\begin{array}{r}
G A U N T \\
O I L E R \\
\hline
R G U O E I
\end{array}
$$

155. BEESWAX

The word BEESWAX represents a number in a criminal's secret code, but the police had no clue until they discovered among his papers the following sum:

$$
\begin{array}{r}
E A S\ E\ B\ S B S X \\
B P W W K S E T Q \\
\hline
K P E\ P\ W E K K Q
\end{array}
$$

The detectives assumed that it was an addition sum and utterly failed to solve it. Then one man hit on the brilliant idea that perhaps it was a case of subtraction. This proved to be correct, and by substituting a different figure for each letter, so that it worked out correctly, they obtained the secret code. What number does BEESWAX represent?

156. WRONG TO RIGHT

"Two wrongs don't make a right," said somebody at the breakfast table.
"I am not so sure about that," Colonel Crackham remarked. "Take this as

an example. Each letter represents a different digit, and no 0 is allowed."

$$
\begin{array}{c}
\text{W R O N G} \\
\text{W R O N G} \\
\hline
\text{R I G H T}
\end{array}
$$

"If you substitute correct figures the little addition sum will work correctly. There are several ways of doing it."

157. LETTER MULTIPLICATION

In this little multiplication sum the five letters represent five different digits. What are the actual figures? There is no 0.

$$
\begin{array}{c}
\text{S E A M} \\
\text{T} \\
\hline
\text{M E A T S}
\end{array}
$$

158. THE CONSPIRATORS' CODE

A correspondent (G. P.) sends this interesting puzzle. Two conspirators had a secret code. Their letters sometimes contained little arithmetical sums relating to some quite plausible discussion, and having an entirely innocent appearance. But in their code each of the ten digits represented a different letter of the alphabet. Thus, on one occasion, there was a little sum in simple addition which, when the letters were substituted for the figures, read as follows:

$$
\begin{array}{c}
\text{F L Y} \\
\text{F O R} \\
\text{Y O U R} \\
\hline
\text{L I F E}
\end{array}
$$

It will be found an interesting puzzle to reconstruct the addition sum with the help of the clue that I and O stand for the figures 1 and 0 respectively.

159. LETTER-FIGURE PUZZLE

A correspondent (C. E. B.) sends the following. It is not difficult, if properly attacked:

$A \times B = B$, $B \times C = AC$, $C \times D = BC$, $D \times E = CH$, $E \times F = DK$, $F \times H = CJ$, $H \times J = KJ$, $J \times K = E$, $K \times L = L$, $A \times L = L$. Every letter represents a different digit, and, of course, AC, BC, etc., are two-figure numbers. Can you find the values in figures of all the letters?

160. THE MILLER'S TOLL

Here is a very simple puzzle, yet I have seen people perplexed by it for a few minutes. A miller was accustomed to take as toll one-tenth of the flour that he ground for his customers. How much did he grind for a man who had just one bushel after the toll had been taken?

161. EGG LAYING

The following is a new variation of an old friend. Though it looks rather complicated and difficult, it is absurdly easy if properly attacked. If a hen and a half lays an egg and a half in a day and a half, how many and a half who lay better by half will lay half a score and a half in a week and a half?

162. THE FLOCKS OF SHEEP

Four brothers were comparing the number of sheep that they owned. It was found that Claude had ten more sheep than Dan. If Claude gave a quarter of his sheep to Ben, then Claude and Adam would together have the same number as Ben and Dan together. If, then, Adam gave one-third to Ben, and Ben gave a quarter of what he then held to Claude, who then passed on a fifth of his holding to Dan, and Ben then divided one-quarter of the number he then possessed equally amongst Adam, Claude, and Dan, they would all have an equal number of sheep.

How many sheep did each son possess?

163. SELLING EGGS

A woman took a certain number of eggs to market and sold some of them. The next day, through the industry of her hens, the number left over had been doubled, and she sold the same number as the previous day. On the third day the new remainder was trebled, and she sold the same number as before. On the fourth day the remainder was quadrupled, and her sales the same as before. On the fifth day what had been left over were quintupled, yet she sold exactly the same as on all the previous occasions and so disposed of her entire stock.

What is the smallest number of eggs she could have taken to market the first day, and how many did she sell daily?

164. PUSSY AND THE MOUSE

"There's a mouse in one of these barrels," said the dog.

"Which barrel?" asked the cat.

"Why, the five hundredth barrel."

"What do you mean by the five hundredth? There are only five barrels in all."

"It's the five hundredth if you count backwards and forwards in this way."

And the dog explained that you count like this:

```
 1  2  3  4  5
 9  8  7  6
   10 11 12 13
```

So that the seventh barrel would be the one marked 3 and the twelfth barrel the one numbered 4.

"That will take some time," said the cat, and she began a laborious count. Several times she made a slip and had to begin again.

"Rats!" exclaimed the dog. "Hurry up or you will be too late!"

"Confound you! You've put me out again, and I must make a fresh start."

Meanwhile the mouse, overhearing the conversation, was working madly at enlarging a hole, and just succeeded in escaping as the cat leapt into the correct barrel.

"I knew you would lose it," said the dog. "Your education has been sadly neglected. A certain amount of arithmetic is necessary to every cat, as it is to every dog. Bless me! Even some snakes are adders!"

Which was the five hundredth barrel? Can you find a quick way of arriving at the answer without making the actual count?

165. ARMY FIGURES

A certain division in an army was composed of a little over twenty thousand men, made up of five brigades. It was known that one-third of the first brigade, two-sevenths of the second brigade, seven-twelfths of the third, nine-thirteenths of the fourth, and fifteen-twenty-seconds of the fifth brigade happened in every case to be the same number of men. Can you discover how many men there were in every brigade?

166. A CRITICAL VOTE

A meeting of the Amalgamated Society of Itinerant Askers (better known as the "Tramps' Union") was held to decide whether the members should strike for reduced hours and larger donations. It was arranged that during the count those in favor of the motion should remain standing, and those who voted against should sit down.

"Gentlemen," said the chairman in due course, "I have the pleasure to announce that the motion is carried by a majority equal to exactly a quarter of the opposition." (Loud cheers.)

"Excuse me, guv'nor," shouted a man at the back, "but some of us over here couldn't sit down."

"Why not?"

" 'Cause there ain't enough chairs."

"Then perhaps those who wanted to sit down but couldn't will hold up their hands. . . . I find there are a dozen of you, so the motion is lost by a majority of one." (Hisses and disorder.)

How many members voted at that meeting?

167. THE THREE BROTHERS

The discussion arose before one of the tribunals as to which of a tradesman's three sons could best be spared for service in the Army. "All I know as to their capacities," said the father, "is this: Arthur and Benjamin can do a certain quantity of work in eight days, which Arthur and Charles will do in nine days, and which Benjamin and Charles will take ten days over."

Of course, it was at once seen that as more time was taken over the job whenever Charles was one of the pair, he must be the slowest worker. This was all they wanted to know, but it is an interesting puzzle to ascertain just how long each son would require to do that job alone.

168. THE HOUSE NUMBER

A man said the house of his friend was in a long street, numbered on his side one, two, three, and so on, and that all the numbers on one side of him added up exactly the same as all the numbers on the other side of him. He said he knew there were more than fifty houses on that side of the street, but not so many as five hundred.

Can you discover the number of that house?

169. A NEW STREET PUZZLE

Brown lived in a street which contained more than twenty houses, but fewer than five hundred, all numbered one, two, three, four, etc., throughout. Brown discovered that all the numbers from one upwards to his own number inclusive summed to exactly half the sum of all the numbers from one up to, and including, the last house. What was the number of his house?

170. ANOTHER STREET PUZZLE

A long street in Brussels has all the odd numbers of the houses on one side and all the even numbers on the other—a method of street numbering quite common in our own country.

(1) If a man lives in an odd-numbered house and all the numbers on one side of him, added together, equal the numbers on the other side, how many houses are there, and what is the number of his house?

(2) If a man lives on the even side and all the numbers on one side of him equal those on the other side, how many houses are there, and what is his number?

We assume that there are more than fifty houses on each side of the street and fewer than five hundred.

171. CORRECTING AN ERROR

Hilda Wilson was given a certain number to multiply by 409, but she made a blunder that is very common with children when learning the elements of simple arithmetic: she placed the first figure of her product by 4 below the second figure from the right instead of below the third. We have all done that as youngsters when there has happened to be a 0 in the multiplier. The result of Hilda's mistake was that her answer was wrong by 328,320, entirely in consequence of that little slip. What was the multiplicand—the number she was given to multiply by 409?

172. THE SEVENTEEN HORSES

"I suppose you all know this old puzzle," said Jeffries. "A farmer left seventeen horses to be divided among his three sons in the following proportions: To the eldest, one-half; to the second, one-third; and to the youngest, one-ninth. How should they be divided?"

"Yes; I think we all know that," said Robinson, "but it can't be done. The answer always given is a fallacy."

"I suppose you mean," Prodgers suggested, "the answer where they borrow another chap's horse to make eighteen for the purpose of the division. Then the three sons take 9, 6, and 2 respectively, and return the borrowed horse to the lender."

"Exactly," replied Robinson, "and each son receives more than his share."

"Stop!" cried Benson. "That can't be right. If each man received more than his share the total must exceed seventeen horses, but 9, 6, and 2 add up to 17 correctly."

"At first sight that certainly looks queer," Robinson admitted, "but the explanation is that if each man received his true fractional share, these fractions would add up to less than seventeen. In fact, there would be a fraction left undistributed. The thing can't really be done."

"That's just where you are all wrong," said Jeffries. "The terms of the will can be exactly carried out, without any mutilation of a horse."

To their astonishment, he showed how it was possible. How should the horses be divided in strict accordance with the directions?

173. EQUAL PERIMETERS

Rational right-angled triangles have been a fascinating subject for study since the time of Pythagoras, before the Christian era. Every schoolboy knows that the sides of these, generally expressed in whole numbers, are such that the square of the hypotenuse is exactly equal to the sum of the squares of the other two sides. Thus, in the case of Diagram A, the square of 30 (900), added to the square of 40 (1600), is the square of 50 (2500), and similarly with B and C. It will be found that the three triangles shown have each the same perimeter. That is the three sides in every case add up to 120.

Can you find six rational right-angled triangles each with a common perimeter, and the smallest possible? It is not a difficult puzzle like my "Four Princes" (in *The Canterbury Puzzles*), in which you had to find four such triangles of equal *area*.

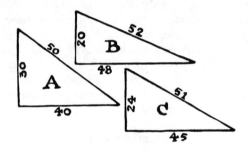

174. COUNTING THE WOUNDED

When visiting with a friend one of our hospitals for wounded soldiers, I was informed that exactly two-thirds of the men had lost an eye, three-fourths had lost an arm, and four-fifths had lost a leg.

"Then," I remarked to my friend, "it follows that at least twenty-six of the men must have lost all three—an eye, an arm, and a leg."

That being so, can you say exactly how many men were in the hospital? It is a simple calculation, but I have no doubt it will perplex many readers.

175. A COW'S PROGENY

"Supposing," said my friend Farmer Hodge, "that cow of mine to have a she calf at the age of two years, and supposing she goes on having the like every year, and supposing every one of her young to have a she calf at the age of two years, and afterwards every year likewise, and so on. Now, how many do you suppose would spring from that cow and all her descendants in the space of twenty-five years?" I understood from Hodge that we are to count from the birth of the original cow, and it is obvious that the family can produce no feminine beef or veal during the period stated.

176. SUM EQUALS PRODUCT

"This is a curious thing," a man said to me. "There are two numbers whose sum equals their product. That is, they give the same result whether you add them together or multiply them together. They are 2 and 2, for if you add them or multiply them, the result is 4." Then he tripped badly, for he added, "These are, I find, the only two numbers that have this peculiarity."

I asked him to write down any number, as large as he liked, and I would immediately give him another that would give a like result by addition or multiplication. He selected the number 987,654,321, and I promptly wrote down the second number. What was it? The fact is, no matter what number you may select there is always another to which that peculiarity applies in combination with it. If this is new to the reader it cannot fail to be interesting to him. He should try to find the rule.

177. SQUARES AND CUBES

Can you find two whole numbers, such that the difference of their squares is a cube and the difference of their cubes is a square? What is the answer in the smallest possible numbers?

178. CONCERNING A CUBE

What is the length in feet of the side of a cube when (1) the surface area equals the cubical contents; (2) when the surface area equals the square of the cubical contents; (3) when the square of the surface area equals the cubical contents?

179. A COMMON DIVISOR

Here is a puzzle that has been the subject of frequent inquiries by correspondents, only, of course, the actual figures are varied considerably. A country newspaper stated that many schoolmasters have suffered in health in their attempts to master it! Perhaps this is merely a little journalistic exaggeration, for it is really a simple question if only you have the cunning to hit on the method of attacking it.

This is the question: Find a common divisor for the three numbers, 480,608; 508,811; and 723,217 so that the remainder shall be the same in every case.

180. CURIOUS MULTIPLICATION

I have frequently been asked to explain the following, which will doubtless interest many readers who have not seen it. If a person can add correctly but is incapable of multiplying or dividing by a number higher than 2, it is possible to obtain the product of any two numbers in this curious way. Multiply 97 by 23.

97	23
48	(46)
24	(92)
12	(184)
6	(368)
3	736
1	1,472
	2,231

In the first column we divide by 2, rejecting the remainders, until 1 is reached. In the second column we multiply 23 by 2 the same number of times. If we now strike out those products that are opposite to the even numbers in the first column (we have enclosed these in parentheses for convenience in printing) and add up the remaining numbers we get 2,231, which is the correct answer. Why is this?

181. THE REJECTED GUN

Here is a little military puzzle that may not give you a moment's difficulty. It is such a simple question that a child can understand it and no knowledge of artillery is required. Yet some of my readers may find themselves perplexed for quite five minutes.

An inventor offered a new large gun to the committee appointed by our government for the consideration of such things. He declared that when once loaded it would fire sixty shots at the rate of a shot a minute. The War Office put it to the test and found that it fired sixty shots an hour, but declined it, "as it did not fulfill the promised condition."

"Absurd," said the inventor, "for you have shown that it clearly does all that we undertook it should do."

"Nothing of the sort," said the experts. "It has failed."

Can you explain this extraordinary mystery? Was the inventor, or were the experts, right?

182. TWENTY QUESTIONS

I am reminded of an interesting old game I used to play as a bachelor. Somebody thinks of an object—say Big Ben, or the knocker on the front door, or the gong of the clock in the next room, or the top button of his friend's coat, or Mr. Baldwin's pipe. You have then to discover the object, by putting not more than twenty questions, each of which must be answered by "yes" or "no." You have to word your questions discreetly, because if you ask, for example, "Is it animal, vegetable, or mineral?" you might get the unsatisfactory answer "Yes," and so waste a question. We found that the expert rarely failed to get an exact solution, and I have known some most remarkably difficult cases solved by the twenty questions.

A novel limitation of the game is suggested to me, which will call for some ingenuity, and the puzzle will doubtless be attacked in various ways by different persons. It is simply this. I think of a number containing six figures. Can you discover what it is by putting to me twenty questions, each of which can only be answered by "yes" or "no"? After the twentieth question you must give the number.

183. A CARD TRICK

Take an ordinary pack of playing cards and regard all the picture cards as tens. Now, look at the top card—say it is a seven—place it on the table face downwards and play more cards on top of it, counting up to twelve. Thus, the bottom card being seven, the next will be eight, the next nine, and so on, making six cards in that pile. Then look again at the top card of the pack—say it is a queen—then count 10, 11, 12 (three cards in all), and complete the second pile. Continue this, always counting up to twelve, and if at last you have not sufficient cards to complete a pile, put these apart.

Now, if I am told how many piles have been made and how many unused cards remain over, I can at once tell you the sum of all the bottom cards in the piles. I simply multiply by 13 the number of piles less 4, and add the number of cards left over. Thus, if there were 6 piles and 5 cards over, then 13 times 2 (i.e., 6 less 4) added to 5 equals 31, the sum of the bottom cards. Why is this? That is the question.

184. THE QUARRELSOME CHILDREN

A man married a widow, and they each already had children. Ten years later there was a pitched battle engaging the present family of twelve children. The mother ran to the father and cried, "Come at once! Your children and my children are fighting our children!"

As the parents now had each nine children of their own, how many were born during the ten years?

185. SHARING THE APPLES

While the Crackhams were having their car filled with gasoline, in a pleasant village, eight children on their way to school stopped to look at them. They had a basket containing thirty-two apples, which they were taking into the village to sell. Aunt Gertrude, in a generous mood, bought the lot, and said the children might divide them among themselves.

Dora asked the names of all the children and said, later in the day (though she was drawing a little on her imagination), "Anne got one apple, Mary two, Jane three, and Kate four. But Ned Smith took as many as his sister, Tom Brown twice as many as his sister, Bill Jones three times as many as his sister, and Jack Robinson four times as many as his sister. Now which of you can give me the full names of the girls?"

186. BUYING RIBBON

Here is a puzzle that appears to bear a strong family resemblance to others given in the past. But it really requires an entirely different method of working. The author is unknown.

Four mothers, each with one daughter, went into a shop to buy ribbon. Each mother bought twice as many yards as her daughter, and each person bought as many yards of ribbon as the number of cents she paid for each yard. Mrs. Jones spent 76¢ more than Mrs. White; Nora bought three yards less than Mrs. Brown; Gladys bought two yards more than Hilda, who spent 48¢ less than Mrs. Smith. What is the name of Mary's mother?

187. SQUARES AND TRIANGULARS

What is the third lowest number that is both a triangular number and a square? Of course the numbers 1 and 36 are the two lowest that fulfill the conditions. What is the next number?

188. PERFECT SQUARES

Find four numbers such that the sum of every two and the sum of all four may be perfect squares.

189. ELEMENTARY ARITHMETIC

This is the kind of question that was very popular in Venice and elsewhere about the middle of the sixteenth century. Nicola Fontana, generally known as "Tartaglia" (the stammerer) was largely responsible for the invention.

If a quarter of twenty is four, what would a third of ten be?

190. TRANSFERRING THE FIGURES

If we wish to multiply 571,428 by 5 and divide by 4, we need only transfer the 5 from the beginning to the end for the correct answer, 714,285. Can you find a number that we can multiply by 4 and then divide the product by 5 in the same simple manner, by moving the first figure to the end?

Of course 714,285, just given, would do if we were allowed to transfer from the end to the beginning. But it must be from the beginning to the end.

191. A QUEER ADDITION

Colonel Crackham asked the junior members of his household at the breakfast table to write down five odd figures so that they will add up and make fourteen. Only one of them did it.

192. SIX SIMPLE QUESTIONS

(1) Deduct four thousand eleven hundred and a half from twelve thousand twelve hundred and twelve.

(2) Add 3 to 182, and make the total less than 20.

(3) What two numbers multiplied together will produce seven?

(4) What three figures multiplied by five will make six?

(5) If five times four are 33, what is the fourth of 20?

(6) Find a fraction whose numerator is less than its denominator, but which, turned upside down, shall remain of the same value.

193. THE THREE DROVERS

As the Crackhams were approaching a certain large town they met and were delayed in passing first a flock of sheep, then a drove of oxen, and afterwards some men leading a number of horses. They ascertained that it was a special market day at the town. George seized the occasion to construct the following puzzle:

"Three drovers with varied flocks met on the highway," he proposed. "Said Jack to Jim: 'If I give you six pigs for a horse then you will have twice as many animals in your drove as I will have in mine.' Said Dan to Jack: 'If I give you fourteen sheep for a horse, then you'll have three times as many animals as I have got.' Said Jim to Dan: 'But if I give you four cows for a horse, then you'll have six times as many animals as I.' There were no deals; but can you tell me just how many animals there were in the three droves?"

194. PROPORTIONAL REPRESENTATION

When stopping at Mangleton-on-the-Bliss the Crackhams found the inhabitants of the town excited over some little local election. There were ten names of candidates on a proportional representation ballot. Voters should place No. 1 against the candidate of their first choice. They might also place No. 2 against the candidate of their second choice, and so on until all the ten candidates have numbers placed against their names.

The voters must mark their first choice, and any others may be marked or not as they wish. George proposed that they should discover in how many different ways the ballot might be marked by the voter.

195. A QUESTION OF CUBES

Professor Rackbrane pointed out one morning that the cubes of successive numbers, starting from 1, would sum to a square number. Thus the cubes of 1, 2, 3 (that is, 1, 8, 27), add to 36, which is the square of 6. He stated that if you are forbidden to use the 1, the lowest answer is the cubes of 23, 24, and 25, which together equal 204^2. He proposed to seek the next lowest number, using more than three consecutive cubes and as many more as you like, but excluding 1.

196. TWO CUBES

"Can you find," Professor Rackbrane asked, "two consecutive cube numbers in integers whose difference shall be a square number? Thus the cube of 3 is 27, and the cube of 2 is 8, but the difference, 19, is not here a square number. What is the smallest possible case?"

197. CUBE DIFFERENCES

If we wanted to find a way of making the number 1,234,567 the difference between two squares, we could at once write down 617,284 and 617,283— a half of the number plus ½ and minus ½ respectively to be squared. But it will be found a little more difficult to discover two cubes the difference of which is 1,234,567.

198. ACCOMMODATING SQUARES

Can you find two three-figure square numbers (no zeros) that, when put together, will form a six-figure square number? Thus, 324 and 900 (the squares of 18 and 30) make 324,900, the square of 570, only there it happens there are two zeros. There is only one answer.

199. MAKING SQUARES

Professor Rackbrane asked his young friends the other morning if they could find three whole numbers in arithmetical progression, the sum of every two of which shall be a square.

200. FIND THE SQUARES

"What number is that," Colonel Crackham asked, "which, added separately to 100 and 164, will make them both perfect square numbers?"

201. FORMING SQUARES

"An officer arranged his men in a solid square," said Dora Crackham, "and had thirty-nine men over. He then started increasing the number of men on a side by one, but found that fifty new men would be needed to complete the new square. Can you tell me how many men the officer had?"

202. SQUARES AND CUBES

Find two different numbers such that the sum of their squares shall equal a cube, and the sum of their cubes equal a square.

203. MILK AND CREAM

Professor Rackbrane, when helping himself to cream at the breakfast table, put the following question:

"An honest dairyman found that the milk supplied by his cows was 5 per cent cream and 95 per cent skimmed milk. He wanted to know how much skimmed milk he must add to a quart of whole milk to reduce the percentage of cream to 4 per cent."

204. FEEDING THE MONKEYS

A man went to the zoo monkey house with a bag of nuts. He found that if he divided them equally among the eleven monkeys in the first cage he would have one nut over; if he divided them equally among the thirteen monkeys in the second cage there would be eight left; if he divided them among the seventeen monkeys in the last cage three nuts would remain.

He also found that if he divided them equally among the forty-one monkeys in all three cages, or among the monkeys in any two cages, there would always be some left over.

What is the smallest number of nuts that the man could have had in his bag?

205. SHARING THE APPLES

Dora Crackham the other morning asked her brother this question: "If three boys had a hundred and sixty-nine apples which they shared in the ratio of one-half, one-third, and one-fourth, how many apples did each receive?"

206. SAWING AND SPLITTING

Colonel Crackham, one morning at the breakfast table, said that two men of his acquaintance can saw five cords of wood per day, or they can split eight cords of wood when sawed. He wanted to know how many cords must they saw in order that they may be occupied for the rest of the day in splitting it.

207. THE BAG OF NUTS

George Crackham put five paper bags on the breakfast table. On being asked what they contained, he said:

"Well, I have put a hundred nuts in these five bags. In the first and second there are altogether fifty-two nuts; in the second and third there are forty-three; in the third and fourth, thirty-four; in the fourth and fifth, thirty."

How many nuts are there in each bag?

208. DISTRIBUTING NUTS

Aunt Martha bought some nuts. She gave Tommy one nut and a quarter of the remainder; Bessie then received one nut and a quarter of what were left; Bob, one nut and a quarter of the remainder; and, finally, Jessie received one nut and a quarter of the remainder. It was then noticed that the boys had received exactly 100 nuts more than the girls.

How many nuts had Aunt Martha retained for her own use?

209. JUVENILE HIGHWAYMEN

Three juvenile highwaymen, returning from the market town movie house, called upon an apple woman "to stand and deliver." Tom seized half of the apples, but returned ten to the basket; Ben took one-third of what were left, but returned two that he did not fancy; Jim took half of the remainder, but threw back one that was worm eaten. The woman was then left with only twelve in her basket.

How many apples had she before the raid was made?

210. BUYING DOG BISCUITS

A salesman packs his dog biscuits (all of one quality) in boxes containing 16, 17, 23, 24, 39, and 40 lbs. respectively, and he will not sell them in any other way, or break into a box. A customer asked to be supplied with 100 lbs. of the biscuits.

Could you have carried out the order? If not, how near could you have got to making up the 100 lbs.? Of course, he has an ample supply of boxes of each size.

211. THE THREE WORKMEN

"Me and Bill," said Casey, "can do the job for you in ten days, but give me Alec instead of Bill, and we can get it done in nine days."

"I can do better than that," said Alec. "Let me take Bill as a partner, and we will do the job for you in eight days."

Then how long would each man take over the job alone?

212. WORKING ALONE

Alfred and Bill together can do a piece of work in twenty-four days. If Alfred can do only two-thirds as much as Bill, how long will it take each of them to do the work alone?

213. THE FIRST "BOOMERANG" PUZZLE

One of the most ancient forms of arithmetical puzzle is that which I call the "Boomerang." Everybody has been asked at some time or another to "Think of a number," and, after going through some process of private calculation, to state the result, when the questioner promptly tells you the number you thought of. There are hundreds of varieties of the puzzle.

The oldest recorded example appears to be that given in the *Arithmetica* of Nicomachus, who died about the year 120. He tells you to think of any whole number between 1 and 100 and then divide it successively by 3, 5, and 7, telling him the remainder in each case. On receiving this information he promptly discloses the number you thought of.

Can the reader discover a simple method of mentally performing this feat? If not, he will perhaps be interested in seeing how the ancient mathematician did it.

214. LONGFELLOW'S BEES

When Longfellow was Professor of Modern Languages at Harvard College he was accustomed to amuse himself by giving more or less simple arithmetical puzzles to the students. Here is an example:

If one-fifth of a hive of bees flew to the ladamba flower, one-third flew to the slandbara, three times the difference of these two numbers flew to an arbor, and one bee continued to fly about, attracted on each side by the fragrant ketaki and the malati, what was the number of bees?

215. LILIVATI, 1150 A.D.

Here is a little morning problem from *Lilivati* (1150 A.D.).

Beautiful maiden, with beaming eyes, tell me which is the number that, multiplied by 3, then increased by three-fourths of the product, divided by 7, diminished by one-third of the quotient, multiplied by itself, diminished by 52, the square root found, addition of 8, division by 10, gives the number 2?

This, like so many of those old things, is absurdly easy if properly attacked.

216. BIBLICAL ARITHMETIC

If you multiply the number of Jacob's sons by the number of times which the Israelites compassed Jericho on the seventh day, and add to the product the number of measures of barley which Boaz gave Ruth, divide this by the number of Haman's sons, subtract the number of each kind of clean beasts that went into the Ark, multiply by the number of men that went to seek Elijah after he was taken to Heaven, subtract from this Joseph's age at the time he stood before Pharaoh, add the number of stones in David's bag when he killed Goliath, subtract the number of furlongs that Bethany was distant from Jerusalem, divide by the number of anchors cast out when Paul was shipwrecked, subtract the number of persons saved in the Ark, and the answer will be the number of pupils in a certain Sunday school class.

How many pupils are in the class?

217. THE PRINTER'S PROBLEM

A printer had an order for 10,000 bill forms per month, but each month the name of the particular month had to be altered: that is, he printed 10,000 "JANUARY," 10,000 "FEBRUARY," 10,000 "MARCH," etc.; but as the particular types with which these words were to be printed had to be specially obtained and were expensive, he only purchased just enough movable types to enable him, by interchanging them, to print in turn the whole of the months of the year.

How many separate types did he purchase? Of course, the words were printed throughout in capital letters, as shown.

218. THE SWARM OF BEES

Here is an example of the elegant way in which Bhaskara, in his great work, *Lilivati,* in 1150, dressed his little puzzles:

The square root of half the number of bees in a swarm has flown out upon a jessamine bush; eight-ninths of the whole swarm has remained behind; one female bee flies about a male that is buzzing within the lotus flower into which he was allured in the night by its sweet odor, but is now imprisoned in it. Tell me the number of bees.

219. BLINDNESS IN BATS

A naturalist, who was trying to pull the leg of Colonel Crackham, said that he had been investigating the question of blindness in bats.

"I find," he said, "that their long habit of sleeping in dark corners during the day, and only going abroad at night, has really led to a great prevalence of blindness among them, though some had perfect sight and others could see out of one eye. Two of my bats could see out of the right eye, just three of them could see out of the left eye, four could not see out of the left eye, and five could not see out of the right eye."

He wanted to know the smallest number of bats that he must have examined in order to get these results.

220. A MENAGERIE

A travelling menagerie contained two freaks of nature—a four-footed bird and a six-legged calf. An attendant was asked how many birds and beasts there were in the show, and he said:

"Well, there are 36 heads and 100 feet altogether. You can work it out for yourself."

How many were there?

221. SHEEP STEALING

Some sheep stealers made a raid and carried off one-third of the flock of sheep and one-third of a sheep. Another party stole one-fourth of what remained and one-fourth of a sheep. Then a third party of raiders carried off one-fifth of the remainder and three-fifths of a sheep, leaving 409 behind. What was the number of sheep in the flock?

222. SHEEP SHARING

A correspondent (C. H. P.) puts the following little question:
An Australian farmer dies and leaves his sheep to his three sons. Alfred is to get 20 per cent more than John, and 25 per cent more than Charles. John's share is 3,600 sheep. How many sheep does Charles get? Perhaps readers may like to give this a few moments' consideration.

223. THE ARITHMETICAL CABBY

The driver of the taxicab was wanting in civility, so Mr. Wilkins asked him for his number.
"You want my number, do you?" said the driver. "Well, work it out for yourself. If you divide my number by 2, 3, 4, 5, or 6 you will find there is always 1 over; but if you divide it by 11 there ain't no remainder. What's more, there is no other driver with a lower number who can say the same."
What was the fellow's number?

224. THE LENGTH OF A LEASE

"I happened to be discussing the tenancy of a friend's property," said the Colonel, "when he informed me that there was a 99 years' lease. I asked him how much of this had already expired, and expected a direct answer. But his reply was that two-thirds of the time past was equal to four-fifths of the time to come, so I had to work it out for myself."

225. MARCHING AN ARMY

A body of soldiers was marching in regular column, with five men more in depth than in front. When the enemy came in sight the front was increased by 845 men, and the whole was thus drawn up in five lines. How many men were there in all?

226. THE YEAR 1927

A French correspondent sends the following little curiosity. Can you find values for p and q so that $p^q - q^p = 1927$? To make it perfectly clear, we will give an example for the year 1844, where $p = 3$, and $q = 7$:

$$3^7 - 7^3 = 1844.$$

Can you express 1927 in the same curious way?

227. BOXES OF CORDITE

Cordite charges (writes W. H. J.) for 6-inch howitzers were served out from ammunition dumps in boxes of 15, 18, and 20.

"Why the three different sizes of boxes?" I asked the officer on the dump.

He answered, "So that we can give any battery the number of charges it needs without breaking a box."

This was an excellent system for the delivery of a large number of boxes, but failed in small cases, like 5, 10, 25, and 61. What is the biggest number of charges that cannot be served out in whole boxes of 15, 18, and 20? It is not a very large number.

228. THE ORCHARD PROBLEM

A market gardener was planting a new orchard. The young trees were arranged in rows so as to form a square, and it was found that there were 146 trees unplanted. To enlarge the square by an extra row each way he had to buy 31 additional trees.

How many trees were there in the orchard when it was finished?

229. BLOCKS AND SQUARES

Here is a curious but not easy puzzle whose author is not traced.

Three children each possess a box containing similar cubic blocks, the same number of blocks in every box. The first girl was able, using all her blocks, to make a hollow square, as indicated by A. The second girl made a larger square, as B. The third girl made a still larger square, as C, but had four blocks left over for the corners, as shown. Each girl used all her blocks at each stage. What is the smallest number of blocks that each box could have contained?

The diagram must not be taken to truly represent the proportion of the various squares.

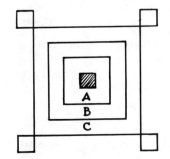

230. FIND THE TRIANGLE

The sides and height of a triangle are four consecutive whole numbers. What is the area of the triangle?

231. COW, GOAT, AND GOOSE

A farmer found that his cow and goat would eat all the grass in a certain field in forty-five days, that the cow and the goose would eat it in sixty days, but that it would take the goat and the goose ninety days to eat it down. Now, if he had turned cow, goat, and goose into the field together, how long would it have taken them to eat all the grass?

Sir Isaac Newton showed us how to solve a puzzle of this kind with the grass growing all the time; but, for the sake of greater simplicity, we will assume that the season and conditions were such that the grass was not growing.

232. THE POSTAGE STAMPS PUZZLE

A youth who collects postage stamps was asked how many he had in his album, and he replied:

"The number, if divided by 2, will give a remainder 1; divided by 3, a remainder 2; divided by 4, a remainder 3; divided by 5, a remainder 4; divided by 6, a remainder 5; divided by 7, a remainder 6; divided by 8, a remainder 7; divided by 9, a remainder 8; divided by 10, a remainder 9. But there are fewer than 3,000."

Can you tell how many stamps there were in the album?

233. MENTAL ARITHMETIC

To test their capacities in mental arithmetic, Rackbrane asked his pupils the other morning to do this:

Find two whole numbers (each less than 10) such that the sum of their squares, added to their product, will make a square.

The answer was soon found.

234. SHOOTING BLACKBIRDS

Twice four and twenty blackbirds
Were sitting in the rain;
I shot and killed a seventh part,
How many did remain?

235. THE SIX ZEROS

A	B	C
111	111	100
333	333	000
555	500	005
777	077	007
999	090	999
2,775	1,111	1,111

Write down the little addition sum A, which adds up 2,775. Now substitute six zeros for six of the figures, so that the total sum shall be 1,111. It will be seen that in the case B five zeros have been substituted, and in case C nine zeros. But the puzzle is to do it with six zeros.

236. MULTIPLICATION DATES

In the year 1928 there were four dates which, written in a well-known manner, the day multiplied by the month will equal the year. These are 28/1/28, 14/2/28, 7/4/28, and 4/7/28. How many times in this century—1901–2000, inclusive—does this so happen? Or, you can try to find out which year in the century gives the largest number of dates that comply with the conditions. There is one year that beats all the others.

237. SHORT CUTS

We have from time to time given various short cuts in mental arithmetic. Here is an example that will interest those who are unfamiliar with the process.

Can you multiply 993 by 879 mentally?

It is remarkable that any two numbers of two figures each, where the tens are the same, and the sum of the units digits make 10, can always be multiplied mentally thus: $97 \times 93 = 9,021$. Multiply the 7 by 3 and set it down, then add 1 to the 9 and multiply by the other 9, $9 \times 10 = 90$.

This is very useful for squaring any number ending in 5, as $85^2 = 7,225$. With two fractions, when we have the whole numbers the same and the sum of the fractions equal unity, we get an easy rule for multiplying them. Take $7\frac{1}{4} \times 7\frac{3}{4} = 56\frac{3}{16}$. Multiply the fractions $= \frac{3}{16}$, add 1 to one of the 7's, and multiply by the other, $7 \times 8 = 56$.

238. MORE CURIOUS MULTIPLICATION

Here is Professor Rackbrane's latest:

What number is it that, when multiplied by 18, 27, 36, 45, 54, 63, 72, 81, or 99, gives a product in which the first and last figures are the same as those in the multiplier, but which when multiplied by 90 gives a product in which the last two figures are the same as those in the multiplier?

239. CROSS-NUMBER PUZZLE

On the following page is a cross-number puzzle on lines similar to those of the familiar cross-word puzzle. The puzzle is to place numbers in the spaces across and down, so as to satisfy the following conditions:

Across—1. a square number; 4. a square number; 5. a square number; 8. the digits sum to 35; 11. square root of 39 across; 13. a square number; 14. a square number; 15. square of 36 across; 17. square of half 11 across; 18. three similar figures; 19. product of 4 across and 33 across; 21. a square number; 22. five times 5 across; 23. all digits alike, except the central one; 25. square of 2 down; 27. see 20 down; 28. a fourth power; 29. sum of 18 across and 31 across; 31. a triangular number; 33. one more than 4 times 36 across; 34. digits sum to 18, and the three middle numbers are 3; 36. an odd number; 37. all digits even, except one, and their sum is 29; 39. a fourth power; 40. a cube number; 41. twice a square.

Down—1. reads both ways alike; 2. square root of 28 across; 3. sum of 17 across and 21 across; 4. digits sum to 19; 5. digits sum to 26; 6. sum of 14 across and 33 across; 7. a cube number; 9. a cube number; 10. a square number; 12. digits sum to 30; 14. all similar figures; 16. sum of digits is 2 down; 18. all similar digits except the first, which is 1; 20. sum of 17 across and 27 across; 21. a multiple of 19; 22. a square number; 24. a square number; 26. square of 18 across; 28. a fourth power of 4 across; 29. twice 15 across; 30. a triangular number; 32. digits sum to 20 and end with 8; 34. six times 21 across; 35. a cube number; 37. a square number; 38. a cube number.

240. COUNTING THE LOSS

An officer explained that the force to which he belonged originally consisted of a thousand men, but that it lost heavily in an engagement, and the survivors surrendered and were marched down to a prisoner of war camp.

On the first day's march one-sixth of the survivors escaped; on the second day one-eighth of the remainder escaped, and one man died; on the third day's march one-fourth of the remainder escaped. Arrived in camp, the rest were set to work in four equal gangs.

How many men had been killed in the engagement?

241. THE TOWER OF PISA

"When I was on a little tour in Italy, collecting material for my book on *Improvements in the Cultivation of Macaroni,*" said the Professor, "I happened to be one day on the top of the Leaning Tower of Pisa, in company with an American stranger. 'Some lean!' said my companion. 'I guess we can build a bit straighter in the States. If one of our skyscrapers bent in this way there would be a hunt round for the architect.'

"I remarked that the point at which we leant over was exactly 179 feet from the ground, and he put to me this question: 'If an elastic ball was dropped from here, and on each rebound rose exactly one-tenth of the height from which it fell, can you say what distance the ball would travel before it came to rest?' I found it a very interesting proposition."

242. A MATCHBOARDING ORDER

A man gave an order for 297 ft. of matchboarding of usual width and thickness. There were to be sixteen pieces, all measuring an exact number of feet —no fractions of a foot. He required eight pieces of the greatest length, the remaining pieces to be 1 ft., 2 ft., or 3 ft. shorter than the greatest length.

How was the order carried out? Supposing the eight of greatest length were 15 ft. long, then the others must be made up of pieces of 14 ft., 13 ft., or 12 ft. lengths, though every one of these three lengths need not be represented.

243. GEOMETRICAL PROGRESSION

Professor Rackbrane proposed, one morning, that his friends should write out a series of three or more different whole numbers in geometrical progression, starting from 1, so that the numbers should add up to a square. Thus, $1 + 2 + 4 + 8 + 16 + 32 = 63$.

But this is just one short of being a square. I am only aware of two answers in whole numbers, and these will be found easy to discover.

244. A PAVEMENT PUZZLE

Two square floors had to be paved with stones each 1 ft. square. The number of stones in both together was 2,120, but each side of one floor was 12 ft.

more than each side of the other floor. What were the dimensions of the two floors?

245. THE MUDBURY WAR MEMORIAL

The worthy inhabitants of Mudbury-in-the-Marsh recently erected a war memorial, and they proposed to enclose a piece of ground on which it stands with posts. They found that if they set up the posts 1 ft. apart they would have too few by 150. But if they placed them a yard apart there would be too many by 70.

How many posts had they in hand?

246. MONKEY AND PULLEY

Here is a funny tangle. It is a mixture of Lewis Carroll's "Monkey and Pulley," Sam Loyd's "How old was Mary?" and some other trifles. But it is quite easy if you have a pretty clear head.

A rope is passed over a pulley. It has a weight at one end and a monkey at the other. There is the same length of rope on either side and equilibrium is maintained. The rope weighs four ounces per foot. The age of the monkey and the age of the monkey's mother together total four years. The weight of the monkey is as many pounds as the monkey's mother is years old. The monkey's mother is twice as old as the monkey was when the monkey's mother was half as old as the monkey will be when the monkey is three times as old as the monkey's mother was when the monkey's mother was three times as old as the monkey. The weight of the rope and the weight at the end was half as much again as the difference in weight between the weight of the weight and the weight and the weight of the monkey. Now, what was the length of the rope?

247. UNLUCKY BREAKDOWNS

On an occasion of great festivities a considerable number of townspeople banded together for a day's outing and pleasure. They pressed into service nearly every wagon in the place, and each wagon was to carry the same number of persons. Half-way ten of these wagons broke down, so it was necessary for every remaining wagon to carry one more person. Unfortunately, when they started for home, it was found that fifteen more wagons were in such bad condition that they could not be used; so there were three more persons in every wagon than when they started out in the morning.

How many persons were there in the party?

248. PAT IN AFRICA

Some years ago ten of a party of explorers fell into the hands of a savage chief, who, after receiving a number of gifts, consented to let them go after half of them had been flogged by the Chief Medicine Man. There were five Britons and five native carriers, and the former planned to make the flogging fall on the five natives. They were all arranged in a circle in the order shown in the illustration, and Pat Murphy (No. 1) was given a number to count round and round in the direction he is pointing. When that number fell on a man he was to be taken out for flogging, while the counting went on from where it left off until another man fell out, and so on until the five had been selected for punishment.

If Pat had remembered the number correctly, and had begun at the right man, the flogging would have fallen upon all the five natives. But poor Pat mistook the number and began at the wrong man, with the result that the Britons all got the flogging and the natives escaped.

Can you find (1) the number the Irishman selected and the man at whom he began to count, and (2) the number he ought to have used and the man at whom the counting ought to have begun? The smallest possible number is required in each case.

249. BLENDING THE TEAS

A grocer buys two kinds of tea—one at 32¢ per pound, and the other, a better quality, at 40¢ a pound. He mixes together some of each, which he proposes to sell at 43¢ a pound, and so make a profit of 25 per cent on the cost. How many pounds of each kind must he use to make a mixture of a hundred pounds weight?

250. THE WEIGHT OF THE FISH

The Crackhams had contrived that their tour should include a certain place where there was good fishing, as Uncle Jabez was a good angler and they wished to give him a day's sport. It was a charming spot, and they made a picnic of the occasion. When their uncle landed a fine salmon trout there was some discussion as to its weight. The Colonel put it into the form of a puzzle, saying:

"Let us suppose the tail weighs nine ounces, the head as much as the tail and half the body, and the body weighs as much as the head and tail together. Now, if this were so, what would be the weight of the fish?"

251. CATS AND MICE

One morning, at the breakfast table, Professor Rackbrane's party were discussing organized attempts to exterminate vermin, when the Professor suddenly said:

"If a number of cats killed between them 999,919 mice, and every cat killed an equal number of mice, how many cats must there have been?"

Somebody suggested that perhaps one cat killed the lot; but Rackbrane replied that he said "cats." Then somebody else suggested that perhaps 999,919 cats each killed one mouse, but he protested that he used the word "mice." He added, for their guidance, that each cat killed more mice than there were cats. What is the correct answer?

252. THE EGG CABINET

A correspondent (T. S.) informs us that a man has a cabinet for holding birds' eggs. There are twelve drawers, and all—except the first drawer, which only holds the catalog—are divided into cells by intersecting wooden strips, each running the entire width or length of a drawer. The number of cells in any drawer is greater than that of the drawer above. The bottom drawer, No. 12, has twelve times as many cells as strips, No. 11 has eleven times as many cells as strips, and so on.

Can you show how the drawers were divided—how many cells and strips in each drawer? Give the smallest possible number in each case.

253. THE IRON CHAIN

Two pieces of iron chain were picked up on the battlefield. What purpose they had originally served is not certain, and does not immediately concern us. They were formed of circular links (all of the same size) out of metal half an inch thick. One piece of chain was exactly 3 ft. long, and the other 22 in. in length. Assuming that one piece contained six links more than the other, how many links were there in each piece of chain?

254. LOCATING THE COINS

"Do you know this?" said Dora to her brother. "Just put a dime in one of your pockets and a nickel in the pocket on the opposite side. Now the dime represents 10¢ and the nickel, 5¢. I want you to triple the value of the coin in your right pocket, and double the value of the coin in your left pocket. Add those two products together and tell me whether the result is odd or even."

He said the result was even, and she immediately told him that the dime was in the right pocket and the nickel in the left one. Every time he tried it she told him correctly how the coins were located. How did she do it?

255. THE THREE SUGAR BASINS

The three basins on the following page each contain the same number of lumps of sugar, and the cups are empty. If we transfer to each cup one-

eighteenth of the number of lumps that each basin contains, we then find that each basin holds twelve more lumps than each of the cups. How many lumps are there in each basin before they are removed?

256. A RAIL PROBLEM

There is a garden railing similar to our design. In each division between two uprights there is an equal number of ornamental rails, and a rail is divided in halves and a portion stuck on each side of every upright, except that the uprights at the ends have not been given half rails. Idly counting the rails from one end to the other, we found that there were 1,223 rails, counting two halves as one rail. We also noticed that the number of those divisions was five more than twice the number of *whole* rails in a division.

How many rails were there in each division?

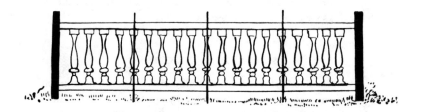

Geometrical
Problems

Geometrical Problems

257. MAKING A PENTAGON

"I am about to start on making a silk patchwork quilt," said a lady, "all composed of pieces in the form of a pentagon. How am I to cut out a true pentagon in cardboard, the sides of which must measure exactly an inch? Of course, I can draw a circle and then by trial with the compass find five points equidistant on the circumference" (see the illustration), "but unless I know the correct size of my circle the pentagon is just as it happens, and the sides are always a little more, or a little less, than an exact inch."

Could you show her a simple and direct way of doing it without any trial?

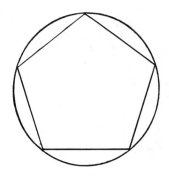

258. WITH COMPASSES ONLY

Can you show how to mark off the four corners of a square, using the compasses only? You simply use a sheet of paper and the compasses, and there is no trick, such as folding the paper.

259. LINES AND SQUARES

Here is a simple question. With how few straight lines can you make exactly one hundred squares?

Thus, in the first diagram it will be found that with nine straight lines I

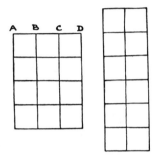

have made twenty squares (twelve with sides of the length A B, six with sides A C, and two with sides of the length A D). In the second diagram, although I use one more line, I only get seventeen squares. So, you see, everything depends on how the lines are drawn. Remember there must be exactly one hundred squares—neither more nor fewer.

260. MR. GRINDLE'S GARDEN

"My neighbor," said Mr. Grindle, "generously offered me, for a garden, as much land as I could enclose with four straight walls measuring 7, 8, 9, and 10 rods in length respectively."

"And what was the largest area you were able to enclose?" asked his friend.

Perhaps the reader can discover Mr. Grindle's correct answer. You see, in the case of three sides the triangle can only enclose one area, but with four sides it is quite different. For example, it is obvious that the area of Diagram A is greater than that of B, though the sides are the same.

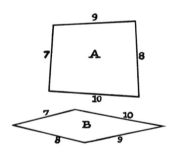

261. THE GARDEN PATH

This is an old puzzle that I find frequently cropping up. Many find it perplexing, but it is easier than it looks. A man has a rectangular garden, 55 yds. by 40 yds., and he makes a diagonal path, one yard wide, exactly in the man-

ner indicated in the diagram. What
is the area of the path?

Dimensions for the garden are generally
given that only admit of an
approximate answer, but I select figures
that will give an answer that is
quite exact. The width of the path is
exaggerated in the diagram for the
sake of clearness.

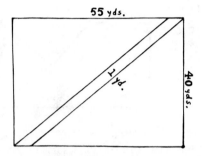

262. THE GARDEN BED

Here is quite a simple little puzzle.
A man has a triangular lawn of the
proportions shown, and he wants to
make the largest possible rectangular
flower bed without enclosing the tree.
How is he to do it?

This will serve to teach the uninitiated
a simple rule that may prove
useful on occasion. For example, it
would equally apply to the case of a
carpenter who had a triangular board
and wished to cut out the largest possible
rectangular table top without including
a bad knot in the wood.

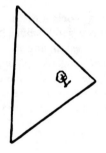

263. A PROBLEM FOR SURVEYORS

There are tricks in every trade, and the science of numbers contains an infinite
number of them. In nearly every vocation of life there are little wrinkles
and short cuts that are most useful when known. For example, a man bought
a little field, and on page 86 is the scale map (one inch to the rod) that was
given to me. I asked my surveyor to tell me the area of the field, but he said

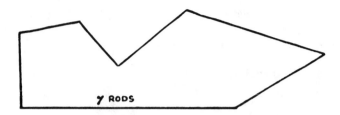

it was impossible without some further measurements; the mere length of one side, seven rods, was insufficient.

What was his surprise when I showed him in about two minutes what was the area! Can you tell how it is to be done?

264. A FENCE PROBLEM

This is a problem that is very frequently brought to my notice in various forms. It is generally difficult, but in the form in which I present it it should be easy to the cunning solver. A man has a square field, 60 feet by 60 feet, with other property, adjoining the highway. For some reason he put up a straight fence in the line of the three trees, as shown, and the length of fence from the middle tree to the tree on the road was just 91 feet.

What is the distance in exact feet from the middle tree to the gate on the road?

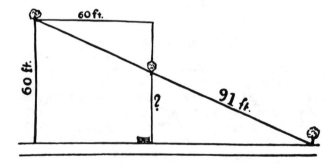

265. THE FOUR CHECKERS

Here is a queer new puzzle that I know will interest my readers considerably. The four checkers are shown exactly as they stood on a square checkered board—not necessarily eight squares by eight—but the board was drawn with vanishing ink, so that all the diagram except the men has disappeared. How many squares were there in the board and how am I to reconstruct it?

I know that each man stood in the middle of a square, one on the edge of each side of the board and no man in a corner. It is a real puzzle, until you hit on the method of solution, and then to get the correct answer is absurdly easy.

266. A MILITARY PUZZLE

An officer wished to form his men into twelve rows, with eleven men in every row, so that he could place himself at a point that would be equidistant from every row.

"But there are only one hundred and twenty of us, sir," said one of the men. Was it possible to carry out the order?

267. THE HIDDEN STAR

The illustration on page 88 represents a square tablecloth of choice silk patchwork. This was put together by the members of a family as a little

birthday present for one of its number. One of the contributors supplied a portion in the form of a perfectly symmetrical star, and this has been worked in exactly as it was received. But the triangular pieces so confuse the eye that it is quite a puzzle to find the hidden star.

Can you discover it, so that, if you wished, by merely picking out the stitches, you could extract it from the other portions of the patchwork?

268. A GARDEN PUZZLE

The four sides of a garden are known to be 20, 16, 12, and 10 rods, and it has the greatest possible area for those sides. What is the area?

269. A TRIANGLE PUZZLE

In the solution to Puzzle No. 230, we said that "there is an infinite number of rational triangles composed of three consecutive numbers such as 3, 4, 5, and 13, 14, 15." We here show these two triangles. In the first case the area (6) is half of 3 × 4, and in the second case, the height being 12, the area (84) is a half of 12 × 14.

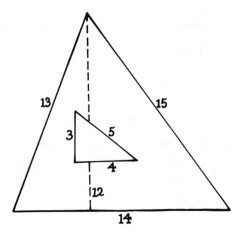

It will be found interesting to discover such a triangle with the smallest possible three consecutive numbers for its sides, that has an area that may be exactly divided by twenty without remainder.

270. THE DONJON KEEP WINDOW

In *The Canterbury Puzzles* Sir Hugh de Fortibus calls his chief builder and, pointing to a window, says: "Methinks yon window is square, and measures, on the inside, one foot every way, and is divided by the narrow bars into four lights, measuring half a foot on every side." See our Figure A. "I desire that another window be made higher up, whose four sides shall also be each one foot, but it shall be divided by bars into eight lights, whose sides shall be all equal." This the craftsman was unable to do,

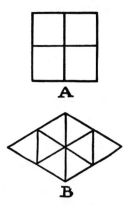

so Sir Hugh showed him our Figure B, which is quite correct. But he added, "I did not tell thee that the window must be square, as it is most certain it never could be."

Now, an ingenious correspondent, Mr. George Plant, found a flaw in Sir Hugh's conditions. Something that was understood is not actually stated, and the window may, as the conditions stand, be perfectly square. How is it to be done?

271. THE SQUARE WINDOW

Crackham told his family that a man had a window a yard square, and it let in too much light. He blocked up one half of it, and still had a square window a yard high and a yard wide. How did he do it?

272. DIVIDING THE BOARD

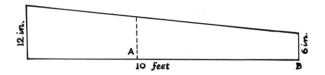

A man had a board measuring 10 feet in length, 6 inches wide at one end, and 12 inches wide at the other, as shown in the illustration. How far from B must the straight cut at A be made in order to divide it into two pieces of equal area?

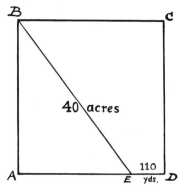

273. A RUNNING PUZZLE

ABCD is a square field of forty acres. The line BE is a straight path, and E is 110 yards from D. In a race Adams runs direct from A to D, but Brown has to start from B, go from B to E, and thence to D. Each keeps to a uniform speed throughout, and when Brown reaches E, Adams is 30 yards ahead of him. Which wins the race, and by how much?

274. THREE TABLECLOTHS

Mrs. Crackham at the breakfast table recently announced that she had had as a gift from an old friend three beautiful new tablecloths, each of which is exactly four feet square. She asked the members of her family if they could tell her the length of the side of the largest square table top that these three cloths will together cover. They might be laid in any way so long as they cover the surface, and she only wanted the answer to the nearest inch.

275. AN ARTIST'S PUZZLE

An artist wished to obtain a canvas for a painting which would allow for the picture itself occupying 72 square inches, a margin of 4 inches on top and on bottom, and 2 inches on each side. What are the smallest dimensions possible for such a canvas?

276. IN A GARDEN

"My friend Tompkins loves to spring on you little puzzling questions on every occasion, but they are never very profound," said the Colonel. "I was walking round his garden with him the other day when he pointed to a rectangular flower bed, and said: 'If I had made that bed 2 feet broader and 3 feet longer it would have been 64 square feet larger; but if it had been 3 feet broader and 2 feet longer it would then have been 68 square feet larger. What is its length and breadth?'"

277. COUNTING THE TRIANGLES

Professor Rackbrane has just given me the following puzzle as an example of those that interested his party at Christmas. Draw a pentagon, and connect each point with every other point by straight lines, as in the diagram.

How many different triangles are contained in this figure? To make it quite clear, AFB, AGB, ACB, BFG,

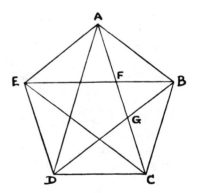

BFC, and BGC, are six such triangles. It is not a difficult count if you proceed with some method, but otherwise you are likely to drop triangles or include some more than once.

278. A HURDLES PUZZLE

The answers given in the old books to some of the best-known puzzles are often clearly wrong. Yet nobody ever seems to detect their faults. Here is an example. A farmer had a pen made of fifty hurdles, capable of holding a hundred sheep only. Supposing he wanted to make it sufficiently large to hold double that number, how many additional hurdles must he have?

279. THE ROSE GARDEN

"A friend of mine," said Professor Rackbrane, "has a rectangular garden, and he wants to make exactly one-half of it into a large bed of roses, with a gravel path of uniform width round it. Can you find a general rule that will apply equally to any rectangular garden, no matter what its proportions? All the measurements must be made in the garden. A plain ribbon, no shorter than the length of the garden, is all the material required."

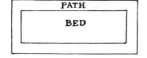

280. CORRECTING A BLUNDER

Mathematics is an exact science, but first-class mathematicians are apt, like the rest of humanity, to err badly on occasions. On refering to Peter Barlow's valuable work on *The Theory of Numbers,* we hit on this problem:

"To find a triangle such that its three sides, perpendicular, and the line drawn from one of the angles bisecting the base may be all expressed in rational numbers." He gives as his answer the triangle 480, 299, 209, which is wrong and entirely unintelligible.

Readers may like to find a correct solution when we say that all the five measurements may be in whole numbers, and every one of them less than a hundred. It is apparently intended that the triangle must not itself be right angled.

281. THE RUSSIAN MOTORCYCLISTS

Two Army motorcyclists, on the road at Adjbkmlprzll, wish to go to Brczrtwxy, which, for the sake of brevity, are marked in the accompanying map as A and B. Now, Pipipoff said: "I shall go to D, which is six miles, and

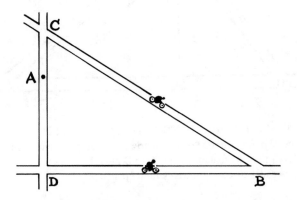

then take the straight road to B, another fifteen miles." But Sliponsky thought he would try the upper road by way of C. Curiously enough, they found on reference to their cyclometers that the distance either way was exactly the same. This being so, they ought to have been able easily to answer the General's simple question, "How far is it from A to C?"

It can be done in the head in a few moments, if you only know how. Can the reader state correctly the distance?

282. THOSE RUSSIAN CYCLISTS AGAIN

Here is another little experience of the two Russian Army motorcyclists that I described in our last puzzle. In the section from a map given in our illustration on page 94 we are shown three long straight roads, forming a right-angled triangle. The General asked the two men how far it was from A to B. Pipipoff replied that all he knew was that in riding right round the triangle, from A to B, from there to C and home to A, his cyclometer registered exactly sixty miles, while Sliponsky could only say that he happened to know that C was exactly

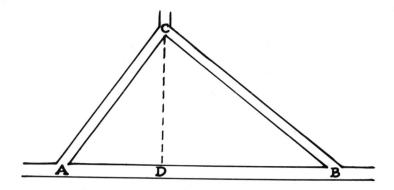

twelve miles from the road A to B—that is, to the point D, as shown by the dotted line. Whereupon the General made a very simple calculation in his head and declared that the distance from A to B must be ———.

Can the reader discover so easily how far it was?

283. THE PRICE OF A GARDEN

Professor Rackbrane informed his friends one morning that a neighbor told him that he had been offered a piece of ground for a garden. He said it was triangular in shape, with the dimensions as shown in our diagram. As the price proposed was ten dollars per square yard, what will the cost be?

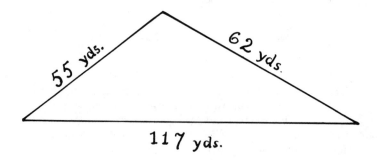

284. CHOOSING A SITE

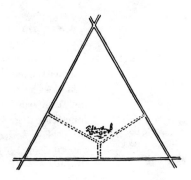

A man bought an estate enclosed by three straight roads forming an equilateral triangle, as shown in the illustration. Now, he wished to build a house somewhere on the estate so that if he should have a straight driveway made from the front to each of the three roads he might be put to the least expense. The diagram shows one such position. Where should he build the house?

285. THE COUNTER CROSS

Arrange twenty counters in the form of a cross, in the manner shown in the diagram. Now, in how many different ways can you point out four counters that will form a perfect square if considered alone? Thus the four counters composing each arm of the cross, and also the four in the center, form squares. Squares are also formed by the four counters marked A, the four marked B, and so on.

How may you remove six counters so that not a single square can be so indicated from those that remain?

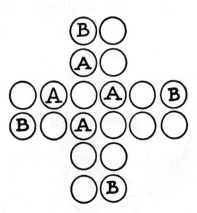

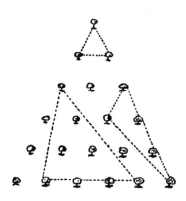

286. THE TRIANGULAR PLANTATION

A man had a plantation of twenty-one trees set out in the triangular form shown in our diagram. If he wished to enclose a triangular piece of ground with a tree at each of the three angles, how many different ways of doing it are there from which he might select? The dotted lines show three ways of doing it. How many are there altogether?

287. THE CIRCLE AND DISCS

During a recent visit to a fair we saw a man with a table, on the oilcloth covering of which was painted a large red circle, and he invited the public to cover this circle entirely with five tin discs which he provided, and offered a substantial prize to anybody who was successful. The circular discs were all of the same size, and each, of course, smaller than the red circle. The diagram, where three discs are shown placed, will make everything clear.

He showed that it was "quite easy when you know how" by covering up the circle himself without any apparent difficulty, but many tried over and over again and failed every time. I should explain that it was a condition that when once you had placed any disc you were not allowed to shift it, otherwise, by sliding them about after they had been placed, it might be tolerably easy to do.

Let us assume that the red circle is six inches in diameter. What is the smallest possible diameter (say, to the nearest half-inch) for the five discs in order to make a solution possible?

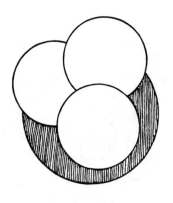

288. THE THREE FENCES

"A man had a circular field," said Crackham, "and he wished to divide it into four equal parts by three fences, each of the same length. How might this be done?"

"Why did he want them of the same length?" asked Dora.

"That is not recorded," replied the Colonel, "nor are we told why he wished to divide the field into four parts, nor whether the fence was of wood or iron, nor whether the field was pasture or arable. I cannot even tell you the man's name, or the color of his hair. You will find that these points are not essential to the puzzle."

289. SQUARING THE CIRCLE

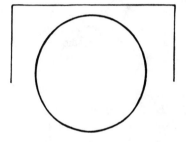

The problem of squaring the circle depends on finding the ratio of the diameter to the circumference. This cannot be found in numbers with exactitude, but we can get it near enough for all practical purposes.

It is equally impossible, by Euclidean geometry, to draw a straight line equal to the circumference of a given circle. You can roll a penny carefully on its edge along a straight line on a sheet of paper and get a pretty exact result, but such a thing as a circular garden bed cannot be so rolled.

The line shown, when straightened out, is very nearly the exact length of the circumference of the accompanying circle. The horizontal part of the line is half the circumference. Could you have found it by a simple method, using only pencil, compasses, and ruler?

290. THE CIRCLING CAR

The outside wheels of a car, running on a circular track, are going twice as fast as the inside ones.

What is the length of the circumference described by the outer wheels? The wheels are five feet apart on the two axles.

291. SHARING A GRINDSTONE

Three men bought a grindstone twenty inches in diameter. How much must each grind off so as to share the stone equally, making an allowance of four inches off the diameter as waste for the aperture? We are not concerned with the unequal value of the shares for practical use—only with the actual equal quantity of stone each receives.

292. THE WHEELS OF THE CAR

"You see, sir," said the automobile salesman, "at present the fore wheel of the car I am selling you makes four revolutions more than the rear wheel in going 120 yards; but if you have the circumference of each wheel reduced by three feet, it would make as many as six revolutions more than the rear wheel in the same distance."

Why the buyer wished that the difference in the number of revolutions between the two wheels should not be increased does not concern us. The puzzle is to discover the circumference of each wheel in the first case. It is quite easy.

293. A WHEEL FALLACY

Here is a curious fallacy that I have found to be very perplexing to many people. The wheel shown in the illustration makes one complete revolution in passing from A to B. It is therefore obvious that the line (AB) is exactly equal in length to the circumference of the wheel. What that length is cannot be stated with accuracy for any diameter, but we can get it near enough for all practical purposes. Thus, if it is a bicycle wheel with a diameter of 28 inches, we can multiply by 22 and divide by 7, and get the length—88 inches. This is a trifle too much, but if we multiply by 355 and divide by 113 we get 87.9646, which is nearer; or by multiplying by 3.1416 we get 87.9648, which is still more nearly exact. This is just by the way.

Now the inner circle (the large hub in the illustration) also makes one complete revolution along the imaginary dotted line (CD) and, since the line (CD) is equal to the line (AB), the circumference of the larger and smaller circles are the same! This is certainly not true, as the merest child can see at a glance. Yet, wherein lies the fallacy?

Try to think it out. There can be no question that the hub makes one complete revolution in passing from C to D. Then why does not CD equal in length its circumference?

294. A FAMOUS PARADOX

There is a question that one is perpetually hearing asked, but to which I have never heard or read an answer that was satisfactory or really convincing to the ordinary man. It is this, "When a bicycle is in motion, does the upper part of each wheel move faster than the bottom part near the ground?" People who are not accustomed to the habit of exact thought will invariably dismiss the subject with a laugh, and the reply, "Of course not!" They regard it as too absurd for serious consideration. A wheel, they say is a rigid whole, revolving round a central axis, and if one part went faster than another it would simply break in pieces.

Then you draw attention of your skeptic to a passing cart and ask him to observe that, while you can clearly distinguish the spokes as they pass the bottom, and count them as they go by, those at the top are moving so fast that they are quite indistinguishable. In fact, a wheel in motion looks something like our rough sketch, and artists will draw it in this way. Our friend has to admit that it is so, but as he cannot explain it he holds to his original opinion, and probably says, "Well, I suppose it is an optical illusion."

I invite the reader to consider the matter: Does the upper part of a wheel move faster than the lower part?

295. ANOTHER WHEEL PARADOX

Two cyclists were resting on a railway bridge somewhere in Sussex, when a railway train went by.

"That's a London train, going to Brighton," said Henderson.

"Most of it is," replied Banks, "but parts of it are going direct towards London."

"What on earth are you talking about?"

"I say that if a train is going from London to Brighton, then parts of that train are all the time going in the opposite direction—from Brighton to London."

"You seriously tell me that while I am cycling from Croydon to Eastbourne, parts of my machine are flying back to Croydon?"

"Steady on, old man," said Banks calmly. "I said nothing about bicycles. My statement was confined to railway trains."

Henderson thought it was a mere catch and suggested the smoke or steam of the engine, but his friend pointed out that there might be a strong wind in the direction the train was going. Then he tried "the thoughts of the passengers," but here there was no evidence, and these would hardly be parts of the train! At last he gave it up. Can the reader explain this curious paradox?

296. A MECHANICAL PARADOX

A remarkable mechanical paradox, invented by James Ferguson* about the year 1751, ought to be known by everyone, but, unfortunately, it is not. It was contrived by him as a challenge to a skeptical watchmaker during a metaphysical controversy. "Suppose," Ferguson said, "I make one wheel as thick as three others and cut teeth in them all, and then put the three wheels all loose upon one axis and set the thick wheel to turn them, so that its teeth may take into those of the three thin ones. Now, if I turn the thick wheel round, how must it turn the others?" The watchmaker replied that it was obvious that all three must be turned the contrary way. Then Ferguson produced his simple machine, which anybody can make in a few hours, showing that, turning the thick wheel which way you would, one of the thin wheels revolved the *same way*, the second the *contrary way*, and the third *remained*

[* Ferguson was an eccentric self-educated Scottish astronomer of the 18th-century, well known in his day as the "Peasant-Boy Philosopher." For a biographical sketch, see *The Encyclopaedia Britannica*, 11th edition.—M. G.]

stationary. Although the watchmaker took the machine away for careful examination, he failed to detect the cause of the strange paradox.

297. THE FOUR HOUSEHOLDERS

Here is a square plot of land with four houses, four trees, a well (W) in the center, and hedges planted across with four gateways (G).

Can you divide the ground so that each householder shall have an equal portion of land, one tree, one gateway, an equal length of hedge, and free access to the well without trespass?

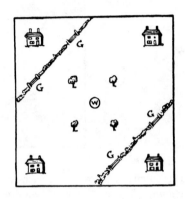

298. THE FIVE FENCES

A man owned a large, square, fenced-in field in which were sixteen oak trees, as depicted in the illustration. He wished, for some eccentric reason, to put up five straight fences, so that every tree should be in a separate enclosure.

How did he do it? Just take your pencil and draw five straight strokes across the field, so that every tree shall be fenced off from all the others.

299. THE FARMER'S SONS

A farmer once had a square piece of ground on which stood twenty-four trees, exactly as shown in the illustration on the following page. He left

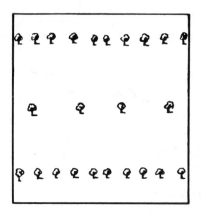

instructions in his will that each of his eight sons should receive the same amount of ground and the same number of trees. How was the land to be divided in the simplest possible manner?

300. AVOIDING THE MINES

Here we have a portion of the North Sea thickly sown with mines by the enemy. A cruiser made a safe passage through them from south to north in two straight courses, without striking a single mine. Take your pencil and try to discover how it is done. Go from the bottom of the chart to any point you like on the chart in a straight line, and then from that point to the top in another straight line without touching a mine.

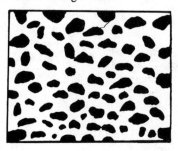

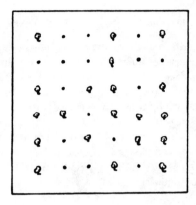

301. SIX STRAIGHT FENCES

A man had a small plantation of thirty-six trees, planted in the form of a square. Some of these died and had to be cut down in the positions indicated by the dots in our illustration. How is it possible to put up six straight fences across the field, so that every one of the remaining twenty trees shall be in a separate enclosure? As a matter of fact, twenty-two trees might be so enclosed by six straight fences if their positions were a little more accommodating, but we have to deal with the trees as they stand in regular formation, which makes all the difference.

Just take your pencil and see if you can make six straight lines across the field so as to leave every tree separately enclosed.

302. DISSECTING THE MOON

In how large a number of pieces can this crescent moon be cut with five straight cuts of the knife? The pieces may not be piled or shifted after a cut.

303. DRAWING A STRAIGHT LINE

If we want to describe a circle we use an instrument that we call a pair of compasses, but if we need a straight line we use no such instrument—we employ a ruler or other straight edge. In other words, we first seek a straight line to produce our required straight line, which is equivalent to using a coin, saucer, or other circular object to draw a circle. Now, imagine yourself to be in such a position that you cannot obtain a straight edge—not even a piece of thread. Could you devise a simple instrument that would draw your straight line, just as the compasses describe a circle?

It is an interesting abstract question, but, of course, of no practical value. We shall continue to use the straightedge.

304. DRAWING AN ELLIPSE

I suppose a large proportion of my readers **are familiar** with this trick for drawing an ellipse. It is very useful if you have **to cut** a mount for a portrait or to make an oval flower bed. You drive in two pins or nails (or, in the case of the flower bed, two stakes) and enclose them with an endless band of thread or string, as shown in our diagram, where the pins are at A and B, and the pencil point, at C, stretches the loop of thread. If you keep the thread taut and pass the pencil all round until you come back to the starting point you will describe the perfect oval shown.

But I have sometimes heard the complaint that the method is too haphazard: that it was only by a lot of trials that you can draw an ellipse of the exact dimensions required. This is a delusion, and it will make an interesting little

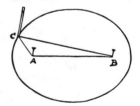

puzzle to show at what distance apart the pins should be placed, and what length the string should be, to draw an ellipse, say, twelve inches in length by eight inches in breadth.

Can you discover the simple rule for doing this?

305. THE BRICKLAYER'S TASK

When a man walked in his estate, one of the walls was partly level and partly over a small rise or hill, precisely as shown in the drawing herewith,

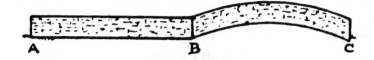

wherein it will be observed that the distance from A to B is the same as from B to C. Now, the contractor desired and claimed that he should be paid more for the part that was on the hill than for the part that was level, since (at least, so he held) it demanded the use of more material. But the employer insisted that he should pay less for that part.

It was a nice point, over which they nearly had recourse to the law. Which of them was in the right?

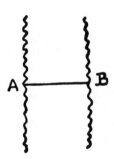

306. MEASURING THE RIVER

A traveller reaches a river at the point A, and wishes to know the width across to B. As he has no means of crossing the river, what is the easiest way of finding its width?

307. PAT AND HIS PIG

Our diagram represents a field 100 yards square. Pat and the pig that he wishes to catch are in opposite corners, 100 yards apart. The pig runs straight for the gateway in the top left-hand corner. As the Irishman can run just twice as fast as the pig, you would expect that he would first make straight for the gate and close it. But this is not Pat's way of doing things. He goes directly for the pig all the time, thus taking a curved course.

Does the pig escape, or does Pat catch it? And if he catches it, exactly how far does the pig run?

308. THE LADDER

There was some talk at the breakfast table about a ladder that was needed for some domestic purposes, when Professor Rackbrane interrupted the discussion with this little puzzle:

"A ladder was fastened on end against a high wall of a building. A man unfastened it and pulled it out four yards at the bottom. It was then found that the top of the ladder had descended just one-fifth of the length of the ladder. What was the length of the ladder?"

309. A MAYPOLE PUZZLE

During a gale a maypole was broken in such a manner that it struck the level ground at a distance of twenty feet from the base of the pole, where it entered the earth. It was repaired, and broken by the wind a second time at a point five feet lower down, and struck the ground at a distance of thirty feet from the base.

What was the original height of the pole? In neither case did the broken part become actually detached.

310. THE BELL ROPE

A bell rope, passing through the ceiling above, just touches the belfry floor, and when you pull the rope to the wall, keeping the rope taut, it touches a point just three inches above the floor, and the wall was four feet from the rope when it hung at rest. How long was the rope from floor to ceiling?

311. THE DISPATCH RIDER IN FLANDERS

A dispatch rider on horseback, somewhere in Flanders, had to ride with all possible speed from the position in which he is shown to the spot indicated by the tent. The distances are marked on the plan. Now, he can ride just twice as fast over the soft turf (the shaded ground) as he can ride over the loose sand. Can you show what is the quickest possible route for him to take? This is just one of those practical problems with which the soldier is faced from day to day when on active service. Important results may hang on the rider taking the right or the wrong route.

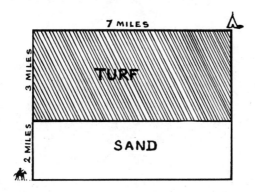

Which way would you have gone? Of course, the turf and the sand extend for miles to the right and the left with the same respective depths of three miles and two miles, so there is no trick in the puzzle.

312. THE SIX SUBMARINES

Readers may remember a puzzle, to place five pennies so that every penny shall touch every other penny, that is given in my book, *Amusements in Mathematics,* and a correspondent has suggested that as many as six coins can be placed under the conditions if we arrange them as shown in the upper diagram—that is, with A, B, and C in the form of a triangle, and D, E, and F respectively on the top of A, B, and C. If we take a section of the coins at XY (see the lower

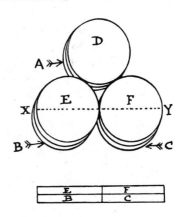

diagram), he held that E and C and also B and F meet at a "mathematical point," and are therefore in contact. But he was wrong, for if E touches C a barrier is set up between B and F. If B touches F, then E cannot touch C. It is a subtle fallacy that I know will interest my readers. When we say that a number of things meet at a point (like the spokes of a wheel) only three can be in contact (each with each) on the same plane.

This has led me to propound a new "touching" problem. If five submarines, sunk on the same day, all went down at the same spot where another had previously been sunk, how might they all lie at rest so that every one of the six U-boats should touch every other one? To simplify we will say, place six ordinary wooden matches so that every match shall touch every other match. No bending or breaking allowed.

313. ECONOMY IN STRING

Owing to the scarcity of string a lady found herself in this dilemma. In making up. a parcel for her son, a prisoner in Germany, she was limited to using twelve feet of string, exclusive of knots, which passed round the parcel once lengthways and twice round its girth, as shown in the illustration.

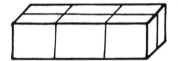

What was the largest rectangular parcel that she could make up, subject to these conditions?

314. THE STONE PEDESTAL

In laying the base and cubic pedestal for a certain public memorial, the stonemason used cubic blocks of stone all measuring one foot on every side. There was exactly the same number of these blocks (all uncut) in the pedestal as in the square base on the center of which it stood.

Look at the sketch and try to determine the total number of blocks actually used. The base is only a single block in depth.

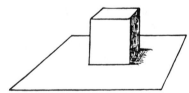

315. A CUBE PARADOX

I had two solid cubes of lead, one very slightly larger than the other, just as shown in the illustration. Through one of them I cut a hole (without destroying the continuity of its four sides) so that the other cube could be passed right through it. On weighing them afterwards it was found that the larger cube was still the heavier of the two! How was this possible?

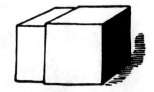

316. THE CARDBOARD BOX

Readers must have often remarked on the large number of little things that one would have expected to have been settled generations ago, and yet never appear to have been considered. Here is a case that has just occurred to me.

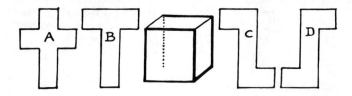

If I have a closed cubical cardboard box, by running the penknife along seven of the twelve edges (it must always be seven) I can lay it out in one flat piece in various shapes. Thus, in the diagram, if I pass the knife along the darkened edges and down the invisible edge indicated by the dotted line, I get the shape A. Another way of cutting produces B or C. It will be seen that D is simply C turned over, so we will not call that a different shape. How many different shapes can be produced?

317. THE AUSTRIAN PRETZEL

On the next page is a twisted Vienna bread roll, known as a pretzel. The twist, like the curl in a pig's tail, is entirely for ornament. The Wiener pretzel, like some other things, is doomed to be cut up or broken, and the interest lies in the number of resultant pieces.

Suppose you had the pretzel depicted in the illustration lying on the table before you, what is the greatest number of pieces into which you could cut it with a single straight cut of a knife? In what direction would you make the cut?

318. CUTTING THE CHEESE

Here is a simple question that will require just a few moments' thought to get an exact answer. I have a piece of cheese in the shape of a cube. How am I to cut it in two pieces with one straight cut of the knife so that the two new surfaces produced by the cut shall each be a perfect hexagon?

Of course, if cut in the direction of the dotted line the surfaces would be squares. Now produce hexagons.

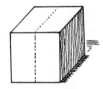

319. THE FLY'S JOURNEY

A fly, starting from the point A, can crawl round the four sides of the base of this cubical block in four minutes. Can you say how long it will take it to crawl from A to the opposite upper corner B?

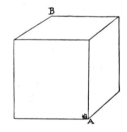

320. THE TANK PUZZLE

The area of the floor of a tank is 6 square feet, the water in it is 9 inches deep. How much does the water rise (1) if a 1-foot metal cube is put in it; (2) how much farther does it rise if another cube like it is put in by its side?

321. THE NOUGAT PUZZLE

A block of nougat is 16 inches long, 8 inches wide, and 7½ inches deep. What is the greatest number of pieces that I can cut from it measuring 5 inches by 3 inches by 2½ inches?

322. AN EASTER EGG PROBLEM

"Here is an appropriate Easter egg problem for you," said Professor Rackbrane at the breakfast table. "If I have an egg measuring exactly three inches in length, and three other eggs all similar in shape, having together the same contents as the large egg, can you give me exact measurements for the lengths of the three smaller ones?"

323. THE PEDESTAL PUZZLE

An eccentric man had a block of wood measuring 3 feet by 1 foot by 1 foot, which he gave to a wood turner with instructions to turn from it a pedestal, saying that he would pay him a certain sum for every cubic inch of wood taken from the block in process of turning. The ingenious turner weighed the block and found it to contain 30 pounds. After he had finished the pedestal it was again weighed, and found to contain 20 pounds. As the original block contained 3 cubic feet, and it had lost just one-third of its weight, the turner asked payment for 1 cubic foot. But the gentleman objected, saying that the heart of the wood might be heavier or lighter than the outside.

How did the ingenious turner contrive to convince his customer that he had taken not more and not less than 1 cubic foot from the block?

324. THE SQUIRREL'S CLIMB

A squirrel goes spirally up a cylindrical post, making the circuit in four feet. How many feet does it travel to the top if the post is sixteen feet high and three feet in circumference?

325. THE FLY AND THE HONEY

I have a cylindrical cup four inches high and six inches in circumference. On the inside of the vessel, one inch from the top, is a drop of honey, and on the opposite side of the vessel, one inch from the bottom on the outside, is a fly. Can you tell exactly how far the fly must walk to reach the honey?

326. PACKING CIGARETTES

A manufacturer sends out his cigarettes in boxes of 160; they are packed in eight rows of 20 each, and exactly fill the box. Could he, by packing differently, get more cigarettes than 160 into the box? If so, what is the greatest number that he could add? At first sight it sounds absurd to expect to get more cigarettes into a box that is already exactly filled, but a moment's consideration should give you the key to the paradox.

327. A NEW CUTTING-OUT PUZZLE

Cut the figure into four pieces that will fit together and form a square.

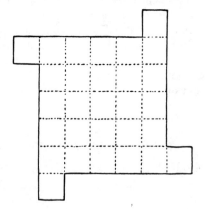

328. THE SQUARE TABLE TOP

A man had three pieces of beautiful wood, measuring 12 inches, 15 inches, and 16 inches square respectively. He wanted to cut these into the fewest pieces possible that would fit together and form a small square table top 25 inches by 25 inches. How was he to do it? I have found several easy solutions in six pieces, very pretty, but have failed to do it in five pieces. Perhaps the latter is not possible. I

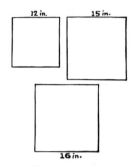

know it will interest my readers to examine the question.

329. THE SQUARES OF VENEER

A man has two square pieces of valuable veneer, each measuring 25 inches by 25 inches. One piece he cut, in the manner shown in our illustration, in four parts that will form two squares, one 20 inches by 20 inches and the other 15 inches by 15 inches. Simply join C to A and D to B. How is he to cut the other square into four pieces that will form again two other squares with sides in exact inches, but not 20 and 15 as before?

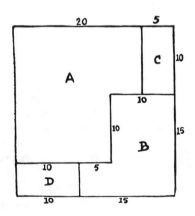

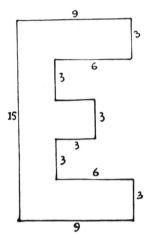

330. DISSECTING THE LETTER E

Can you cut this letter E into only five pieces so that they will fit together to form a perfect square? I have given all the measurements in inches so that there should be no doubt as to the correct proportions of the letter. In this case you are not allowed to turn over any piece.

After you have solved the problem, see if you can reduce the number of pieces to four, with the added freedom to turn over any of the pieces.

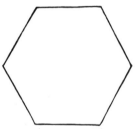

331. HEXAGON TO SQUARE

Can you cut this perfect hexagon into five pieces that will fit together and form a square?

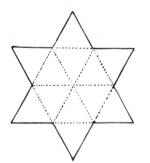

332. SQUARING A STAR

This six-pointed star can be cut into as few as five pieces that will fit together and form a perfect square. To perform the feat in seven pieces is quite easy, but to do it in five is more difficult. I introduce the dotted lines merely to show the true proportions of the star, which is thus built up of twelve equilateral triangles.

333. THE MUTILATED CROSS

Here is a symmetrical Greek Cross from which has been cut a square piece exactly equal to one of the arms of the cross. The puzzle is to cut what remains into four pieces that will fit together and form a square. This is a pleasing but particularly easy cutting-out puzzle.

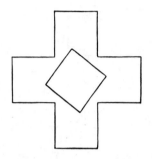

334. THE VICTORIA CROSS

We have shown elsewhere how innumerable puzzles may be devised on the Greek, St. George, or Red Cross, so familiar to us all, composed as it is of five equal squares assembled together. Let us now do homage to the Maltese or Victoria Cross. Cut the cross shown into seven pieces that will fit together and form a perfect square. Of course, there must be no trickery or waste of material.

In order that the reader may have no doubt as to the exact proportions of the cross as given, I have inserted the dotted lines. As the pieces A and B will fit together to form one of those little squares, it is clear that the area

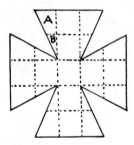

of the cross is equal to seventeen such squares.

335. SQUARING THE SWASTIKA

Cut out the swastika on page 116 and then cut it up into four pieces that will fit together and form a square. There can be no question as to the proportions

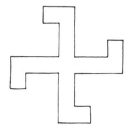

of the figure if we regard it as built up of seventeen equal squares. You can divide it up into these seventeen squares with your pencil without difficulty. Now try to cut it into four pieces to form a single square.

336. THE MALTESE CROSS

Can you cut the star into four pieces and place them inside the frame so as to show a perfect Maltese Cross?

337. THE PIRATES' FLAG

Here is a flag taken from a band of pirates on the high seas. The twelve

stripes represented the number of men in the band, and when a new man was admitted or dropped out a new stripe was added or one removed, as the case might be. Can you discover how the flag should be cut into as few pieces as possible so that they may be put together again and show only ten stripes? No part of the material may be wasted, and the flag must retain its oblong shape.

338. THE CARPENTER'S PUZZLE

Here is a well-known puzzle, given in all the old books. A ship's carpenter had to stop a hole twelve inches square, and the only piece of wood that was available measured 9 inches in breadth by 16 inches in length. How did he cut it into only two pieces that would exactly fit the hole? The answer is based on what I call the "step principle," as shown in the diagram. If you move the piece marked B up one step to the left, it will exactly fit on A and form a perfect square measuring twelve inches on every side.

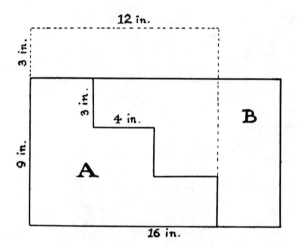

This is very simple and obvious. But nobody has ever attempted to explain the general law of the thing. As a consequence, the notion seems to have got abroad that the method will apply to any rectangle where the proportion of length to breadth is within reasonable limits. This is not so, and I have had to expose some bad blunders in the case of published puzzles that were supposed to be solved by an application of this step principle, but were really impossible of solution.* Let the reader take different measurements, instead of 9 in. by 16 in., and see if he can find other cases in which this trick will work in two pieces and form a perfect square.

[* See Dudeney's *Amusements in Mathematics,* Problem 150, where he catches Sam Loyd in such a blunder.—M. G.]

339. THE CRESCENT AND THE STAR

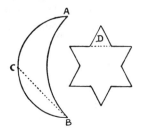

Here is a little puzzle on the Crescent and the Star. Look at the illustration, and see if you can determine which is the larger, the Crescent or the Star. If both were cut out of a sheet of solid gold, which would be the more valuable?

As it is very difficult to guess by the eye, I will state that the outer arc, A C B, is a semicircle; the radius of the inner arc is equal to the straight line B C; the distance in a straight line from A to B is twelve inches; and the point of the star, D, contains three square inches. It is quite easy to settle the matter at a glance—when you know how.

340. THE PATCHWORK QUILT

Here is a patchwork quilt that was produced by two young ladies for some charitable purpose. When they came to join their work it was found that each lady had contributed a portion of exactly the same size and shape. It is an amusing puzzle to discover just where these two portions are joined together. Can you divide the quilt into two parts, simply by cutting the stitches, so that the portions shall be of the same size and shape? You may think you have solved it in a few minutes, but—wait and see!

341. THE IMPROVISED CHECKERBOARD

Some Englishmen at the front during the Great War wished to pass a restful hour at a game of checkers. They had coins and small stones for the men, but no board. However, one of them found a piece of linoleum as shown in

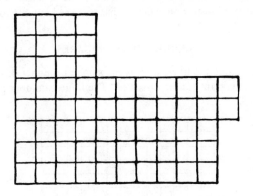

the illustration, and, as it contained the right number of squares, it was decided to cut it and fit the pieces together to form a board, blacking some of the squares afterwards for convenience in playing.

An ingenious Scotsman showed how this could be done by cutting the stuff in two pieces only, and it is a really good puzzle to discover how he did it. Cut the linoleum along the lines into two pieces that will fit together and form the board, eight by eight.

342. TESSELLATED PAVEMENTS

The reader must often have noticed, in looking at tessellated pavements and elsewhere, that a square space had sometimes to be covered with square tiles under such conditions that a certain number of the tiles have to be

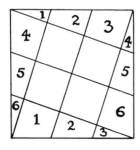

a square has been formed with ten square tiles. As ten is not a square number a certain number of tiles must be cut. In this case it is six. It will be seen that the pieces 1 and 1 are cut from one tile, 2 and 2 from another, and so on.

cut in two parts. A familiar example is shown in our illustration, where

If you had to cover a square space with exactly twenty-nine square tiles of equal size, how would you do it? What is the smallest number of tiles that you need cut in two parts?

343. SQUARE OF SQUARES

Cutting only along the lines, what is the smallest number of square pieces into which the diagram can be dissected? The largest number possible is, of

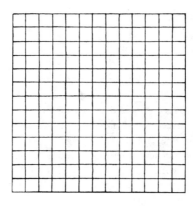

course, 169, where all the pieces will be of the same size—one cell—but we want the smallest number. We might cut away the border on two sides, leaving one square 12 × 12, and cutting the remainder in 25 little squares, making 26 in all. This is better than 169, but considerably more than the fewest possible.

344. STARS AND CROSSES

This puzzle calls for a certain amount of ingenuity on account of the awkward position of the cross in the corner.

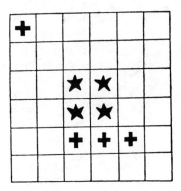

The puzzle is to cut the square into four parts by going along the lines, so that each part shall be exactly the same size and shape, and each part contain a star and a cross.

345. GREEK CROSS PUZZLE

Here is a puzzle for our younger readers. Cut a square into four pieces in the manner shown, then put these four pieces together so as to form a symmetrical Greek cross.

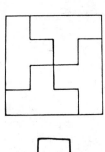

346. SQUARE AND CROSS

Cut a symmetrical Greek cross into five pieces, so that one piece shall be a smaller symmetrical Greek cross, entire, and so that the remaining four pieces will fit together and form a perfect square.

347. THREE GREEK CROSSES FROM ONE

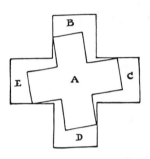

In *Amusements in Mathematics* (page 168) is given this elegant solution for cutting two symmetrical Greek crosses of the same size from a larger cross. Of course A is cut out entire, and the reader will have no difficulty in placing the other four pieces together to form a similar cross. It was then added:

"The difficult question now presents itself—how are we to cut three Greek crosses from one in the fewest possible pieces? As a matter of fact this problem may be solved in as few as thirteen pieces; but as I know many of my readers, advanced geometricians, will be glad to have something to work at of which they are not shown the solution, I leave the mystery for the present undisclosed."

Only one correspondent has ever succeeded in solving the problem, and his method is exceedingly complex and difficult. Of course the three crosses must be all of one size.

348. MAKING A SQUARE

Here is an elegant, but not difficult, little cutting-out puzzle that will interest readers (sent by E. B. E.).* Cut the figure into four pieces, each of the same size and shape, that will fit together and form a perfect square.

[* Edward B. Escott. See footnote to solution for Problem 332.—M. G.]

349. TABLE TOP AND STOOLS

Most people are familiar with the old puzzle of the circular table top cut into pieces to form two oval stools, each with a hand hole. The old solution was in eight pieces, but an improved version was given in only six pieces in *Amusements in Mathematics,* No. 157.

Those who remember the puzzle will be interested in a solution in as few as four pieces by the late Sam Loyd. Can you cut the circle into four pieces that will fit together (two and two) and form two oval stool tops, each with a hand hole?

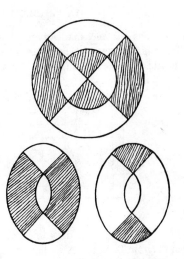

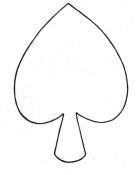

350. TRIANGLE AND SQUARE

Can you cut each of the equilateral triangles into three pieces, so that the six pieces will fit together and form a perfect square?

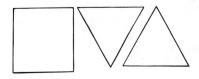

351. CHANGING THE SUIT

You are asked to cut the spade into three pieces that will fit together and form a heart. Of course no part of the material may be wasted, or it would be absurd, since it would be necessary merely to cut away the stem of the spade.

352. PROBLEM OF THE EXTRA CELL

Here is a fallacy that is widely known but imperfectly understood. Doubtless many readers will recognize it, and some of them have probably been not a little perplexed. In Figure A the square resembling a chessboard is cut into

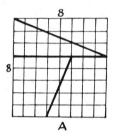
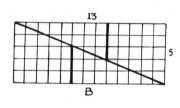

four pieces along the dark lines, and these four pieces are seen reassembled in diagram B. But in A we have sixty-four of these little square cells, whereas in B we have sixty-five. Where does the additional cell come from?

Examine it carefully and see if you can discover how that extra square creeps in, and whether it is really possible that you can increase the size of a slice of bread and butter by merely cutting it in pieces and putting them together again differently.

353. PROBLEM OF THE MISSING CELL

Can you arrange the four pieces of the previous puzzle in another way so that instead of gaining a square we have lost one, the new figure apparently containing only 63 cells?

354. A HORSESHOE PUZZLE

Here is an easy little puzzle, but we have seen people perplexed by it for some time. Given a paper horseshoe, similar to the one in the illustration, can you cut it into seven pieces, with two straight clips of the scissors, so that each part shall contain a nail hole? There is no objection to your shifting the pieces and putting them together after the first cut, only you must not bend or fold the paper in any way.

355. SQUARE TABLE TOP

From a square sheet of paper or cardboard, divided into smaller squares, 7 × 7, as in the diagram, cut out the eight pieces in the manner indicated. The shaded parts are thrown away. A cabinetmaker had to fit together these eight pieces of veneer to form a small square table top, 6 × 6, and he stupidly cut that piece number eight into three parts.

How would you form the square without cutting any one of the pieces?

356. TWO SQUARES IN ONE

Two squares of any relative size can be cut into five pieces, in the manner shown below, that will fit together and form a larger square. But this involves cutting the smaller square. Can you show an easy method of doing it without in any way cutting the smaller square?

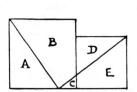

357. CUTTING THE VENEER

A cabinetmaker had a 7 × 7 square checkerboard of beautiful veneer which he wished to cut into six pieces to form three separate squares, all different sizes. How can this be done without any waste, and by cutting only along the lattice lines?

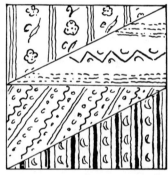

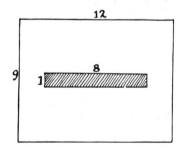

358. IMPROVISED CHESSBOARD

A good cutting-out puzzle in as few as two pieces is not often forthcoming. Here is one that I think cannot fail to interest readers. Cut this piece of checkered linoleum into only two pieces, that will fit together and form a perfect chessboard, without disturbing the checkering of black and white. Of course, it would be easy to cut off those two overhanging white squares and put them in the vacant places, but this would be doing it in three pieces.

359. THE PATCHWORK CUSHION

A lady had twenty pieces of silk, all of the same triangular shape and size. She found that four of these would fit together and form a perfect square, as in the illustration. How was she to fit together these twenty pieces to form a perfectly square patchwork cushion? There must be no waste, and no allowance need be made for turnings.

360. THE DAMAGED RUG

A lady had a valuable Persian rug 12 feet by 9 feet, which was badly damaged by fire. So she cut from the middle a strip 8 feet by 1 foot, as shown in the illustration, and then cut the remainder into two pieces that fitted together and made a perfectly square rug 10 feet by 10 feet. How did she do it? Of course, no allowance is to be made for turnings.

361. FOLDING A HEXAGON

Paper folding is a branch of puzzledom both instructive and interesting. I do not refer to folding paper into the forms of boxes, boats, frogs, and such things, for these are toys rather than puzzles, but to the solving of certain geometrical problems with paper and fingers alone.

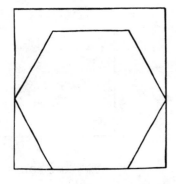

I will give a comparatively easy example. Suppose you are given a perfectly square piece of paper, how are you going to fold it so as to indicate by creases a regular hexagon, as shown in the illustration, all ready to be cut out? Of course, you must use no pencil, measure, or instrument of any kind whatever. The hexagon may be in any position in the square.

362. FOLDING A PENTAGON

Here is another puzzle in paper folding of a rather more difficult character than the hexagon example that we have considered. If you are given a perfectly square piece of paper, how are you to fold it so as to indicate by creases a regular pentagon, as in our illustration all ready to be cut out? Remember that you must use your fingers alone, without any instrument or measure whatever.

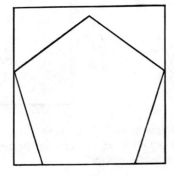

363. FOLDING AN OCTAGON

Can you cut the regular octagon from a square piece of paper without using compasses or ruler, or anything but scissors? You can fold the paper so as to make creases.

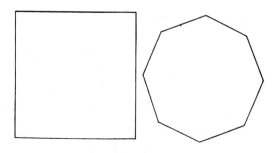

364. SQUARE AND TRIANGLE

Take a perfectly square piece of paper, and so fold it as to form the largest possible equilateral triangle. A triangle in which the sides are the same length

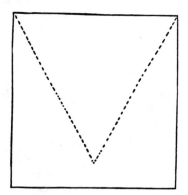

as those of the square, as shown in our diagram, will not be the largest possible. Of course, no markings or measurements may be made except by the creases themselves.

365. STRIP TO PENTAGON

Given a ribbon of paper, as in the illustration, of any length—say more than four times as long as broad—it can all be folded into a perfect pentagon, with

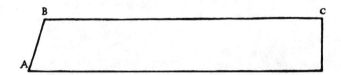

every part lying within the boundaries of the figure. The only condition is that the angle ABC must be the correct angle of two contiguous sides of a regular pentagon. How are you to fold it?

366. A CREASE PROBLEM

Fold a page, so that the bottom outside corner touches the inside edge and the crease is the shortest possible. That is about as simple a question as we

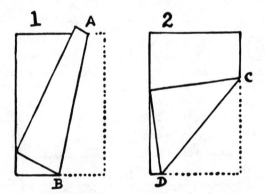

could put, but it will puzzle a good many readers to discover just where to make that fold. I give two examples of folding. It will be seen that the crease AB is considerably longer than CD, but the latter is not the shortest possible.

367. FOLDING POSTAGE STAMPS

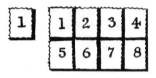

If you have eight postage stamps, 4 by 2, as in the diagram, it is very interesting to discover the various ways in which they can be folded so that they will lie under one stamp, as shown. I will say at once that they can actually be folded in forty different ways so that number 1 is face upwards and all the others invisible beneath it. Numbers 5, 2, 7, and 4 will always be face downwards, but you may arrange for any stamp except number 6 to lie next to number 1, though there are only two ways each in which numbers 7 and 8 can be brought into that position. From a little law that I discovered, I was convinced that they could be folded in the order 1, 5, 6, 4, 8, 7, 3, 2, and also 1, 3, 7, 5, 6, 8, 4, 2, with number 1 at the top, face upwards, but it puzzled me for some time to discover how.

Can the reader so fold them without, of course, tearing any of the perforation? Try it with a piece of paper well creased like the diagram, and number the stamps on both sides for convenience. It is a fascinating puzzle. Do not give it up as impossible!

368. COUNTER SOLITAIRE

This simplification of the board of the old game of solitaire lends itself to many entertaining little pastimes of patience. Copy the simple diagram on a sheet of paper or cardboard and use sixteen counters, numbered and placed as shown. The puzzle is to remove all but one counter by a succession of leaps. A counter can leap over another adjoining it to the next square beyond, if vacant, and in making the leap you remove the one jumped over. But no leap can be made in a diagonal direction.

The following is a solution in eight moves: 5–13, (6–14, 6–5), 16–15, (3–11, 3–6), 2–10, (8–7, 8–16, 8–3), (1–9, 1–2, 1–8), (4–12, 4–1). This means that 5 leaps over 13 and 13 is removed, 6 then leaps over 14 and 14 is removed, and so on. The leaps within parentheses count as one move, because the leaps are made with the same counter in succession. It will be seen that number 4 makes the last leap. Now try to find a solution, in seven moves, in which number 1 makes the last leap.

369. A NEW LEAP-FROG PUZZLE

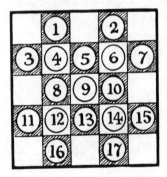

Make a rough board, as shown, and place seventeen counters on the squares indicated. The puzzle is to remove all but one by a series of leaping moves, as in checkers or solitaire. A counter can be made to leap over another to the next square beyond, if vacant, and you then remove the one jumped over. It will be seen that the first leap must be made by the central counter, number 9, and one has the choice of eight directions. A continuous series of leaps with the same counter will count as a single move. It is required to take off sixteen counters in four moves, leaving the number 9 on its original central square. Every play must be a leap.

370. TRANSFERRING THE COUNTERS

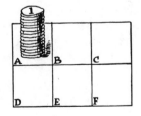

Divide a sheet of paper into six compartments, as shown in the illustration, and place a pile of fifteen counters, numbered consecutively 1, 2, 3 ... 15 downwards, in compartment A. The puzzle is to transfer the complete pile, in the fewest possible moves, to compartment F. You can move the counters one at a time to any compartment, but may never place a counter on one that bears a smaller number than itself. Thus, if you place 1 on B and 2 on C, you can then place 1 on 2, but not 2 on 1.

371. MAGIC FIFTEEN PUZZLE

This is Sam Loyd's famous 14–15 puzzle, in which you were asked to get the 14 and 15 in their proper order by sliding the blocks about in the box. It was, of course, impossible of solution. I now propose to slide them about until they shall form a perfect magic square in which the four columns, four rows, and two diagonals all add up to 30.

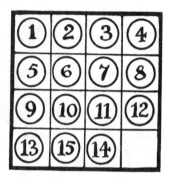

It will be found convenient to use numbered counters in place of the blocks. What are your fewest possible moves?

372. TRANSFERRING THE COUNTERS

Place ten counters on the squares of a chessboard as here shown, and transfer them to the other corner as indicated by the ten crosses. A counter may jump over any counter to the next square beyond, if vacant, either horizontally or vertically, but not diagonally, and there are no captures and no simple moves—only leaps.

Not to waste the reader's time it can be conclusively proved that this is impossible. You are now asked to add two more counters so that it may be done.

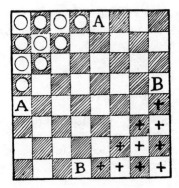

If you place these, say, on AA, they must, in the end, be found in the corresponding positions BB. Where will you place them?

373. ODDS AND EVENS

Place eight counters in a pile on the middle circle so that they shall be in proper numerical order, with 1 on the top and 8 at the bottom. It is required to transfer 1, 3, 5, 7 to the circle marked ODDS, and 2, 4, 6, 8 to the circle marked EVENS. You can only move one counter at a time from circle to circle, and you must never place a number on a smaller number, nor an odd and an even number together on the same circle. That is to say, you may

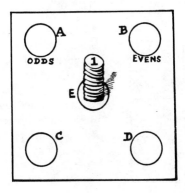

place the 1 on the top of the 3, or the 3 on the top of the 7, or the 2 on the 6, or the 2 on the 4, but you must not place the 1 on the 2, or the 4 on the 7, as that would be an odd and even together.

What are the fewest possible moves?

374. RAILWAY SHUNTING

How are the two trains in our illustration to pass one another, and proceed with their engines in front? The small sidetrack is only large enough to hold one engine or one car at a time, and no tricks, such as ropes and flying switches, are allowed. Every reversal—that is, change of direction—of an

engine is counted as a move in the solution. What is the smallest number of moves necessary?

To work on the problem, make a sketch of the track, and on it place a nickel and three pennies (heads up) for the engine and three cars on the left, and a nickel and two pennies (tails up) for the engine and two cars on the right.

375. ADJUSTING THE COUNTERS

7	24	10	19	3
12	20	8	22	23
2	15	25	18	13
11	21	5	9	16
17	4	14	1	6

Place twenty-five counters in a square in the order shown. Then it is a good puzzle to put them all into regular order so that the first line reads 1 2 3 4 5, and the second 6 7 8 9 10, and so on to the end, by taking up one counter in each hand and making them change places. Thus you might take up 7 and 1 and replace them as 1 and 7. Then take up 24 and 2 and make them also change places, when you will have the first two counters properly placed. The puzzle is to determine the fewest possible exchanges in which this can be done.

376. NINE MEN IN A TRENCH

Here are nine men in a trench. Number 1 is the sergeant, who wishes to place himself at the other end of the line—at point 1—all the other men returning to their proper places as at present. There is no room to pass in the trench, and for a man to attempt to climb over another would be a dangerous exposure. But it is not difficult with those three recesses, each of which will hold a man.

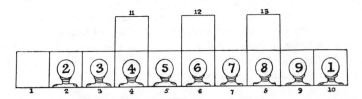

How is it to be done with the fewest possible moves? A man may go any distance that is possible in a move.

377. BLACK AND WHITE

One morning Rackbrane showed his friends this old puzzle. Place four white and four black counters alternately in a row as here shown. The puzzle is to transfer two contiguous counters to one end then move two contiguous counters to the vacant space, and so on until in four such moves they form a continuous line of four black counters followed by four white ones. Remember that two counters moved must always be contiguous ones.

"Now," he said, "as you know how to do that, try this variation. The conditions are exactly the same, only in moving a contiguous pair you must make them change sides. Thus, if you move 5, 6, to the end, you must replace them in the order 6, 5. How many moves will you now require?"

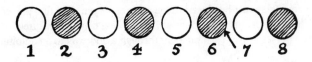

378. THE ANGELICA PUZZLE

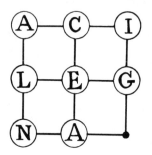

the intersecting points eight lettered counters as shown in our illustration. The puzzle is to move the counters, one at a time, along the lines from point to vacant point until you get them in the order ANGELICA thus:

A   N   G
E   L   I
C   A   .

Here is a little puzzle that will soon become quite fascinating if you attempt it. Draw a square with three lines in both directions and place on

Try to do this in the fewest possible moves. It is quite easy to record your moves, as you merely have to write the letters thus, as an example: A E L N, etc.

379. THE FLANDERS WHEEL

Place eight lettered counters on the wheel as shown. Now move them one at a time along the lines from circle to circle until the word FLANDERS can be correctly read round the rim of the wheel as at present, only that the F is in the upper circle now occupied by the N. Of course two counters cannot be in a circle at the same time. Find the fewest possible moves.

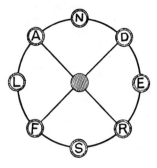

380. CATCHING THE PRISONERS

Make a rough diagram on a sheet of paper, and use counters to indicate the two warders (the men in peaked caps) and the two prisoners. At the beginning the counters must be placed in the squares shown. The first player moves each of the warders through a doorway to the next cell, in any direction. Then the second player moves each prisoner through a doorway to an adjoining cell;

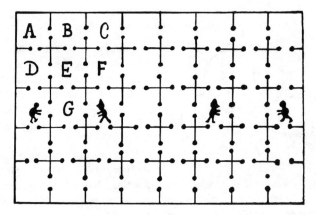

and so on until each warder captures his prisoner. If one warder makes a capture, both he and his captive are out of the game, and the other pair continue alone.

Thus (taking only one side, just for illustration of the moves), the warder on the left may go to F, then the prisoner to D, then the warder to E, then the prisoner to A, the warder to B, the prisoner to D, and so on. You may come to the conclusion that it is a hopeless chase, but it can really be done if you use a little cunning.

381. GRASSHOPPERS' QUADRILLE

It is required to make the white men change places with the black men in the fewest possible moves. There is no diagonal play or captures. The white men can only move to the right or downwards, and the black men to the left or upwards, but they may leap over one of the opposite color, as in checkers. It is quite easy when once you have hit on the method of solution.

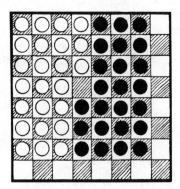

382. THE FOUR PENNIES

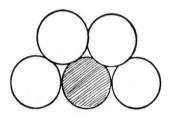

Take four pennies and arrange them on the table without the assistance of another coin or any other means of measurement, so that when a fifth penny is produced it may be placed in exact contact with each of the four (without moving them) in the manner shown in the illustration. The shaded circle represents the fifth penny.

If you trust to the eye alone you will probably fail to get the four in correct position, but it can be done with absolute exactitude. How should you proceed?

383. THE SIX PENNIES

Lay six pennies on the table, and then arrange them as shown by the six white circles in the illustration, so that if a seventh penny (the black circle) were produced it could be dropped in the center and exactly touch each of the six. It is required to get it exact, without any dependence on the eye. In this case you are not allowed to lift any penny off the table—otherwise there would be no puzzle at all—nor can any measuring

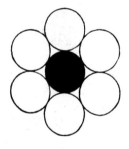

or marking be employed. You require only the six pennies.

Combinatorial

&

Topological Problems

Combinatorial & Topological Problems

384. AN IRREGULAR MAGIC SQUARE

Here we have a perfect magic square composed of the numbers 1 to 16 inclusive. The rows, columns, and two long diagonals all add up 34. Now, supposing you were forbidden to use the two numbers 2 and 15, but allowed, in their place, to repeat any two numbers already used, how would you construct your square so that rows, columns, and diagonals should still add up 34? Your success will de-

1	14	7	12
15	4	9	6
10	5	16	3
8	11	2	13

pend on which two numbers you select as substitutes for the 2 and 15.

385. A MAGIC SQUARE DELUSION

Here is a magic square of the fifth order. I have found that a great many

17	24	1	8	15
23	5	7	14	16
4	6	13	20	22
10	12	19	21	3
11	18	25	2	9

people who have not gone very profoundly into these things believe that the central number in all squares of this order must be 13. One correspondent who had devoted years to amusing himself with this particular square was astounded when I told him that any number from 1 to 25 might be in the center. I will show that this is so. Try to form such a magic square with 1 in the central cell.

141

386. DIFFERENCE SQUARES

4	3	2
7	1	9
6	5	8

Can you rearrange the nine digits in the square so that in all the eight directions the difference between one of the digits and the sum of the remaining two shall always be the same? In the example shown it will be found that all the rows and columns give the difference 3; (thus 4 + 2 − 3, and 1 + 9 − 7, and 6 + 5 − 8, etc.), but the two diagonals are wrong, because 8 − (4 + 1) and 6 − (1 + 2) is not allowed: the sum of two must not be taken from the single digit, but the single digit from the sum. How many solutions are there?

387. SWASTIKA MAGIC SQUARE

A correspondent sent me this little curiosity. It is a magic square, the rows, columns, and two diagonals all adding up 65, and all the prime numbers that occur between 1 and 25 (viz., 1, 2, 3, 5, 7, 11, 13, 17, 19, 23) are to be found within the swastika except 11. "This number," he says, "in occult lore is ominous and is associated with the eleven Curses of Ebal, so it is just as well it does not come into this potent charm of good fortune."

He is clearly under the impression that 11 cannot be got into the swastika with the other primes. But in this he is wrong, and the reader may like to try to reconstruct the square so that the swastika contains all the ten prime numbers and yet forms a correct magic square, for it is quite possible.

24	3	17	11	10
12	6	25	4	18
5	19	13	7	21
8	22	1	20	14
16	15	9	23	2

388. IS IT VERY EASY?

Here is a simple magic square, the three columns, three rows, and two diagonals adding up 72. The puzzle is to convert it into a multiplying magic square, in which the numbers in all the eight lines if *multiplied* together give the same product in every case. You are not allowed to change, or add to, any of the figures in a cell or use any arithmetical sign whatever! But you may shift the two figures within a cell. Thus, you may write 27 as 72, if you like. These simple conditions make the puzzle absurdly easy, if you once hit on the idea; if you miss it, it

27	20	25
22	24	26
23	28	21

will appear to be an utter impossibility.

389. MAGIC SQUARE TRICK

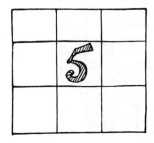

Here is an advertising trick that appeared in America many years ago. Place in the empty squares such figures (different in every case, and no two squares containing the same figure) so that they shall add up 15 in as many straight directions as possible. A large prize was offered, but no correct solution received. Can the reader guess the trick?

390. A FOUR-FIGURE MAGIC SQUARE

Because every cell in this square contains the same number, 1234, the three columns, three rows, and two long diagonals naturally add up alike. The puzzle is to form and place nine different four-figure numbers (using the same figures) so that they also shall form a perfect magic square. Remember that the numbers together

1234	1234	1234
1234	1234	1234
1234	1234	1234

must contain nine of each figure 1, 2, 3, 4, and that they must be four-square numbers without fractions or trick of any kind.

391. PROGRESSIVE SQUARES

This is a magic square, adding up 287 in every row, every column, and each of the two diagonals. If we remove the outer margin of numbers we have another square giving sums of 205. If we again remove the margin there is left a magic square adding up 123. Now fill up the vacant spaces in the diagram with such numbers from 1 to 81 inclusive as have not already been given, so that there shall be formed a magic square adding up 369 in each of twenty directions.

	20	55	30	57	28	71	26	
	14	31	50	29	60	35	68	
	58	46	38	45	40	36	24	
	65	33	43	41	39	49	17	
	64	48	42	37	44	34	18	
	10	47	32	53	22	51	72	
	56	27	52	25	54	11	62	

392. CONDITIONAL MAGIC SQUARE

Though there is nothing new to be said about the mere construction of a perfect magic square, and the subject has a very large, though scattered, literature of its own, a little variation that has some fresh condition is generally welcome. Here is a not difficult example.

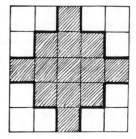

Can you form a magic square with all the columns, rows, and two long diagonals, adding up alike, with the numbers 1 to 25 inclusive, placing only the odd numbers on the shaded squares in our diagram, and the even numbers on the other squares? There are a good many solutions. Can you find one of them?

393. THE FIVE-POINTED STAR

There is something very fascinating about star puzzles. I give an example, taking the case of the simple five-pointed star. It is required to place a different number in every circle so that the four circles in a line shall add up to 24 in all the five directions. No solution is possible with ten consecutive numbers, but you can use any whole numbers you like.

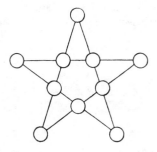

394. THE SIX-POINTED STAR

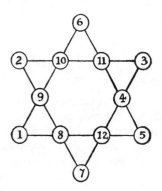

We have considered the question of the five-pointed star. We shall now find the six-pointed star even more interesting. In this case we can always use the twelve consecutive numbers 1 to 12 and the sum of the four numbers in every line will always be 26. The numbers at the six points of the star may add up to any even number from 24 to 54 inclusive, except 28 and 50, which are impossible. It will be seen that in the example I have given the six points add up to 24. If for every number in its present position you substitute its difference from 13 you will get another solution, its complementary, with the points adding up 54, which is 78 less 24. The two complementary totals will always sum to 78.

I will give the total number of different solutions and point out some of the pretty laws which govern the problem, but I will leave the reader this puzzle to solve. There are six arrangements, and six only, in which all the lines of four and the six points also add up to 26. Can you find one or all of them?

395. THE SEVEN-POINTED STAR

We have already dealt briefly with stars of five and six points. The case of the seven-pointed star is particularly interesting. All you have to do is to place the numbers 1, 2, 3, up to 14 in the fourteen disks so that every line of four disks shall add up to 30.

If you make a rough diagram and use numbered counters, you will soon find it difficult to break away from the fascination of the thing. Possibly, however, not a single reader will hit upon a simple method of solution; his answer, when found, will be obtained by mere patience and luck. Yet, like those of the large majority of the puzzles given in these pages, the solution is subject to law, if you can unravel it.

396. TWO EIGHT-POINTED STARS

The puzzles of stars with five, six, and seven points that I have given lead us to the eight-pointed star. The star may be formed in two different ways, as shown in our illustration, and the first example is a solution. The numbers 1 to 16 are so placed that every straight line of four adds up to 34. If you substitute for every number its difference from 17 you will get the complementary solution.

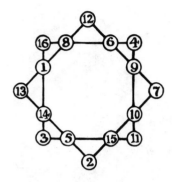
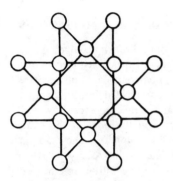

Let the reader try to discover some of the other solutions, and he will find it a very hard nut, even with this one to help him. But I will present the puzzle in an easy and entertaining form. When you know how, every arrangement in the first star can be transferred to the second one automatically. Every line of four numbers in the one case will appear in the other, only the *order* of the numbers will have to be changed. Now, with this information given, it is not a difficult puzzle to find a solution for the second star.

397. FORT GARRISONS

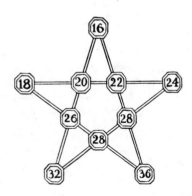

Here we have a system of fortifications. It will be seen that there are ten forts, connected by lines of outworks, and the numbers represent the strength of the small garrisons. The General wants to dispose these garrisons afresh so that there shall be 100 men in every one of the five lines of four forts. Can you show how it can be done?

The garrisons must be moved bodily —that is to say, you are not allowed to break them up into other numbers. It is quite an entertaining little puzzle with counters, and not very difficult.

398. THE CARD PENTAGON

Make a rough pentagon on a large sheet of paper. Then throw down the ten non-court cards of a suit at the places indicated in the illustration, so that the pips on every row of three cards on the sides of the pentagon shall add up alike. The example will be found faulty. After you have found the rule you will be able to deal the cards into their places without any thought. And there are very few ways of placing them.

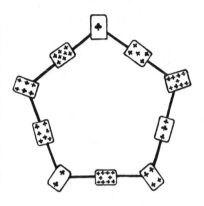

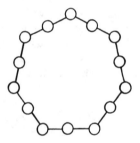

399. A HEPTAGON PUZZLE

Using the fourteen numbers, 1, 2, 3, up to 14, place a different number in every circle so that the three numbers in every one of the seven sides add up to 19.

400. ROSES, SHAMROCKS, AND THISTLES

Place the numbers 1 to 12 (one number in every design) so that they shall add up to the same sum in the following seven different ways—viz., each of the two center columns, each of the two central rows, the four roses together, the four shamrocks together, and the four thistles together.

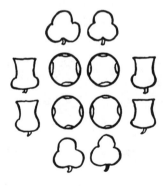

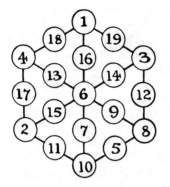

401. THE MAGIC HEXAGON

In the illustration it will be seen how we have arranged the numbers 1 to 19 so that all the twelve lines of three add up to 23. Six of these lines are, of course, the six sides, and the other six lines radiate from the center. Can you find a different arrangement that will still add up to 23 in all the twelve directions? There is only one such arrangement to be found.

402. THE WHEEL PUZZLE

Place the numbers 1 to 19 in the 19 circles, so that wherever there are three in a straight line they shall add up to 30. It is, of course, very easy.

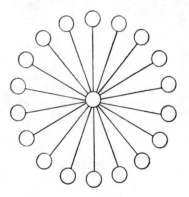

403. AT THE BROOK

In introducing liquid measuring puzzles in my book *Amusements in Mathematics,* I have said, "It is the general opinion that puzzles of this class can only be solved by trial, but I think formulas can be constructed for the solution generally of certain related cases. It is a practically unexplored field for investigation."

So far as I know, the hint has not been taken and the field is still unexplored, so I recently took advantage of a little unexpected leisure to look into the matter. The result, as I thought probable, was that I struck some new and very interesting things. For example, let us take the simplest possible case of a man who goes to a brook with only two vessels with which to measure a given quantity of water. When we are dealing, say, with a barrel of wine we may have complications arising from the barrel being full or empty, from its capacity and contents being known or unknown, from waste of wine being permitted or not permitted, and from pouring back into the barrel being allowed. All these points are eliminated. Is it then possible that any puzzle remains? Let us see.

A man goes to the brook with two measures of 15 pints and 16 pints. How is he to measure exactly 8 pints of water, in the fewest possible transactions? Filling or emptying a vessel or pouring any quantity from one vessel to another counts as a transaction.

The puzzle is not difficult, but I think the reader will find it very entertaining and instructive. I need hardly add that no tricks, such as marking or tilting the vessels, are allowed.

404. A PROHIBITION POSER

Let us now take another step and look at those cases where we are still allowed any amount of waste, though

the liquid is now limited to a stated quantity.

The American prohibition authorities discovered a full barrel of beer, and were about to destroy the liquor by letting it run down a drain when the owner pointed to two vessels standing by and begged to be allowed to retain in them a small quantity for the immediate consumption of his household. One vessel was a 7-quart and the other a 5-quart measure. The officer was a wag, and, believing it to be impossible, said that if the man could measure an exact quart into each vessel (without any pouring back into the barrel) he might do so.

How was it to be done in the fewest possible transactions without any marking or other tricks? Perhaps I should state that an American barrel of beer contains exactly 120 quarts.

405. PROHIBITION AGAIN

Let us now try to discover the fewest possible manipulations under the same conditions as in the last puzzle, except that we may now pour back into the barrel.

406. THE KEG OF WINE

A man had a 10-gallon keg of wine and a jug. One day he drew off a jugful of wine and filled up the keg with water. Later on, when the wine and water had got thoroughly mixed, he drew off another jugful, and again filled up the keg with water. The keg then contained equal quantities of wine and water. What was the capacity of the jug?

407. WATER MEASUREMENT

A maid was sent to the brook with two vessels that exactly measured 7 pints and 11 pints respectively. She had to bring back exactly 2 pints of water. What is the smallest possible number of transactions necessary? A "transaction" is filling a vessel, or emptying it, or pouring from one vessel to another.

408. MIXING THE WINE

A glass is one-third full of wine, and another glass, with equal capacity, is one-fourth full of wine. Each is filled with water and their contents mixed in a jug. Half of the mixture is poured into one of the glasses. What proportion of this is wine and what part water?

409. THE STOLEN BALSAM

Three men robbed a gentleman of a vase containing 24 ounces of balsam. While running away, they met in a forest a glass seller, of whom, in a great hurry, they purchased three vessels. On reaching a place of safety they wished to divide the booty, but they found that their vessels contained 5, 11, and 13 ounces respectively. How could they divide the balsam into equal portions?

410. DELIVERING THE MILK

A milkman one morning was driving to his dairy with two 10-gallon cans full of milk, when he was stopped by two countrywomen, who implored him to sell them a quart of milk each. Mrs. Green had a jug holding exactly 5 pints, and Mrs. Brown a jug holding exactly 4 pints, but the milkman had no measure whatever.

How did he manage to put an exact quart into each of the jugs? It was the second quart that gave him all the difficulty. But he contrived to do it in as few as nine transactions—and by a "transaction" we mean the pouring from a can into a jug, or from one jug to another, or from a jug back to the can. How did he do it?

411. THE WAY TO TIPPERARY

The popular bard assures us that "it's a long, long way to Tipperary." Look at the accompanying chart and

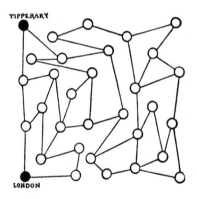

see if you can discover the best way from London to "the sweetest girl I know." The lines represent stages from town to town, and it is necessary to get from London to Tipperary in an even number of stages.

You will find no difficulty in getting there in 3, 5, 7, 9, or 11 stages, but these are odd numbers and will not do. The reason they are odd is that they all omit the sea passage, a very necessary stage. If you get to your destination in an even number of stages, it will be because you have crossed the Irish Sea. Which stage is the Irish Sea?

412. MARKING A TENNIS COURT

The lines of our tennis court are faint and need remarking. My marker is of such a kind that, though I can start anywhere and finish anywhere, it cannot be lifted off the lines when working without making a mess. I have therefore to go over some of the lines twice.

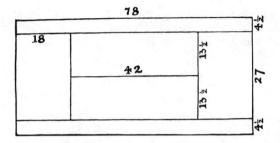

Where should I start and what route should I take, without lifting the marker, to mark the court completely and yet go over the minimum distance twice? I give the correct proportions of a tennis court in feet. What is the best route?

413. WATER, GAS, AND ELECTRICITY

I think I receive, on an average, about ten letters a month from unknown correspondents respecting this puzzle which I published some years ago under the above title. They invariably say that someone has shown it to them who did not know the answer, and they beg me to relieve their minds by telling them whether there is, or is not, any possible solution. As many of my readers may have come across the puzzle and be equally perplexed, I will try to clear up the mystery for them in a more complete way than I have done in *Amusements in Mathematics*. First of all here is the thing, as I originally gave it, for their consideration.

It is required to install water, gas, and electricity from W, G, and E to each

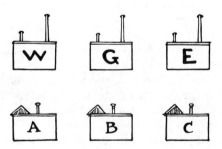

of the three houses, A, B, and C, without any pipe crossing another. Take your pencil and draw lines showing how this should be done. You will soon find yourself landed in difficulties.

414. CROSSING THE LINES

There is a little puzzle about which, for many years, I have perpetually received enquiries as to its possibility of solution. You are asked to draw the diagram in Figure 1 (exclusive of the little crosses) with three continuous strokes of the pencil, with out removing the pencil from the paper during a stroke, or going over a line twice.

As generally understood, it is quite impossible. Wherever I have placed a cross there is an "odd node," and the law for all such cases is that half as many lines will be necessary as there are odd nodes—that is, points from which you can depart in an odd number of ways. Here we have, as indicated,

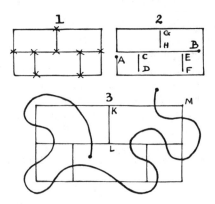

eight nodes, from each of which you can proceed in three directions (an odd number), and, therefore, *four* lines will be required. But, as I have shown in my book of *Amusements,* it may be solved by a trick, overriding the conditions as understood. You first fold the paper, and with a thick lead pencil draw CD and EF, in Figure 2, with a single stroke. Then draw the line from A to B as the second stroke, and GH as the third!

During the last few years this puzzle has taken a new form. You are given the same diagram and asked to start where you like and try to pass through every short line comprising the figure, once and once only, without crossing your own path. Figure 3 will make quite clear what is meant. It is an attempted solution, but it fails because the line from K to L has not been crossed. We might have crossed it instead of KM, but that would be no better.

Is it possible? Many who write to me about the puzzle say that though they have satisfied themselves as a "pious opinion" that it cannot be done, yet they see no way whatever of *proving* the impossibility, which is quite another matter. I will show my way of settling the question.

415. THE NINE BRIDGES

The illustration represents the map of a district with a peculiar system of irrigation. The lines are waterways enclosing the four islands, A, B, C, and D, each with its house, and it will be seen that there are nine bridges available.

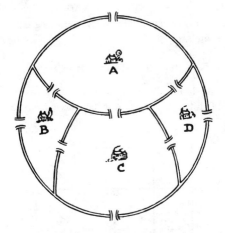

Whenever Tompkins leaves his house to visit his friend Johnson, who lives in one of the others, he always carries out the eccentric rule of crossing every one of the bridges once, and once only, before arriving at his destination.

How many different routes has he to select from? You may choose any house you like as the residence of Tompkins.

416. SINKING THE FISHING-BOATS

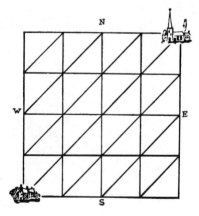

There are forty-nine fishing-boats in the North Sea. How could an enemy ram and sink the lot in twelve straight courses, starting from the place shown and finishing up at the same place?

417. GOING TO CHURCH

A man living in the house shown in the diagram wants to know what is the greatest number of different routes by which he can go to the church. The

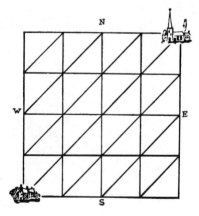

possible roads are indicated by the lines, and he always walks either due N, due E, or NE; that is, he goes so that every step brings him nearer to the church. Can you count the total number of different routes from which he may select?

418. THE SUBMARINE NET

The illustration is supposed to represent a portion of a long submarine net, and the puzzle is to make as few cuts as possible from top to bottom, to divide the net into two parts, and so make an opening for a submarine to pass through.

Where would you make the cuts? No cuts can be made through the knots. Remember that the cuts must be made from the top line to the bottom.

419. THE TWENTY-TWO BRIDGES

We have a rough map on page 158 of a district with an elaborate system of irrigation, as the various waterways and numerous bridges will show. A man set out from one of the lettered departments to pay a visit to a friend living

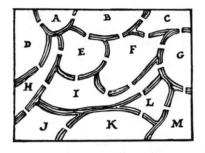

in a different department. For the purpose of pedestrian exercise he crossed every one of the bridges once, and once only.

The puzzle is to show in which two departments their houses are situated. It is exceedingly easy if you give it a few moments' thought. You must not, of course, go outside the borders of the diagram.

420. FOOTPRINTS IN THE SNOW

Four schoolboys, living respectively in the houses A, B, C, and D, attended different schools. After a snowstorm one morning their footprints were examined, and it was found that no boy had ever crossed the track of another boy, or gone outside the square boundary. Take your pencil and continue their tracks, so that the boy A goes to the school A, the boy B to the school B, and so on, without any line crossing another line.

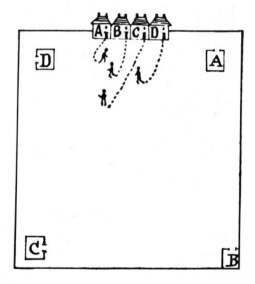

421. A MONMOUTH TOMBSTONE

```
E   I   N   E   R   N   H   O   J   S   J   O   H   N   R   E   N   I   E
I   N   E   R   N   H   O   J   S   E   S   J   O   H   N   R   E   N   I
N   E   R   N   H   O   J   S   E   I   E   S   J   O   H   N   R   E   N
E   R   N   H   O   J   S   E   I   L   I   E   S   J   O   H   N   R   E
R   N   H   O   J   S   E   I   L   E   L   I   E   S   J   O   H   N   R
N   H   O   J   S   E   I   L   E   R   E   L   I   E   S   J   O   H   N
H   O   J   S   E   I   L   E   R   E   R   E   L   I   E   S   J   O   H
O   J   S   E   I   L   E   R   E   H   E   R   E   L   I   E   S   J   O
H   O   J   S   E   I   L   E   R   E   R   E   L   I   E   S   J   O   H
N   H   O   J   S   E   I   L   E   R   E   L   I   E   S   J   O   H   N
R   N   H   O   J   S   E   I   L   E   L   I   E   S   J   O   H   N   R
E   R   N   H   O   J   S   E   I   L   I   E   S   J   O   H   N   R   E
N   E   R   N   H   O   J   S   E   I   E   S   J   O   H   N   R   E   N
I   N   E   R   N   H   O   J   S   E   S   J   O   H   N   R   E   N   I
E   I   N   E   R   N   H   O   J   S   J   O   H   N   R   E   N   I   E
```

In the burial ground attached to St. Mary's Church, Monmouth, is this arrangement of letters on one of the tombstones. In how many different ways can these words "HERE LIES JOHN RENIE" be read, starting at the central H and always passing from one letter to another that is contiguous?

422. THE FLY'S TOUR

A fly pitched on the square in the top left-hand corner of a chessboard, and then proceeded to visit every white square. He did this without ever entering a black square or ever passing through the same intersection (where a horizontal and a vertical line meet) more than once. Can you show his route? It can be done in seventeen continuous straight courses.

423. INSPECTING THE ROADS

A man starting from the town A, has to inspect all the roads shown from town to town. Their respective lengths, 13, 12, and 5 miles, are all shown. What is the shortest possible route he can adopt, ending his journey wherever he likes?

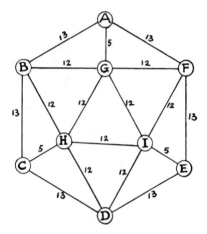

424. RAILWAY ROUTES

The diagram below represents a simplified railway system, and we want to know how many different ways there are of going from A to E, if we never go twice along the same line in any journey.

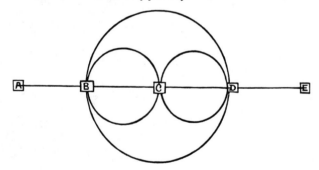

This is a very simple proposition, but practically impossible to solve until you have hit on some method of recording the routes. You see there are many ways of going, from the short route ABDE, taking one of the large loops, up to the long route ABCDBCDBCDE, which takes you over every line on the system and can itself be varied in order in many ways. How many different ways of going are there?

425. A CAR TOUR

A man started in a car from the town A, and wished to make a complete tour of these roads, going along every one of them once, and once only. How many different routes are there from which he can select? It is puzzling unless you can devise some ingenious method. Every route must end at the town A, from which you start, and you must go straight from town to town—never turning off at crossroads.

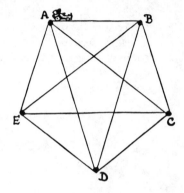

426. MRS. SIMPER'S HOLIDAY TOUR

The illustration represents a plan, very much simplified, of a tour that my friend Mrs. Simper proposes to make next autumn. It will be seen that there are twenty towns all connected by lines of railways. Mrs. Simper lives at the town marked H, and she wants to visit every one of the other towns once, and once only, ending her tour at home.

It may interest the reader to know that there are just sixty different routes from which she may select, counting

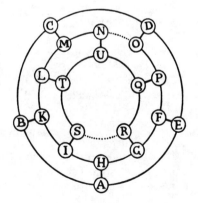

the reverse way of a route as different. There is a tunnel between N and O, and another between R and S, and the good lady objects very much to going through these. She also wants to delay her visit to D as long as possible in order to meet the convenience of a friend who resides there. The puzzle is to show Mrs. Simper her very best route in these circumstances.

427. SIXTEEN STRAIGHT RUNS

A commercial traveller started in his car from the point shown, and wished to go 76 miles in sixteen straight runs, never going along the same road twice. The dots represent towns and villages, and these are one mile apart. The lines show the route he selected. It will be seen that he carried out his plan correctly, but six towns or villages were unvisited.

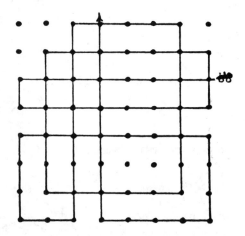

Can you show a better route by which he could have gone 76 miles in sixteen straight runs, and left only three towns unvisited?

428. PLANNING TOURS

The illustration represents a map (considerably simplified for our purposes) of a certain district. The circles are towns and villages, and the lines roads. Can you show how five automobile drivers can go from A to A, from B to B,

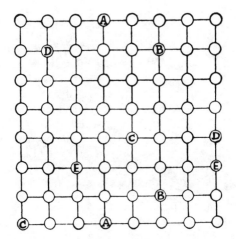

from C to C, from D to D, from E to E, respectively, without one ever crossing the track or going along the same road as another car?

Just take your pencil and mark the routes you propose, and you will probably find it a little puzzling. Of course it makes no difference which of two similar letters is the startingplace, because we are only concerned with the routes joining them. You see, if you take the route straight down from A to A you will have barred out every possible route for the other cars, with the exception of B to B, because, of course, the drivers are restricted to the roads shown on the map.

429. A MADAM PROBLEM

In how many different ways is it possible to read the word "MADAM" in the diagram? You may go as you please, upwards and downwards, forwards and backwards, any way possible along the open paths. But the letters in every case must be contiguous, and you may never pass a letter without using it.

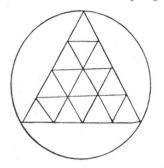

430. THE ENCIRCLED TRIANGLES

Here is a little puzzle that will require some patience and judgment to solve. You have merely to draw the design of circle and triangles in as few continuous strokes as possible. You may go over a line twice if you wish to do so, and begin and end wherever you like.

431. THE SIAMESE SERPENT

The conditions of this puzzle are exceedingly simple. You are asked to draw as much as possible of the serpent in one continuous line. Starting where you like and ending where you like, just see how much of the serpent you can trace without once taking your pencil off the paper or going over the same line twice.

An artful person might dodge the condition of going over a line twice by claiming that he drew half the width of the line going forward and

the other half going back; but he is reminded that a line has no breadth!

432. A BUNCH OF GRAPES

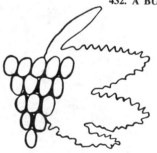

Here is a rough conventionalized sketch of a bunch of grapes. The puzzle is to make a copy of it with one continuous stroke of the pencil, never lifting the pencil from the paper, nor going over a line twice throughout. You can first try tracing it with the pencil until you get some idea of the general method.

433. A HOPSCOTCH PUZZLE

We saw some boys playing the ancient and ever popular game of hopscotch, and we wondered whether the figure that they had marked on the ground could be drawn with one continuous stroke. We found it to be possible. Can the reader draw the hopscotch figure in the illustration without taking his pencil off the paper or going along the same line twice? The curved line is not generally used in the game, but we give the figure just as we saw it.

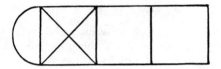

434. A WILY PUZZLE

An unscrupulous advertiser offered a hundred dollars for a correct solution to this puzzle:

"A life prisoner appealed to the king for pardon. Not being ready to favor the appeal, the king proposed a pardon on condition that the prisoner should start from cell A and go in and out of each cell in the prison, coming back to the cell A without going into any cell twice."

Either the advertiser had no answer, and knew he had none, or he was prepared to fall back on some trick or quibble. What is the best answer the reader can devise that may be held to comply with the advertiser's conditions as given?

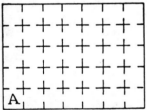

435. A TREE PLANTING PUZZLE

A man planted thirteen trees in the manner shown on the following page, and so formed eight straight rows with four trees in every row. But he was not satisfied with that second tree in the horizontal row. As he quaintly put it, "it was not doing enough work—seemed to be a sort of loafer." It certainly does

appear to be somewhat out of the
game, as the only purpose it serves is
to complete one row. So he set to
work on a better arrangement, and in
the end discovered that he could plant
thirteen trees so as to get nine rows of
four. Can the reader show how it
might be done?

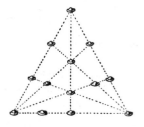

436. THE TWENTY PENNIES

If sixteen pennies are arranged in the form of a square there will be the
same number of pennies in every row, column, and each of the two long
diagonals. Can you do the same with twenty pennies?

437. TRANSPLANTING THE TREES

A man has a plantation of twenty-two trees arranged in the manner here
shown. How is he to transplant only six of the trees so that they shall then
form twenty rows with four trees in every row?

438. A PEG PUZZLE

The illustration represents a square mahogany board with forty-nine holes
in it. There are ten pegs to be placed in the positions shown, and the puzzle

is to remove only three of these pegs to different holes, so that the ten shall form five rows with four pegs in every row. Which three would you move, and where would you place them?

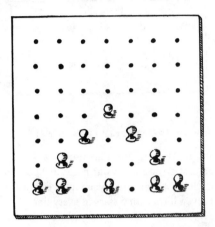

439. FIVE LINES OF FOUR

The illustration shows how ten counters may be placed on the points of the diagram where the lines intersect, so that they form five straight lines with four counters in every line, as indicated by the dotted lines. Can you find a second way of doing this?

Of course a mere reversal or reflection of the given arrangement is not considered different—it must be a new scheme altogether, and of course you cannot increase the dimensions of the diagram or alter its shape.

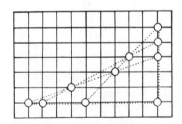

440. DEPLOYING BATTLESHIPS

Ten battleships were anchored in the form shown on page 168. The puzzle is for four ships to move to new positions (the others remaining where they are) until the ten form five straight rows with four ships in every row. How should the admiral do it?

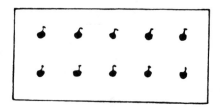

441. CONSTELLATION PUZZLE

The arrangement of stars in the illustration is known as "The British Constellation." It is not given in any star maps or books, and it is very difficult to find on the clearest night for the simple reason that it is not visible. The 21 stars form seven lines with 5 stars in every line.

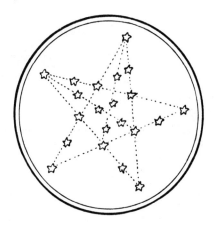

Can you rearrange these 21 stars so that they form eleven straight lines with 5 stars in every line? There are many solutions. Try to find a symmetrical one.

442. THE FOUR-COLOR MAP THEOREM

For just about fifty years various mathematicians, including De Morgan, Cayley, Kempe, Heawood, Heffter, Wernicke, Birkhoff, Franklin, and many others have attempted to prove the truth of this theorem, and in a long and learned article in the *American Mathematical Monthly* for July-August, 1923,

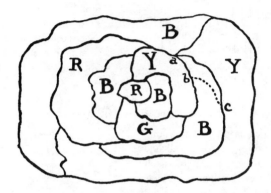

Professor Brahana, of the University of Illinois, states that "the problem is still unsolved." It is simply this, that in coloring any map under the condition that no contiguous countries shall be colored alike, not more than four colors can ever be necessary. Countries only touching at a point, like two Blues and two Yellows at *a* in the diagram, are not contiguous. If the boundary line *ca* had been, instead, at *cb*, then the two Yellows would be contiguous, but that would simply be a different map, and I should have only to substitute Green for that outside Yellow to make it all right. In fact, that Yellow might have been Green as the map at present stands.

I will give, in condensed form, a suggested proof of my own which several good mathematicians to whom I have shown it accept as quite valid. Two others, for whose opinion I have great respect, think it fails for a reason that the former maintain will not "hold water." The proof is in a form that anybody can understand. It should be remembered that it is one thing to be convinced, as everybody is, that the thing is true, but quite another to give a rigid proof of it.

443. A SWASTIKLAND MAP

Here is a puzzle that the reader will probably think he has solved at almost the first glance. But will he be correct? Swastikland is divided in the manner shown in our illustration. The Lord High Keeper of the Maps was ordered so to color this map of the country that there should be a different color on each side of every boundary line. What was the smallest possible number of colors that he required?

444. COLORING THE MAP

Colonel Crackham asked his young son one morning to color all the twenty-six districts in this map in such a way that no two contiguous districts should be of the same color. The lad looked at it for a moment, and replied, "I haven't enough colors by one in my box."

This was found to be correct. How many colors had he? He was not allowed to use black and white—only colors.

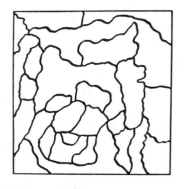

445. PICTURE PRESENTATION

A wealthy collector had ten valuable pictures. He proposed to make a presentation to a public gallery, but could not make up his mind as to how many he would give. So it amused him to work out the exact number of different ways. You see, he could give any one picture, any two, any three, and so on, or give the whole ten.

The reader may think it a long and troublesome calculation, but I will give a little rule that will enable him to get the answer in all such cases without any difficulty and only trivial labor.

446. A GENERAL ELECTION

In how many different ways may a Parliament of 615 members be elected if there are only four parties: Conservatives, Liberals, Socialists, and Independents? You see you might have C. 310, L. 152, S. 150, I. 3; or C. 0, L. 0, S. 0, I. 615; or C. 205, L. 205, S. 205, I. 0; and so on. The candidates are indistinguishable, as we are only concerned with the party numbers.

447. THE MAGISTERIAL BENCH

A friend at Singapore asked me some time ago to give him my solution to this problem. A bench of magistrates (he does not say where) consists of two Englishmen, two Scotsmen, two Welshmen, one Frenchman, one Italian, one Spaniard, and one American. The Englishmen will not sit beside one another, the Scotsmen will not sit beside one another, and the Welshmen also object to sitting together.

In how many different ways may the ten men sit in a straight line so that no two men of the same nationality shall ever be next to one another?

448. CROSSING THE FERRY

Six persons, all related, have to cross a river in a small boat that will only hold two. Mr. Webster, who had to plan the little affair, had quarrelled with his father-in-law and his son, and, I am sorry to say, Mrs. Webster was not on speaking terms with her own mother or her daughter-in-law. In fact, the relations were so strained that it was not safe to permit any of the belligerents to pass over together or to remain together on the same side of the river. And to prevent further discord, no man was to be left with two women or two men with three women.

How are they to perform the feat in the fewest possible crossings? No tricks, such as making use of a rope or current, or swimming across, are allowed.

449. MISSIONARIES AND CANNIBALS

There is a strange story of three missionaries and three cannibals, who had to cross a river in a small boat that would only carry two men at a time.

Being acquainted with the peculiar appetites of the cannibals, the missionaries could never allow their companions to be in a majority on either side of the river. Only one of the missionaries and one of the cannibals could row the boat. How did they manage to get across?

450. CROSSING THE RIVER

During the Turkish stampede in Thrace, a small detachment found itself confronted by a wide and deep river. However, they discovered a boat in which two children were rowing about. It was so small that it would only carry the two children, or one grown person.

How did the officer get himself and his 357 soldiers across the river and leave the two children finally in joint possession of their boat? And how many times need the boat pass from shore to shore?

451. A GOLF COMPETITION PUZZLE

I was asked to construct some schedules for players in American golf competitions. The conditions are:

(1) Every player plays every other player once, and once only.

(2) There are half as many links as players, and every player plays twice on every links except one, on which he plays but once.

(3) All the players play simultaneously in every round, and the last round is the one in which every player is playing on a links for the first time.

I have written out schedules for a long series of even numbers of players up to twenty-six, but the problem is too difficult for this book except in its most simple form—for six players. Can the reader, calling the players A, B, C, D, E, and F, and pairing these in all possible ways, such as AB, CD, EF, AF, BD, CE, etc., complete the above simple little table for six players?

ROUNDS				
1	2	3	4	5

1ST LINKS
2ND LINKS
3RD LINKS

452. FOOTBALL RESULTS

Near the close of a football season a correspondent informed me that when he was returning from Glasgow after the international match between Scotland and England the following table caught his eye in a newspaper:

	Played	Won	Lost	Drawn	Goals For	Goals Against	Points
Scotland	3	3	0	0	7	1	6
England	3	1	1	1	2	3	3
Wales	3	1	1	1	3	3	3
Ireland	3	0	3	0	1	6	0

As he knew, of course, that Scotland had beaten England by 3–0, it struck him that it might be possible to find the scores in the other five matches from the table. In this he succeeded. Can you discover from it how many goals were won, drawn, or lost by each side in every match?

453. THE DAMAGED MEASURE

Here is a new puzzle that is interesting, and it reminds one, though it is really very different, of the classical problem by Bachet concerning the weight that was broken in pieces which would then allow of any weight in pounds being determined from one pound up to the total weight of all the pieces. In the present case a man has a yardstick from which 3 inches have been broken off, so that it is only 33 inches in length. Some of the graduation marks are also obliterated, so that only eight of these marks are legible; yet he is able to measure any given number of inches from 1 inch up to 33 inches. Where are these marks placed?

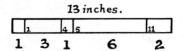

As an example, I give in the illustration the case of a 13-inch rod with four markings. If I want to measure 4 inches, I take 1 and 3; for 8 inches, 6 and 2; for 10 inches, 3, 1, and 6; and so on. Of course, the exact measure must be taken at once on the rod; otherwise the single mark of 1 inch repeated a sufficient number of times would measure any length, which would make the puzzle absurd.

454. THE SIX COTTAGES

A circular road, twenty-seven miles long, surrounds a tract of wild and desolate country, and on this road

are six cottages so placed that one cottage or another is at a distance of one, two, three up to twenty-six miles inclusive from some other cottage. Thus, Brown may be a mile from Stiggins, Jones two miles from Rogers, Wilson three miles from Jones, and so on. Of course, they can walk in either direction as required.

Can you place the cottages at distances that will fulfill these conditions? The illustration is intended to give no clue as to the relative distances.

455. FOUR IN LINE

Here we have a board of thirty-six squares, and four counters are so placed in a straight line that every square of the board is in line horizontally, vertically, or diagonally with at least one counter. In other words, if you regard them as chess queens, every square on the board is attacked by at least one queen. The puzzle is to find in how many different ways the four counters may be placed in a straight line so that every square shall thus be in line with a counter.

Every arrangement in which the counters occupy a different set of four squares is a different arrangement. Thus, in the case of the example given, they can be moved to the next column to the right with equal effect, or they may be transferred to either of the two central rows of the board. This arrangement, therefore, produces four solutions by what we call reversals or reflections of the board. Remember

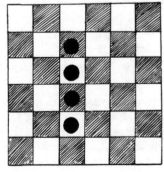

that the counters must always be disposed in a straight line. It will be found an entertaining little puzzle.

456. FLIES ON WINDOW PANES

Here is a window with eighty-one panes. There are nine flies on as many panes, and no fly is in line with another one horizontally, vertically, or diagonally. Six of these flies are very torpid and do not move, but each of the remaining three goes to an adjoining pane. And yet, after this change of station, no fly is in line with another.

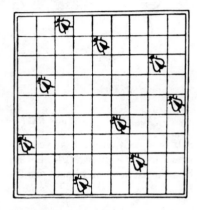

Which are the three lively flies, and to which three panes (at present unoccupied) do they pass?

457. CITY LUNCHEONS

The clerks attached to the firm of Pilkins and Popinjay arranged that three of them would lunch together every day at a particular table so long as they could avoid the same three men sitting down twice together. The same number of clerks of Messrs. Radson, Robson, and Ross decided to do precisely the same, only with four men at a time instead of three. On working it out they found that Radson's staff could keep it up exactly three times as many days as their neighbors.

What is the least number of men there could have been in each staff?

458. THE NECKLACE PROBLEM

How many different necklaces can be made with eight beads, where each bead may be either black or white, the beads being indistinguishable except by color?

We may have eight white or eight black, or seven white and one black, or six white and two black, as in our illustration on page 176. Of course, if

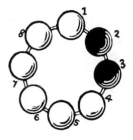

you exchange black number 3 with 4, or with 5, or with 6, you get different necklaces. But if you exchange 3 with 7 it will be the same as 3 with 5, because it is merely turning the necklace over. So we have to beware of counting such repetitions as different. The answer is a much smaller one than the reader may anticipate.

459. AN EFFERVESCENT PUZZLE

In how many different ways can the letters in the word EFFERVESCES be arranged in a line without two E's

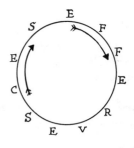

ever appearing together? Of course similar letters, such as FF, have no separate identity, so that to interchange them will make no difference.

When the reader has done this he should try the case where the letters have to be arranged differently in a circle, as shown, with no two E's together. We are here, of course, only concerned with the order of the letters and not with their positions on the circumference, and you must always read in a clockwise direction, as indicated by the arrow.

460. TESSELLATED TILES

Here we have twenty tiles, all colored with the same four colors, and the order of the coloring is indicated by the shadings: thus, the white may represent white; the black, blue; the striped, red; and the dotted, yellow.

The puzzle is to select any sixteen of these tiles that you choose and arrange them in the form of a square, always placing similar colors together—white against white, red against red, and so on. It is quite easy to make the squares

in paper or cardboard, and color them according to taste, but the order of the colors must be exactly as shown in the illustration.

461. THE THIRTY-SIX LETTER PUZZLE

If you try to fill up this square by repeating the letters A, B, C, D, E, F, so that no A shall be in a line, across, downwards or diagonally, with another A, no B with another B, no C with another C, and so on, you will find that it is impossible to get in all the thirty-six letters under these conditions.

A	B	C	D	E	F

The puzzle is to place as many letters as possible. Probably the reader will leave more blank spaces than there need be.

462. THE TEN BARRELS

A merchant had ten barrels of sugar, which he placed in the form of a pyramid, as shown on following page. Every barrel bore a different number, except one, which was not marked. It will be seen that he had accidentally

arranged them so that the numbers in the three sides added up alike—that is, to 16.

Can you rearrange them so that the three sides shall sum to the smallest number possible? Of course the central barrel (which happens to be 7 in the illustration) does not come into the count.

463. LAMP SIGNALLING

Two spies on the opposite sides of a river contrived a method for signalling by night. They each put up a stand, like our illustration, and each possessed three lamps which could show either white, red, or green light. They constructed a code in which every different signal meant a sentence. You will, of course, see that a single lamp hung on any one of the hooks could only mean the same thing, that two lamps hung on the upper hooks 1 and 2 could not be distinguished from two on 4 and 5. Two red lamps on 1 and 5 could be distinguished from two on 1 and 6. And two on

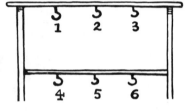

1 and 2 would be different from two on 1 and 3.

Remembering the variations of color as well as of position, what is the greatest number of signals that could be sent?

464. THE HANDCUFFED PRISONERS

Once upon a time there were nine prisoners of particularly dangerous character who had to be carefully watched. Every weekday they were taken out for exercise, handcuffed together, as shown in the sketch made by one of their guards. On no day in any one week were the same two men to

be handcuffed together. It will be
seen how they were sent out on Monday. Can you arrange the nine men
in triplets for the remaining five days?

It will be seen that number 1 cannot again be handcuffed to number 2
(on either side), nor number 2 with
number 3, but, of course, number 1
and number 3 can be put together.
Therefore, it is quite a different problem from the old one of the Fifteen
Schoolgirls, and it will be found to
be a fascinating teaser and amply re-
pay for the leisure time spent on its
solution.

465. SEATING THE PARTY

As the Crackham family were taking their seats on starting out on their tour
Dora asked in how many different ways they could all be seated, as there were
six of them and six seats—one beside the driver, two with their backs to the
driver, and two behind, facing the driver—if no two of the same sex are ever
to sit side by side?

As the Colonel, Uncle Jabez, and George were the only ones who could
drive, it required just a little thinking out. Perhaps the reader will like to
work out the answer concerning which they were all agreed at the end of the
day.

466. QUEER GOLF

A certain links had nine holes, 300, 250, 200, 325, 275, 350, 225, 375, and
400 yards apart. If a man could always strike the ball in a perfectly straight
line and send it exactly one of two distances, so that it would either go
towards the hole, pass over it, or drop into it, what would the two distances
be that would carry him in the least number of strokes round the whole course?

Two very good distances are 125 and 75, which carry you round in twenty-
eight strokes, but this is not the correct answer.

467. THE ARCHERY MATCH

On a target on which the scoring was 40 for the bull's-eye, and 39, 24, 23, 17, and 16 respectively for the rings from the center outwards, as shown in the illustration, three players had a match with six arrows each. The result was: Miss Dora Talbot, 120 points; Reggie Watson, 110 points; Mrs. Finch, 100 points. Every arrow scored, and the bull's-eye was only once hit.

Can you, from these facts, deter-

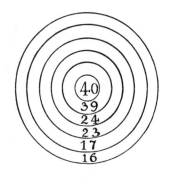

mine the exact six hits made by each competitor?

468. TARGET PRACTICE

Colonel Crackham paid a visit one afternoon by invitation to the Slocomb-on-Sea Toxophilite Club, where he picked up the following little poser.

Three men in a competition had each six shots at a target, and the result is shown in our illustration, where they all hit the target every time. The bull's-eye scores 50, the next ring 25, the next 20, the next 10, the next 5, the next 3, the next 2, and the outside ring scores only 1. It will be seen that the hits on the target are one bull's-eye, two 25's, three 20's, three 10's, three 1's, and two hits in every other ring. Now the three men tied with an equal score.

Next morning the Colonel asked his family to show the exact scoring of each man. Will it take the reader many minutes to find the correct answer?

469. TOM TIDDLER'S GROUND

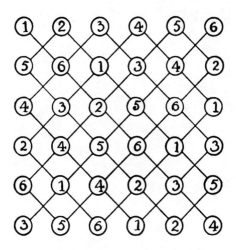

The Crackham family were comfortably accommodated at the "Blue Boar" at Puddlebury. Here they had the luck to come upon another guest who was clearly engaged in solving some sort of puzzle. The Colonel contrived a conversation with him, and learned that the puzzle was called "Tom Tiddler's Ground."

"You know," said the stranger, "the words, 'I am on Tom Tiddler's ground picking up gold and silver.' Here we have a piece of land marked off with 36 circular plots, on each of which is deposited a bag containing as many dollars as the figures indicate in the diagram. I am allowed to pick up as many bags as I like, provided I do not take two lying on the same line. What is the greatest amount of money I can secure?"

470. THE SEVEN CHILDREN

Four boys and three girls are seated in a row at random. What are the chances that the two children at the ends of the row will be girls?

Game Puzzles

Game Puzzles

471. TIC TAC TOE

Every child knows how to play this ancient game. You make a square of nine cells, and each of the two players, playing alternately, puts his mark (a zero or a cross, as the case may be) in a cell with the object of getting three in a line. Whichever player gets three in a line wins. I have said in my book

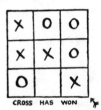

CROSS HAS WON

The Canterbury Puzzles that between two players who thoroughly understand the play every game should be drawn, for neither party could ever win except through the blundering of his opponent. Can you prove this? Can you be sure of not losing a game against an expert opponent?

472. THE HORSESHOE GAME

This little game is an interesting companion to tic tac toe. There are two players. One has two white counters, the other two black. Playing alternately, each places a counter on a vacant point, where he leaves it. When all are played, you slide only, and the player is beaten who is so blocked that he cannot move. In the example, Black has just placed his lower counter. White now slides his lower one to the center, and wins. Black should have played to the

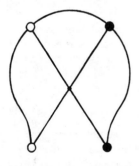

center himself and won. Now, which player ought to win at this game?

185

473. TURNING THE DIE

This is played with a single die. The first player calls any number he chooses, from 1 to 6, and the second player throws the die at hazard. Then

they take it in turns to roll over the die in any direction they choose, but never giving it more than a quarter turn. The score increases as they proceed, and the player wins who manages to score 25 or force his opponent to score beyond 25. I will give an example game. A calls 6, and B happens to throw a 3 (as shown in our illustration), making the score 9. Now A decides to turn up 1, scoring 10; B turns up 3, scoring 13; A turns up 6, scoring 19; B turns up 3, scoring 22; A turns up 1, scoring 23; and B turns up 2, scoring 25 and winning.

What call should A make in order to have the best chance of winning? Remember that the numbers on opposite sides of a correct die always sum to 7, that is, 1–6, 2–5, 3–4.

474. THE THREE DICE

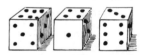

Mason and Jackson were playing with three dice. The player won whenever the numbers thrown added up to one of two numbers he selected at the beginning of the game. As a matter of fact, Mason selected seven and thirteen, and one of his winning throws is shown in the illustration.

What were his chances of winning a throw? And what two other numbers should Jackson have selected for his own throws to make his chances of winning exactly equal?

475. THE 37 PUZZLE GAME

Here is a beautiful new puzzle game, absurdly simple to play but quite fascinating. To most people it will seem to be practically a game of chance—equal for both players—but

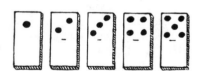

there are pretty subtleties in it, and I will show how to win with certainty.

Place the five dominoes, 1, 2, 3, 4, 5, on the table. There are two players, who play alternately. The first player places a coin on any domino, say the 5, which scores 5; then the second player removes the coin to another domino, say to the 3, and adds that domino, scoring 8; then the first player removes the coin again, say to the 1, scoring 9; and so on. The player who scores 37, or forces his opponent to score more than 37, wins. Remember, the coin must be removed to a different domino at each play.

476. THE 22 GAME

Here is a variation of our little "Thirty-one Game" (*Canterbury Puzzles:* No. 79). Lay out the sixteen cards as shown. Two players alternately turn down a card and add it to the common score, and the player who makes the score of 22, or forces his opponent to go beyond that number, wins. For example, A turns down a 4, B turns down a 3 (counting 7), A turns down a 4

(counting 11), B plays a 2 (counting 13), A plays 1 (14), B plays 3 (17), and whatever A does, B scores the winning 22 next play. Again, supposing the play was 3–1, 1–2, 3–3, 1–2, 1–4, scoring 21, the second player would win again, because there is no 1 left and his opponent must go beyond 22.

Which player should always win, and how?

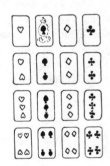

477. THE NINE SQUARES GAME

Make the simple square diagram shown on page 188 and provide a box of matches. The side of the large square is three matches in length. The game is, playing one match at a time alternately, to enclose more of those small squares than your opponent. For every small square that you enclose you not only score one point, but you play again. The illustration shows an illustrative game in progress. Twelve matches are placed, my opponent and myself having made six plays each, and, as I had first play, it is now my turn to place a match.

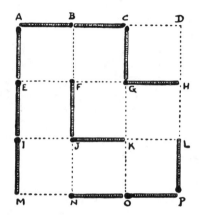

What is my best line of play in order to win most squares? If I play FG my opponent will play BF and score one point. Then, as he has the right to play again, he will score another with EF and again with IJ, and still again with GK. If he now plays CD, I have nothing better than DH (scoring one), but, as I have to play again, I am compelled, whatever I do, to give him all the rest. So he will win by 8 to 1—a bad defeat for me.

What should I have played instead of that disastrous FG? There is room for a lot of skillful play in the game, and it can never end in a draw.

478. THE TEN CARDS

Place any ten playing cards in a row as shown. There are two players. The first player may turn down any single card he chooses. Then the second player can turn down any single card or two adjoining cards. And so on. The player who turns down the last card wins.

Remember that the first player must turn down a single, but afterwards either player can turn down either a single or two adjoining cards, as he pleases. Should the first or second player win?

Domino Puzzles

Domino Puzzles

479. THE DOMINO SWASTIKA

Here is a little puzzle by Mr. Wilfred Bailey. Form a square frame with twelve dominoes, as shown in the illustration. Now, with only four extra dominoes, form within the frame a swastika. The reader may hit on the idea at once, or it may give him considerable trouble. In any case he cannot fail to be pleased with the solution.

480. DOMINO FRACTIONS

Here is a new puzzle with dominoes. Taking an ordinary box, discard all doubles and blanks. Then, substituting figures for the pips, regard the remaining fifteen dominoes as fractions. It will be seen in the illustration that I have so arranged them that the fractions in every row of five dominoes sum to exactly 2½. But I have only used proper fractions. You are allowed to use as many improper fractions (such as ⅔, ½, ⁶⁄₁) as you like, but must make the five dominoes in every rank sum to 10.

$$\frac{3}{4} + \frac{1}{4} + \frac{3}{6} + \frac{1}{2} + \frac{2}{4} = 2\tfrac{1}{2}$$

$$\frac{5}{6} + \frac{2}{6} + \frac{1}{3} + \frac{4}{5} + \frac{1}{5} = 2\tfrac{1}{2}$$

$$\frac{4}{6} + \frac{1}{6} + \frac{2}{3} + \frac{3}{5} + \frac{2}{5} = 2\tfrac{1}{2}$$

481. A NEW DOMINO PUZZLE

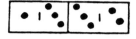

It will be seen that I have selected and placed together two dominoes so that by taking the pips in unbroken conjunction I can get all the numbers from 1 to 9 inclusive. Thus, 1, 2, and 3 can be taken alone; then 1 and 3 make 4; 3 and 2 make 5; 3 and 3 make 6; 1, 3, and 3 make 7; 3, 3, and 2 make

8; and 1, 3, 3, and 2 make 9. It would not have been allowed to take the 1 and the 2 to make 3, nor to take the first 3 and the 2 to make 5. The numbers would not have been in conjunction.

Now try to arrange four dominoes so that you can make the pips in this way sum to any number from 1 to 23 inclusive. The dominoes need not be placed 1 against 1, 2 against 2, and so on, as in play.

482. A DOMINO SQUARE

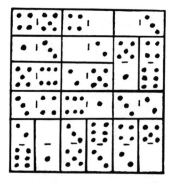

Select any eighteen dominoes you please from an ordinary box, and arrange them any way you like in a square so that no number shall be repeated in any row or any column. The example given is imperfect, for it will be seen that though no number is repeated in any one of the columns yet three of the rows break the condition. There are two 4's and two blanks in the first row, two 5's and two 6's in the third row, and two 3's in the fourth row.

Can you form an arrangement without such errors? Blank counts as a number.

483. A DOMINO STAR

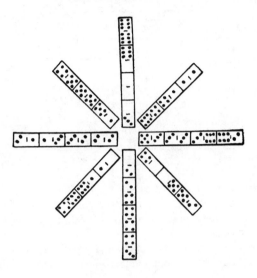

Place the twenty-eight dominoes, as shown in the illustration, so as to form a star with alternate rays of four and three dominoes. Every ray must contain twenty-one pips (in the example only one ray contains this number) and the central numbers must be 1, 2, 3, 4, 5, 6, and two blanks, as at present, and these may be in any order. In every ray the dominoes must be placed according to the ordinary rule, six against six, blank against blank, and so on.

484. DOMINO GROUPS

I wonder how many of my readers know that if you lay out the twenty-eight dominoes in line according to the ordinary rule—six against six, two against two, blank against blank, and so on—the last number must always be the same as the first, so that they will really always form a circle. It is a very ancient trick to conceal one domino (but do not take a double) and then ask him to arrange all the others in line without your seeing. It will astonish him when you tell him, after he has succeeded, what the two end numbers are. They must be those on the domino that you have withdrawn, for that domino com-

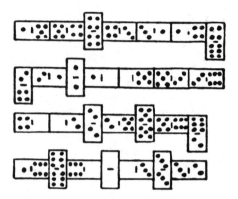

pletes the circle. If the dominoes are laid out in the manner shown in our illustration and I then break the line into four lengths of seven dominoes each, it will be found that the sum of the pips in the first group is 49, in the second 34, in the third 46, and in the fourth 39.

I want to play them out so that all the four groups of seven when the line is broken shall contain the same number of pips. Can you find a way of doing it?

485. LES QUADRILLES

This old French puzzle will, I think, be found very interesting. It is required to arrange a complete set of twenty-eight dominoes so as to form the figure

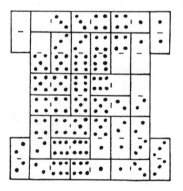

shown in our illustration, with all the numbers forming a series of squares. Thus, in the upper two rows we have a square of blanks, and a square of four 3's, and a square of 4's, and a square of 1's; in the third and fourth rows we have squares of 5, 6, and blank, and so on. This is, in fact, a perfect solution under the conditions usually imposed, but what I now ask for is an arrangement with no blanks anywhere on the outer edge. At present every number from blank to 6 inclusive will be found somewhere on the margin. Can you construct an arrangement with all the blanks inside?

486. DOMINO FRAMES

Take an ordinary set of twenty-eight dominoes and return double 3, double 4, double 5, and double 6 to the box as not wanted. Now, with the remainder

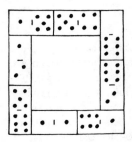

form three square frames, in the manner shown, so that the pips in every side shall add up alike. In the example given the sides sum to 15. If this were to stand, the sides of the two other frames must also sum to 15. But you can take any number you like, and it will be seen that it is not required to place 6 against 6, 5 against 5, and so on, as in play.

487. DOMINO HOLLOW SQUARES

Every game lends itself to the propounding of interesting little puzzles.

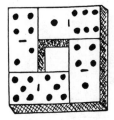

Let us, as an example, take the following poser, devised from an ordinary box of twenty-eight dominoes. It is required with these twenty-eight to form seven hollow squares, all similar to the example given, so that the pips in the four sides of every square shall add up alike. All these seven squares need not have the same sum, and, of course, the example given need not be one of your set.

The reader will probably find it easy to form six of the squares correctly, in many ways, but the trouble generally begins when you come to make the seventh square with the four remaining dominoes.

488. DOMINO SEQUENCES

A boy who had a complete set of dominoes, up to double 9, was trying to arrange them all in sequence, in the usual way—6 against 6, 3 against 3, blank against blank, etc. His father said to him, "You are attempting an impossibility, but if you will let me pick out four dominoes it can then be done. And those that I take shall contain the smallest total number of pips possible in the circumstances."

Now, which dominoes might the father have selected? Remember that the dominoes in common use in this country stop at double 6, but we are here using a set up to double 9.

489. TWO DOMINO SQUARES

Arrange the twenty-eight dominoes as shown in the diagram to form two squares so that the pips in every one of the eight sides shall add up alike. The dominoes being on the table one day recently, we set ourselves the above task, and found it very interesting.

The constant addition must be within limits to make the puzzle possible, and it will be found interesting to find these limits. Of course, the dominoes need not be laid according to the rule, 6 against 6, blank against blank, and so on.

490. DOMINO MULTIPLICATION

We have received the following entertaining puzzle from W. D. W., of Philadelphia, Pa.:

Four dominoes may be so placed as to form a simple multiplication sum if we regard the pips as figures. The example here shown will make everything perfectly clear. Now, the puzzle is, using all the twenty-eight dominoes to arrange them so as to form seven such little sums in multiplication.

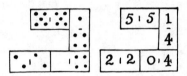

It will be found comparatively easy to construct six such groups, while the four dominoes left over are impossible of arrangement. But it can be done, and the quest will be found amusing. No blank may be placed at the left end of the multiplicand or product.

491. DOMINO RECTANGLE

Here is a new domino puzzle that I hope will be found entertaining. Arrange

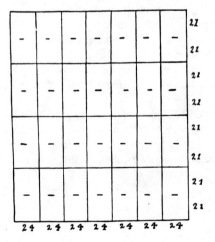

the twenty-eight dominoes exactly as shown in the illustration, where the pips are omitted, so that the pips in every one of the seven columns shall sum to 24, and the pips in every one of the eight rows to 21. The dominoes need not be 6 against 6, 4 against 4, and so on.

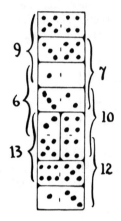

492. THE DOMINO COLUMN

Arrange the twenty-eight dominoes in a column so that the three sets of pips, taken anywhere, shall add up alike on the left side and on the right. Such a column has been started in the diagram. It will be seen that the top three add up to 9 on both sides, the next three add up to 7 on both sides, and so on. This is merely an example, so you can start afresh if you like.

493. ARRANGING THE DOMINOES

Somebody reminded Professor Rackbrane one morning at the breakfast table that he had promised to tell them in how many different ways the set of twenty-eight dominoes may be arranged in a straight line, in accordance with the original rule of the game, left to right and right to left, in any arrangement counting as different ways. Later on he told them that the answer was 7,959,229,931,520 different ways. He said that it was an exceedingly difficult problem.

He then proposed that they should themselves find out in how many different ways the fifteen smaller dominoes (after discarding all those bearing a 5 or a 6) may similarly be arranged in a line. Of course, you always place 1 against 1, 6 against 6, and so on, the two directions counting different.

Match Puzzles

Match Puzzles

494. A NEW MATCH PUZZLE

I have a box of matches. I find that I can form with them any given pair of these four regular figures, using all the matches every time. Thus, if there were eleven matches, I could form with them, as shown, the triangle and pentagon or the pentagon and hexagon, or the square and triangle (by using only three matches in the triangle); but could not with eleven matches form the triangle

and hexagon, or the square and pentagon, or the square and hexagon. Of course there must be the same number of matches in every side of a figure.

What is the smallest number of matches I can have in the box?

495. HURDLES AND SHEEP

This is a little puzzle that you can try with matches. A farmer says that four of his hurdles will form a square enclosure just sufficient for one sheep. That

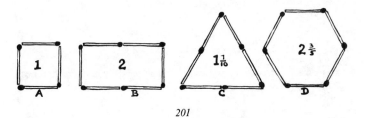

being so, what is the smallest number of hurdles that he will require for enclosing ten sheep? Everything depends on the shape of your enclosure. The only other way of placing the four matches (or hurdles) in A is to form a diamond-shaped figure, and the more attenuated this diamond becomes the smaller will be its area, until the sides meet, when there will be no area enclosed at all.

If you place six matches, as in B, you will have room for two sheep. But if you place them as in C, you will only have room for one sheep, for seven-tenths of a sheep will only exist as mutton. And if you place them as in D, you can still only accommodate two sheep, which is the maximum for six hurdles. How many hurdles do you require for ten sheep?

496. THE TWENTY MATCHES

The illustration shows how twenty matches, divided into two groups of fourteen and six, may form two enclosures so that one space enclosed is exactly three times as large as the other. Now divide the twenty matches into two groups of thirteen and seven, and with them again make two enclosures, one exactly three times as large as the other.

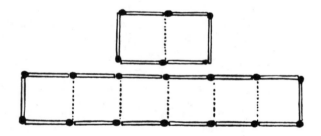

497. A MATCH PUZZLE

The sixteen squares of a chessboard are enclosed by sixteen matches. It is required to place an *odd* number of matches inside the square so as to enclose four groups of four squares each. There are obvious and easy ways of doing it with 8, 10, or 12 matches, but these are *even* numbers.

It may only take the reader a few moments to discover the four distinctive ways (mere reversals and reflections not counting as different) of doing it with an odd number of matches. Of course no duplicated matches are allowed.

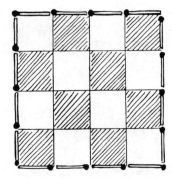

498. AN INGENIOUS MATCH PUZZLE

Place six matches as shown, and then shift one match without touching the others so that the new arrangement shall represent an arithmetical fraction equal to 1. The match forming the horizontal fraction bar must not be the one moved.

499. FIFTY-SEVEN TO NOTHING

After the last puzzle, this one should be easy.

It will be seen that we have arranged six cigarettes (matches will do just as well) so as to represent the number 57. The puzzle is to remove any two of them

you like (without disturbing any of the others) and so replace them as to represent 0, or nothing. Remember that you can only shift two cigarettes. There are two entirely different solutions. Can you find one or both?

500. THE FIVE SQUARES

Here is a new little match puzzle that will perplex a good many readers,

though they will smile when they see the answer. It will be seen that the twelve matches are so arranged that they form four squares. Can you rearrange the same number of matches (all lying flat on the table) so that they enclose five squares?

Every square must be entirely "empty" or the illustration itself will show five squares if we were allowed to count the large square forming the boundary. No duplicated match or loose ends are allowed.

501. A MATCH TRICK

We pulled open a box of matches the other day, and showed some friends that there were only about twelve matches in it. When opened at that end no head was visible. The heads were all at the other end of the box. We told them after we had closed the box in front of them we would give it a shake, and, on reopening, they would find a match turned round with its head visible. They afterwards examined it to see that the matches were all sound. How did we do it?

502. THREE TIMES THE SIZE

Lay out 20 matches in the way shown in our illustration. You will see that the two groups of 6 and 14 matches form two enclosures, so that one space enclosed is exactly three times as large as the other.

Now transfer 1 match from the larger to the smaller group, and with the 7 and 13 enclose two spaces again, one exactly three times as large as the other.

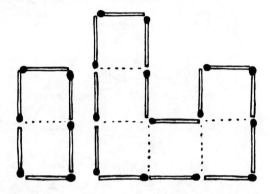

Twelve of the matches must remain unmoved from their present positions—and there must be no duplicated matches or loose ends. The dotted lines are simply to indicate the respective areas.

503. A SIX-SIDED FIGURE

Here are 6 matches arranged so as to form a regular hexagon. Can you take 3 more matches and so arrange the 9 as to show another regular six-sided figure? No duplicated matches or loose ends allowed.

504. TWENTY-SIX MATCHES

Make a rough square diagram, like the one shown on page 206, where the side of every little square is the length of a match, and put the stars and crosses in their given positions. It is required to place 26 matches along the lines so as to enclose two parts of exactly the same size and shape, one part containing two stars, and the other two crosses.

In the example given, each part is correctly of the same size and shape, and each part contains either two stars or two crosses; but, unfortunately, only 20 matches have been used. So it is not a solution. Can you do it with 26 matches?

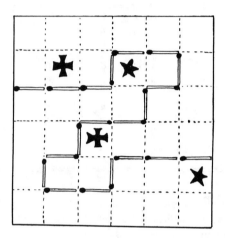

505. THE THREE MATCHES

Can you place 3 matches on the table, and support the matchbox on them, without allowing the heads of the matches to touch the table, to touch one another, or to touch the box?

506. EQUILATERAL TRIANGLES

Here is a little puzzle for young readers:

Place 16 matches, as shown, to form eight equilateral triangles. Now take away 4 matches so as to leave only four equal triangles. No superfluous matches or loose ends to be left.

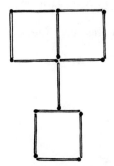

507. SQUARES WITH MATCHES

Arrange 12 matches on the table, as shown in the illustration. Now it is required to remove 6 of these matches and replace them so as to form five squares. Of course 6 matches must remain unmoved, and there must be no duplicated matches or loose ends.

508. HEXAGON TO DIAMONDS

Here is another match puzzle for young readers. With 6 matches form a hexagon, as here shown. Now, by moving only 2 matches and adding 1 more, can you form two diamonds?

509. QUEER ARITHMETIC

Can you show with matches how to take seven-tenths from five so that exactly four remains?

510. COUNTING THE MATCHES

A friend writes to say he bought a little box of midget matches, each one inch in length. He found that he could arrange them all in the form of a triangle whose area was just as many square inches as there were matches. He then used up six of the matches, and found that with the remainder he could again construct another triangle whose area was just as many square inches as there were matches. And using another six matches he could again do precisely the same.

How many matches were there in the box originally? The number is less than forty.

Unclassified Puzzles

Unclassified Puzzles

511. A PUZZLE WITH CARDS

Take from the pack the thirteen cards forming the suit of diamonds and arrange them in this order face downwards with the 3 at the top and 5 at the bottom: 3, 8, 7, ace, queen, 6, 4, 2, jack, king, 10, 9, 5. Now play them out in a row on the table in this way. As you spell "ace" transfer for each letter a card from the top to the bottom of the pack—A-C-E—and play the fourth card on to the table. Then spell T-W-O, while transferring three more cards to the bottom, and place the next card on the table. Then spell T-H-R-E-E, while transferring five to the bottom, and so on until all are laid out in a row, and you will find they will be all in regular order. Of course, you will spell out the knave as J-A-C-K.

Can you arrange the whole pack so that they will play out correctly in order, first all the diamonds, then the hearts, then the spades, and lastly the clubs?

512. CARD SHUFFLING

The rudimentary method of shuffling a pack of cards is to take the pack face downwards in the left hand and then transfer them one by one to the right hand, putting the second on top of the first, the third under, the fourth above, and so on until all are transferred. If you do this with any even number of cards and keep on repeating the shuffle in the same way, the cards will in due time return to their original order.

Try with 4 cards, and you will find the order is restored in three shuffles. In fact, where the number of cards is 2, 4, 8, 16, 32, 64, the number of shuffles required to get them back to the original arrangement is 2, 3, 4, 5, 6, 7 respectively. How many shuffles are necessary in the case of 14 cards?

513. A CHAIN PUZZLE

A man has eighty links of old chain in thirteen fragments, as shown on the following page. It will cost him 1¢ to open a link and 2¢ to weld one together again. What is the lowest price it must cost him to join all the pieces together so as to form an endless chain?

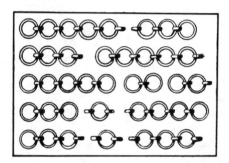

A new chain will cost him 36¢. What is the cheapest method of procedure? Remember that the large and small links must run alternately.

514. A SQUARE WITH FOUR PENNIES

Can you place four English pennies together so as to show a square? They must all lie flat on the table.

515. SIMPLE ADDITION

Can you show that four added to six will make eleven?

516. A CALENDAR PUZZLE

I have stated in my book *Amusements in Mathematics* that, under our present calendar rules, the first day of a century can never fall on a Sunday or a Wednesday or a Friday. As I have not given the proof, I am frequently asked the reason why. I will try to explain the mystery in as simple a way as possible.

517. THE FLY'S TOUR

I had a ribbon of paper, divided into squares on each side, as shown in the illustration. I joined the two ends together to make a ring, which I threw on

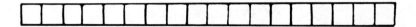

the table. Later I noticed that a fly pitched on the ring and walked in a line over every one of the squares on both sides, returning to the point from which it started, *without ever passing over the edge of the paper!* Its course passed through the centers of the squares all the time. How was this possible?

518. A MUSICAL ENIGMA

Here is an old musical enigma that has been pretty well known in Germany for some years.

519. SURPRISING RELATIONSHIP

ANGELINA: You say that Mr. Tomkins is your uncle?

EDWIN: Yes, and I am his uncle!

ANGELINA: Then—let me see—you must be nephew to each other, of course! Funny, isn't it?

Can you say quite simply how this might be, without any breach of the marriage law or disregard of the Table of Affinity?

520. AN EPITAPH (A.D. 1538)

Two grandmothers, with their two granddaughters;
Two husbands, with their two wives;
Two fathers, with their two daughters;
Two mothers, with their two sons;
Two maidens, with their two mothers;
Two sisters, with their two brothers;
   Yet only six in all lie buried here;
   All born legitimate, from incest clear.
How might this happen?

521. THE ENGINEER'S NAME

Three business men—Smith, Robinson, and Jones—all live in the Leeds-Sheffield district. Three railwaymen of similar names live in the same district. The business man Robinson and the guard live at Sheffield, the business man Jones and the stoker live at Leeds, while the business man Smith and the railway engineer live half-way between Leeds and Sheffield. The guard's namesake earns $10,000.00 per annum, and the engineer earns *exactly* one-third of the business man living nearest to him. Finally, the railwayman Smith beats the stoker at billiards.

What is the engineer's name?

522. STEPPING STONES

The illustration represents eight stepping stones across a certain stream. The puzzle is to start from the lower bank and land twice on the upper bank (stopping there), having returned once to the lower bank. But you must be careful to use each stepping stone the same number of times. In how few steps can you make the crossing?

Make the steps with two fingers in the diagram, and you will see what a

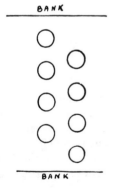

very simple matter it is. Yet it is more than likely that you will at first take a great many more steps than are necessary.

523. AN AWKWARD TIME

"When I told a man the other morning," said Colonel Crackham at the breakfast table, "that I had to catch the 12:50 train, he surprised me by saying that it was a very awkward time for any train to start. I asked him to explain why. Can you guess his answer?"

524. CRYPTIC ADDITION

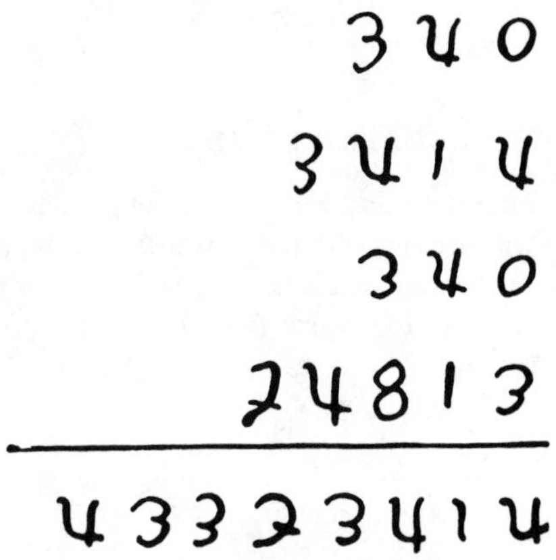

$$
\begin{array}{r}
340 \\
3414 \\
340 \\
24813 \\
\hline
4332 3414
\end{array}
$$

Can you prove that the above addition sum is correct?

525. THE TWO SNAKES

We have been asked this question:
Suppose that two snakes start swallowing one another simultaneously, each

getting the tail of the other in its mouth, so that the circle formed by the snakes becomes smaller and smaller, what will eventually happen?

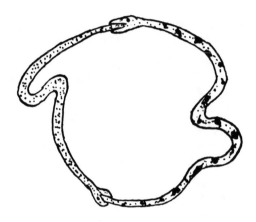

526. TWO PARADOXES

A child may ask a question that will profoundly perplex a learned philosopher, and we are often meeting with paradoxes that demand a little thought before we can explain them in simple language. The following was put to us:

"Imagine a man going to the North Pole. The points of the compass are, as every one knows:

$$
\begin{array}{c}
N \\
W \quad E \\
S
\end{array}
$$

"He reaches the Pole and, having passed over it, must turn about to look North. East is now on his left-hand side, West on his right-hand side, and the points of the compass therefore

$$
\begin{array}{c}
N \\
E \quad W \\
S
\end{array}
$$

which is absurd. What is the explanation?

"We were standing with a child in front of a large mirror that reflected the whole body. 'Why is it,' asked the intelligent youngster, 'that I am turned right round in the mirror, so that right is left and left right, and yet top is not bottom and bottom top? If it reverses sideways, why does it not reverse lengthways? Why am I not shown standing on my head?'"

527. COIN AND HOLE

We have before us a specimen of every American coin from a penny to a dollar. And we have a small sheet of paper with a circular hole cut in it of

exactly the size shown. (It was made by tracing around the rim of a penny.) What is the largest coin I can pass through that hole without tearing the paper?

528. A LEAP YEAR PUZZLE

The month of February in 1928 contained five Wednesdays. There is, of course, nothing remarkable in this fact, but it will be found interesting to discover the last year prior to 1928 and the first year after 1928 that had five Wednesdays in February.

529. BLOWING OUT THE CANDLE

Candles were lighted on Colonel Crackham's breakfast table one foggy morning. When the fog lifted, the Colonel rolled a sheet of paper into the form of a hollow cone, like a megaphone. He then challenged his young friends to use it in blowing out the candles. They failed, until he showed them the trick. Of course, you must blow through the small end.

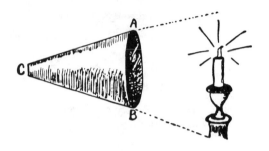

530. RELEASING THE STICK

Here is a puzzle that will often cause a good deal of bewilderment amongst your friends, though it is not so generally known as it deserves to be. I think

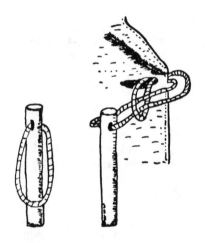

it was invented by Sam Loyd, the American chess and puzzle genius. At any rate, it was he who first showed it to us more than a quarter of a century ago.

It is simply a loop of string passed through one end of a stick as here shown, but not long enough to pass round the other end. The puzzle is to suspend it in the manner shown from the top hole of a man's coat, and then get it free again.

531. THE KEYS AND RING

Colonel Crackham the other day produced a ring and two keys, as here shown, cut out of a solid piece of cardboard, without a break or join anywhere. Perhaps it will puzzle the reader more than it puzzled George, who promptly cut them out.

532. THE ENTANGLED SCISSORS

Here is an old puzzle that many readers, who have forgotten how to put on the string, will be glad to see again. If you start on the loop at the bottom, the string can readily be got into position. The puzzle is, of course, to let some one hold the two ends of the string until you disengage the scissors. A good length of string should be used to give you free play. We would also advise the use of a large pair of scissors and thick cord that will slide easily.

533. INTELLIGENCE TESTS

Nowadays the schools are all out to give their children "Intelligence Tests," and in *The New Examiner,* by Dr. Ballard, there is a fine collection. I have included one here which, although not new, is really worthy of honorable mention.

An English officer, after a gruesome experience during the Boxer rebellion in China some years ago, fell asleep in church during the sermon. He was dreaming that the executioner was approaching him to cut off his head, and just as the sword was descending on the officer's unhappy neck his wife lightly touched her husband on the back of his neck with her fan to awaken him. The shock was too great, and the officer fell forward dead. Now, there is something wrong with this. What is it?

Another good question on similar lines for the scientific boy would be:

If we sell apples by the cubic inch, how can we really find the exact number of cubic inches in, say, a dozen dozen apples?

534. AT THE MOUNTAIN TOP

"When I was in Italy I was taken to the top of a mountain and shown that a mug would hold less liquor at the top of this mountain than in the valley beneath. Can you tell me," asked Professor Rackbrane, at the breakfast table, "what mountain this might be that has so strange a property?"

535. CUPID'S ARITHMETIC

Dora Crackham one morning produced a slip of paper bearing the jumble of figures shown in our illustration. She said that a young mathematician had this poser presented to him by his betrothed when she was in a playful mood.

$$15122 \ 1116 \ 9601621$$

"What am I to do with it?" asked George.

"Just interpret its meaning," she replied. "If it is properly regarded it should not be difficult to decipher."

536. TANGRAMS

Those readers who were interested in the article on "Tangrams" in *Amusements in Mathematics* may be glad to have a further collection of examples of the strikingly realistic figures and designs that can be produced by combining these curious shaped pieces. In diagram 1 the square is shown cut into the seven pieces. If you mark the point B, midway between A and C, on one side of a square of any size, and D, midway between C and E, on an adjoining side, the direction of the cuts is obvious. In the examples given below and on the following page, two complete sets of seven pieces have been combined.

Diagram 2 represents a man riding a bicycle; 3, a man pushing a wheelbarrow; 4, a boy riding a donkey; 5, a motor-car; 6, a house; 7, a dog; 8, a horse; 9, the British lion.

As will be seen, the possibility with these two sets combined is infinite, and many interesting subjects may be produced very successfully.

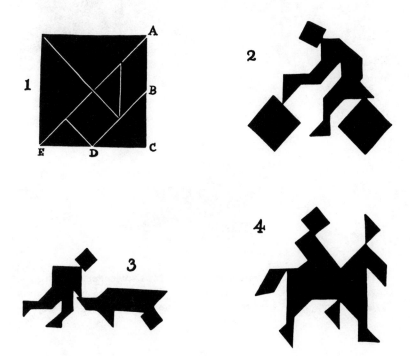

[The reader interested in tangrams will enjoy two excellent new paperbacks: *Tangrams: 330 Puzzles*, by Ronald C. Read (Dover, 1965), and *Tangrams: Picture-making Puzzle Game*, by Peter Van Note (Tuttle, 1966).—M. G.]

Answers

Answers

1. CONCERNING A CHECK

The amount must have been $31.63. He received $63.31. After he had spent a nickel there would remain the sum of $63.26, which is twice the amount of the check.

2. DOLLARS AND CENTS

The man must have entered the store with $99.98 in his pocket.

3. LOOSE CASH

The largest sum is $1.19, composed of a half dollar, quarter, four dimes, and four pennies.

4. GENEROUS GIFTS

At first there were twenty persons, and each received $6.00. Then fifteen persons (five fewer) would have received $8.00 each. But twenty-four (four more) appeared and only received $5.00 each. The amount distributed weekly was thus $120.00.

5. BUYING BUNS

There must have been three boys and three girls, each of whom received two buns at three for a penny and one bun at two for a penny, the cost of which would be exactly 7¢.

6. UNREWARDED LABOR

Weary Willie must have worked 16⅔ days and idled 13⅓ days. Thus the former time, at $8.00 a day, amounts to exactly the same as the latter at $10.00 a day.

7. THE PERPLEXED BANKER

The contents of the ten bags (in dollar bills) should be as follows: $1, 2, 4, 8, 16, 32, 64, 128, 256, 489. The first nine numbers are in geometrical progression, and their sum, deducted from 1,000, gives the contents of the tenth bag.

8. A WEIRD GAME

The seven men, A, B, C, D, E, F, and G, had respectively in their pockets before play the following sums: $4.49, $2.25, $1.13, 57¢, 29¢, 15¢, and 8¢. The answer may be found by laboriously working backwards, but a simpler method is as follows: $7 + 1 = 8$; $2 \times 7 + 1 = 15$; $4 \times 7 + 1 = 29$; and so on, where the multiplier increases in powers of 2, that is, 2, 4, 8, 16, 32, and 64.

9. DIGGING A DITCH

A. should receive one-third of two dollars, and B. two-thirds. Say B. can dig all in 2 hours and shovel all in 4 hours; then A. can dig all in 4 hours and shovel all in 8 hours. That is, their ratio of digging is as 2 to 4 and their ratio of shovelling as 4 to 8 (the same ratio), and A. can dig in the same time that B. can shovel (4 hours), while B. can dig in a quarter of the time that A. can shovel. Any other figures will do that fill these conditions and give two similar ratios for their working ability. Therefore, A. takes one-third and B. twice as much—two-thirds.

10. NAME THEIR WIVES

As it is evident that Catherine, Jane, and Mary received respectively $122.00, $132.00, and $142.00, making together the $396.00 left to the three wives, if John Smith receives as much as his wife Catherine, $122.00; Henry Snooks half as much again as his wife Jane, $198.00; and Tom Crowe twice as much as his wife Mary, $284.00, we have correctly paired these married couples and exactly accounted for the $1,000.00.

11. MARKET TRANSACTIONS

The man bought 19 cows for $950.00, 1 sheep for $10.00, and 80 rabbits for $40.00, making together 100 animals at a cost of $1,000.00.

A purely arithmetical solution is not difficult by a method of averages, the average cost per animal being the same as the cost of a sheep.

By algebra we proceed as follows, working in dollars: Since $x + y + z = 100$, then $\frac{1}{2}x + \frac{1}{2}y + \frac{1}{2}z = 50$.

$$
\begin{array}{r}
50x + 10y + \frac{1}{2}z = 1{,}000 \\
\frac{1}{2}x + \frac{1}{2}y + \frac{1}{2}z = 50 \\
\hline
49\frac{1}{2}x + 9\frac{1}{2}y \phantom{+ \frac{1}{2}z} = 950
\end{array}
$$

by subtraction, or $99x + 19y = 1900$. We have therefore to solve this indeterminate equation. The only answer is $x = 19$, $y = 1$. Then, to make up the 100 animals, z must equal 80.

12. THE SEVEN APPLEWOMEN

Each woman sold her apples at seven for 1¢, and 3¢ each for the odd ones over. Thus, each received the same amount, 20¢. Without questioning the ingenuity of the thing, I have always thought the solution unsatisfactory, because really indeterminate, even if we admit that such an eccentric way of selling may be fairly termed a "price." It would seem just as fair if they sold them at different rates and afterwards divided the money; or sold at a single rate with different discounts allowed; or sold different kinds of apples at different values; or sold the same rate per basketful; or sold by weight, the apples being of different sizes; or sold by rates diminishing with the age of the apples; and so on. That is why I have never held a high opinion of this old puzzle.

In a general way, we can say that n women, possessing $an + (n - 1)$, $n(a + b) + (n - 2)$, $n(a + 2b) + (n - 3), \ldots, n[a + b(n - 1)]$ apples respectively, can sell at n for a penny and b pennies for each odd one over and each receive $a + b(n - 1)$ pennies. In the case of our puzzle $a = 2$, $b = 3$, and $n = 7$.

13. A LEGACY PUZZLE

The legacy to the first son was $55.00, to the second son $275.00, to the third son $385.00, and to the hospital $605.00, making $1,320.00 in all.

14. PUZZLING LEGACIES

The answer is $1,464.00—a little less than $1,500.00. The legacies, in order, were $1,296.00, $72.00, $38.00, $34.00, and $18.00. The lawyer's fee would be $6.00.

15. DIVIDING THE LEGACY

The two legacies were $24.00 and $76.00, for if 8 (one-third of 24) be taken from 19 (one-fourth of 76) the remainder will be 11.

16. A NEW PARTNER

We must take it for granted that the sum Rogers paid, $2,500.00, was one-third of the value of the business, which was consequently worth $7,500.00 before he entered. Smugg's interest in the business had therefore been $4,500.00 (1½ times as much as Williamson), and Williamson's $3,000.00. As each is now to have an equal interest, Smugg will receive $2,000.00 of Rogers's contribution, and Williamson $500.00.

17. POCKET MONEY

When he left home Tompkins must have had $2.10 in his pocket.

18. DISTRIBUTION

The smallest number originally held by one person will be (in cents) one more than the number of persons. The others can be obtained by continually doubling and deducting one. So we get their holdings as 10, 19, 37, 73, 145, 289, 577, 1,153, and 2,305. Let the largest holder start the payment and work backwards, when the number of cents in the end held by each person will be 2^9 or 512—that is, $5.12.

19. REDUCTIONS IN PRICE

It is evident that the salesman's rule was to take off three-eighths of the price at every reduction. Therefore, to be consistent, the motorcycle should be offered at $156.25 after the next reduction.

20. HORSES AND BULLOCKS

We have to solve the indeterminate equation $344x = 265y + 33$. This is easy enough if you know how, but we cannot go into the matter here. Thus x is 252, and y is 327, so that if he buys 252 horses for $344.00 apiece, and 327 bullocks for $265.00 apiece, the horses will cost him in all $33.00 more than the bullocks.

21. BUYING TURKEYS

The man bought 75 turkeys at 80¢ each, making $60.00. After retaining 15 he sold the remaining 60 at 90¢ each, making $54.00, as stated. He thus made a profit of 10¢ each on the 60 birds he resold.

22. THE THRIFTY GROCER

He must have had 168 each of dollar bills, half dollars, and quarters, making a total of $294.00. In each of the six bags there would be 28 of each kind; in each of the seven bags 24 of each kind; and in each of the eight bags, 21 of each kind.

23. THE MISSING PENNY

The explanation is simply this. The two ways of selling are only identical when the number of apples sold at three for a penny and two for a penny is in the proportion of three to two.

Thus, if the first woman had handed over 36 apples, and the second woman 24, they would have fetched 24¢, whether sold separately or at five for 2¢. But if they each held the same number of apples there would be a loss when sold together of 1¢ in every 60 apples. So if they had 60 each there would be a loss of 2¢. If there were 180 apples (90 each) they would lose 3¢, and so on.

The missing penny in the case of 60 arises from the fact that the three a penny woman gains 2¢, and the two a penny woman loses 3¢.

Perhaps the fairest practical division of the 24¢ would be that the first woman receives 9½¢ and the second woman 14½, so that each loses ½¢ on the transaction.

24. THE RED DEATH LEAGUE

The total amount of subscriptions, reduced to cents, is 300,737, which is the product of 311 and 967, each of which is a prime. As we know that the R.D.L. had fewer than 500 members, it follows that there were 311, and they each paid as a subscription 967¢, or $9.67. This is the only possible answer.

25. A POULTRY POSER

The price of a chicken was $2.00, for a duck $4.00, and for a goose $5.00.

26. BOYS AND GIRLS

[Dudeney did not give the smallest answer. The minimal solution, supplied by J. A. H. Hunter is: Each boy starts with 3¢, gives 1¢ to every girl. Each girl starts with 15¢, gives 2¢ to every boy. Each child then has 6¢.— M. G.]

27. THE COST OF A SUIT

The cost of Melville's suit was $150.00, the coat costing $75.00, the trousers $50.00, and the vest $25.00.

28. A QUEER SETTLING UP

Richard had $4.00, and John had $2.50.

29. APPLE TRANSACTIONS

The apples cost 96¢ per 100.

30. PROSPEROUS BUSINESS

He possessed $22,781.25.

31. THE BANKER AND THE COUNTERFEIT BILL

Since the identical counterfeit bill can be traced through all the transactions, these are all invalid. Therefore everybody stands in relation to his debtor just where he was before the banker picked up the note, except that the butcher owes, in addition, $5.00 to the farmer for the calf received.

32. THEIR AGES

Tom's age was seven years and Mary's thirteen years.

33. MRS. WILSON'S FAMILY

The ages must be as follows: Mrs. Wilson, 39; Edgar, 21; James, 18; John, 18; Ethel, 12; Daisy, 9. It is clear that James and John were twins.

34. DE MORGAN AND ANOTHER

De Morgan was born in 1806. When he was 43, the year was the square of his age—1849. Jenkins was born in 1860. He was $5^2 + 6^2$ (61) in the year $5^4 + 6^4$ (1921). Also he was 2×31 (62) in the year 2×31^2 (1922). Again, he was 3×5 (15) in the year 3×5^4 (1875).

35. "SIMPLE" ARITHMETIC

Their ages were, respectively, sixty-four and twenty.

36. ANCIENT PROBLEM

Demochares must be just sixty years of age.

37. FAMILY AGES

The father and mother were both of the same age, thirty-six years old, and the three children were triplets of six years of age. Thus the sum of all their ages is ninety years, and all the other conditions are correctly fulfilled.

38. MIKE'S AGE

Mike's present age is $10^{16}/_{21}$ years, Pat's is $29^{15}/_{21}$, and Biddy's is $24^{20}/_{21}$ years. When the sty was built ($7^9/_{21}$ years ago), Mike was $3^7/_{21}$, Pat was $22^6/_{21}$, and Biddy was $17^{11}/_{21}$. In $11^{11}/_{21}$ years Mike will be $22^6/_{21}$ (as old as Pat was when he built the sty), Pat will be $41^5/_{21}$, and Biddy will be $36^{10}/_{21}$, making 100 years together.

39. THEIR AGES

Thirty years and twelve years, respectively.

40. BROTHER AND SISTER

The boy's age was ten and his sister's four.

41. A SQUARE FAMILY

The ages of the nine children were respectively 2, 5, 8, 11, 14, 17, 20, 23, 26, and the age of the father was 48.

42. IN THE YEAR 1900

The man was born in 1856 and died in 1920, **aged 64** years. Let x = age at death. Then $29x$ = date of birth. The date of **birth** + age = date of death, so that $29x + x = 30x$, or date of death. Now, from the question he was clearly alive in 1900, and dead by 1930. So death occurred during or between those dates, and as the date is $30x$, it is divisible by 30. The date can only be 1920, which, divided by 30, gives 64. So in 1900 he was 44 years of age.

43. FINDING A BIRTHDAY

The man must have been born at midday on February 19, 1873, and at midday on November 11, 1928, he had lived 10,176½ days in each century. Of course, the century ended at midnight on December 31, 1900, which was not a leap year, and his age on November 11, 1928, was 55 years and nearly 9 months.

44. THE BIRTH OF BOADICEA

There were 129 years between the birth of Cleopatra and the death of Boadicea; but, as their united ages amounted to 100 years only, there must have been 29 years when neither existed—that is, between the death of Cleopatra and the birth of Boadicea. Therefore Boadicea must have been born 29 years after the death of Cleopatra in 30 B.C., which would be in the year 1 B.C.

45. ROBINSON'S AGE

Robinson's age must have been 32, his brother's 34, his sister's 38, and his mother's 52.

46. A DREAMLAND CLOCK

The hour indicated would be exactly 23⅓ minutes after four oclock. But because the minute hand moved in the opposite direction, the real time would be 36⅔ minutes after four. You must deduct the number of minutes indicated from 60 to get the real time.

47. WHAT IS THE TIME?

The time is 6¾ minutes past IX, when the hour hand is 45⁹⁄₁₆ (the square of 6¾) minutes past XII. If we allow fractions *less* than a minute point, there is also the solution, five seconds (one-twelfth of a minute) past XII oclock.

48. THE AMBIGUOUS CLOCK

The first time would be 5⁵⁄₁₄₃ minutes past twelve, which might also (the hands being similar) indicate ⁶⁰⁄₁₄₃ minutes past one oclock.

49. THE BROKEN CLOCK FACE

If the clock face be broken or cracked in the manner shown in our illustration, the numerals on each of the four parts will sum to 20. The cunning reader will at once have seen that, as three X's (in IX, X, and XI) are adjacent, two of these must be alone contained in one piece. Therefore there are only two possible cases for trial.

[The first edition of *Puzzles and Curious Problems,* in which this puz-

zle appeared, gave an inferior solution in which it was necessary to view the hour IX upside down and interpret it as XI. (Note that it is so interpreted in the illustration accompanying the statement of the problem.) When a revised second edition of the book was issued, this blemish was removed and the solution shown here was substituted. Actually, there are twelve more legitimate solutions. The reader is invited to see if he can find all of them without checking my *Scientific American* columns for May and June, 1966, in which all thirteen can be found.

It is assumed that the Roman numerals are permanently attached to the rim of the clock face. Lines of breakage may separate the parts of an hour, as shown in Dudeney's solution, but must not go *around* any numerals, separating them from the rim.—M. G.]

50. WHEN DID THE DANCING BEGIN?

The dancing must have begun at $59\frac{83}{143}$ minutes past ten, and the hands were noticed to have changed places at $54\frac{138}{143}$ minutes past eleven.

51. MISTAKING THE HANDS

The time must have been $5\frac{5}{11}$ minutes past two oclock.

52. EQUAL DISTANCES

At $23\frac{1}{13}$ minutes past three oclock.

53. RIGHT AND LEFT

It must be $41\frac{7}{13}$ minutes past three oclock.

54. AT RIGHT ANGLES

To be at right angles the minute hand must always be exactly fifteen minutes either behind or ahead of the hour hand. Each case would happen eleven times in the twelve hours—*i.e.*, every 1 hour $5\frac{5}{11}$ minutes. Starting from nine oclock, the eighth addition will give the case 5 hours $43\frac{7}{11}$ minutes. In the other case, starting from three oclock, the second addition gives 5 hours $10\frac{10}{11}$ minutes.

These are the two cases between five and six, and the latter will, of course, be the sooner.

55. WESTMINSTER CLOCK

The times were 8 hours 23^{7}⁄₁₄₃ minutes, and 4 hours 41^{13}⁄₁₄₃ minutes. We are always allowed to assume that these fractional times can be indicated in clock puzzles.

56. HILL CLIMBING

It must have been 6¾ miles to the top of the hill. He would go up in 4½ hours and descend in 1½ hours.

57. TIMING THE CAR

As the man can walk 27 steps while the car goes 162, the car is clearly going six times as fast as the man. The man walks 3½ miles an hour: therefore the car was going at 21 miles an hour.

58. THE STAIRCASE RACE

If the staircase were such that each man would reach the top in a certain number of full leaps, without taking a reduced number at his last leap, the smallest possible number of steps would, of course, be 60 (that is, $3 \times 4 \times 5$). But the sketch showed us that A. taking three steps at a leap, has one odd step at the end; B. taking four at a leap, will have three only at the end; and C. taking five at a leap, will have four only at the finish. Therefore, we have to find the smallest number that, when divided by 3, leaves a remainder 1, when divided by 4 leaves 3, and when divided by 5 leaves a remainder 4. This number is 19. So there were 19 steps in all, only 4 being left out in the sketch.

59. A WALKING PUZZLE

It will be found (and it is the key to the solution) that the man from B. can walk 7 miles while the man from A. can walk 5 miles. Say the distance between the towns is 24 miles, then the point of meeting would be 14 miles from A. and the man from A. walked $3\frac{3}{7}$ miles per hour, while the man from B. walked $4\frac{4}{5}$ miles per hour. They both arrived at 7 P.M. exactly.

60. RIDING IN THE WIND

He could ride one mile in $3\frac{3}{7}$ minutes, or $\frac{7}{24}$ mile per minute. The wind would help or retard him to the extent of $\frac{1}{24}$ mile per minute. Therefore, with the wind he could ride $\frac{8}{24}$ mile per minute and against the wind, $\frac{6}{24}$ mile per minute; so that is 1 mile in 3 minutes or 4 minutes, respectively, as stated.

61. A ROWING PUZZLE

The correct answer is $3\frac{9}{17}$ minutes. The crew can row $\frac{1}{5}$ of the distance per minute on still water, and the stream does $\frac{1}{12}$ of the distance per minute. The difference and sum of these two fractions are $\frac{7}{60}$ and $\frac{17}{60}$. Therefore, against the stream would take $\frac{60}{7}$ minutes (or $8\frac{4}{7}$ minutes), and with the stream $\frac{60}{17}$ (or $3\frac{9}{17}$ minutes).

62. THE ESCALATOR

If I walk 26 steps I require 30 seconds, and if I walk 34 steps I require only 18 seconds. Multiply 30 by 34 and 26 by 18 and we get 1,020 and 468, the difference between which is 552. Divide this by the difference between 30 and 18 (that is, by 12) and the answer is 46, the number of steps in the stairway, which descends at the rate of 1 step in $1\frac{1}{2}$ seconds. The speed at which I walk on the stairs does not affect the question, as the step from which I alight will reach the bottom at a given moment, whatever I do in the meantime.

63. SHARING A BICYCLE

Let Anderson ride $11\frac{1}{9}$ miles, drop the bicycle, and walk the rest of the way. Brown will walk until he picks up the bicycle and then rides to their destination, getting there at exactly the same time as Anderson. The journey takes them 3 hours 20 minutes. Or you can divide the 20 miles into nine stages of $2\frac{2}{9}$ miles each, and drop the machine at every stage, only you must make

Anderson ride at the start. Anderson will then ride each of his five stages in ⅔ hour and walk each of his four stages in ⅚ hour, making his total time 3⅓ hours. Brown will ride each of his four stages in ⁵⁄₁₈ hour and walk each of his five stages in ⅘ hour, making his total time also 3⅓ hours. The distances that Anderson and Brown ride respectively must be in the proportion of 5 to 4; the distances they walk in the proportion of 4 to 5.

64. MORE BICYCLING

A. rides 7¹¹⁄₂₇ miles, B. rides 1¹³⁄₂₇ miles, and C. rides 11³⁄₂₇ miles, making the 20 miles in all. They may ride in any order, only each man should complete his ride in one mount and the second rider must always walk both before and after riding. They will each take 3⁵⁄₉ hours on the journey, and therefore will all arrive together.

65. A SIDECAR PROBLEM

Atkins takes Clarke 40 miles in his car and leaves him to walk the remaining 12 miles. He then rides back and picks up Baldwin at a point 16 miles from the start and takes him to their destination. All three arrive in exactly 5 hours. Or Atkins might take Baldwin 36 miles and return for Clarke, who will have walked his 12 miles. The sidecar goes 100 miles in all, with no passenger for 24 miles.

66. THE DISPATCH RIDER

The answer is the square root of twice the square of 40, added to 40. This is 96.568 miles, or, roughly, 96½ miles.

67. THE TWO TRAINS

In 5 seconds both trains (together) go 600 feet, or 81⁹⁄₁₁ miles per hour. In 15 seconds the faster train gains 600 feet, or 27³⁄₁₁ miles per hour. From this we get 54⁶⁄₁₁ miles per hour as the rate of the faster train; and it is clear that 27³⁄₁₁ miles per hour is the rate of the other.

68. PICKLEMINSTER TO QUICKVILLE

There are two possible distances that will fit the conditions—210 miles and 144 miles, only I barred the latter by the words, "at an ordinary rate." With 144 miles A would run 140 miles, while B and D ran 4 miles; so if the latter went 2 miles per hour, the former would have to go 70 miles per hour—rates which are certainly not "ordinary"! With 210 miles B and D go half the speed of A, and C goes three-quarters the speed of A, so you can give them reasonable rates.

69. THE DAMAGED ENGINE

The distance from Anglechester to Clinkerton must be 200 miles. The train went 50 miles at 50 m.p.h. and 150 miles at 30 m.p.h. If the accident had occurred 50 miles farther on, it would have gone 100 miles at 50 m.p.h. and 100 miles at 30 m.p.h.

70. THE PUZZLE OF THE RUNNERS

While Brown has only run $\frac{1}{6}$ or $\frac{4}{24}$ of the course, Tompkins has run the remainder $\frac{5}{6}$, less $\frac{1}{8}$, or $\frac{17}{24}$. Therefore Tompkins's pace is $1\frac{1}{4}$ times that of Brown. Brown has now $\frac{5}{6}$ of the course to run, whereas Tompkins has only $\frac{1}{6}$. Therefore Brown must go five times as fast as Tompkins, or increase his own speed to five times $1\frac{1}{4}$, that is, $8\frac{5}{4}$ times as fast as he went at first. But the question was not how many times as fast, but "how much faster," and $8\frac{5}{4}$ times as fast is equal to $8\frac{1}{4}$ times faster than Brown's original speed. The correct answer is therefore $20\frac{1}{4}$ times faster, though in practice probably impossible.

71. THE TWO SHIPS

The error lies in assuming that the average speeds are equal. They are not. The first ship does a mile in $\frac{1}{12}$ hour outwards and in $\frac{1}{8}$ hour homewards. Half of the sum of these fractions is $\frac{5}{48}$. Therefore the ship's average speed for the 400 miles is a mile in $\frac{5}{48}$ hour. The average speed of the second ship is a mile in $\frac{1}{10}$ hour.

72. FIND THE DISTANCE

The distance between the two places must have been 18 miles. The meeting points were 10 miles from A———— and 12 miles from B————. Simply multiply 10 (the first distance) by 3 and deduct the second distance, 12. Could anything be simpler? Try other distances for the meeting points (taking care that the first meeting distance is more than two-thirds of the second) and you will find the little rule will always work.

73. THE MAN AND THE DOG

The dog's speed was 16 miles per hour. The following facts will give the reader clues to the general solution. The distance remaining to be walked side by side with the dog was 81 feet, the fourth power of 3 (for the dog returned four times), and the distance to the end of the road was 625 feet, the fourth power of 5. Then the difference between the speeds (in miles per hour) of man and dog (that is, 12) and the sum of the speeds (20) must be in the same ratio, 3 to 5, as is the case.

74. BAXTER'S DOG

It is obvious that Baxter will overtake Anderson in one hour, for each will be 4 miles from the hotel in the same direction. Then, as the dog has been running uniformly at 10 miles an hour during that hour, he must have run 10 miles! When a friend put this problem before a French professor of mathematics, he exclaimed: *"Mon Dieu, quelle série!"* quite overlooking the simple manner of solution.

75. THE RUNNER'S REFRESHMENT

As the radius is t, the diameter is $2t$. The diameter multiplied by π (the Greek letter *pi*) gives us the circumference, $2t\pi$ miles. As he goes round n times, $2t\pi n$ equals the number of miles run, and, as he drinks s quarts per mile, he consumes $2t\pi ns$ quarts. We can put the factors in any order: therefore the answer is $2\pi nts$ (two pints) or one quart.

76. EXPLORING THE DESERT

The nine men, A, B, C, D, E, F, G, H, J, all go 40 miles together on the 1 gal. in their engine tanks, when A transfers 1 gal. to each of the other eight and has 1 gal. left to return home. The eight go another 40 miles, when B transfers 1 gal. to each of the other seven and has 2 gals. to take him home. The seven go another 40 miles, when C transfers 1 gal. to each of the six others and returns home on the remaining 3 gals. The six go another 40 miles, when D gives each of five 1 gal. and returns home. The five go 40 miles, when E gives each of four 1 gal. and returns home. The four go another 40 miles, when F gives each of three 1 gal. and returns home. The three go 40 miles, when G gives each of two 1 gal. and returns home. The two go 40 miles, when H gives 1 gal. to J and returns home. Finally, the last man, J, goes another 40 miles and then has 9 gals. to take him home. Thus J has gone 360 miles out and home, the greatest distance in a straight line that could be reached under the conditions.

77. EXPLORING MOUNT NEVEREST

Dump 5 rations at 90-mile point and return to base (5 days). Dump 1 at 85 and return to 90 (1 day). Dump 1 at 80 and return to 90 (1 day). Dump 1 at 80, return to 85, pick up 1 and dump at 80 (1 day). Dump 1 at 70 and return to 80 (1 day). Return to base (1 day). We have thus left 1 ration at 70 and 1 at 90. Dump 1 at 5 and return to base (1 day). If he must walk 20 miles he can do so by going to 10 and returning to base. Dump 4 at 10 and return to base (4 days). Dump 1 at 10 and return to 5; pick up 1 and dump at 10 (1 day). Dump 2 at 20 and return to 10 (2 days). Dump 1 at 25 and return to 20 (1 day). Dump 1 at 30, return to 25, pick up 1 and dump at 30 (1 day). March to 70 (2 days). March to base (1½ days). Total, 23½ days.

A few claims have been made for fewer than 23½ days, but they were all based on tricks that were actually, or in spirit, forbidden, such as dumping only portions of the sealed boxes, making the man take a long march fasting, or making him eat his day's ration before starting so as to carry and dump two rations. In the last case he would really be carrying three rations, one inside and two on his back!

If the route had been in a straight march across a desert, the shortest time necessary would be 86 days, as follows:

Dump 42 at 10, return to base (42 days). Dump 1 at 15, return to 10 (1 day). Dump 20 at 20 and return to 10 (20 days). Dump 1 at 20 and return to 15, pick up 1 and dump at 20 (1 day). Dump 10 at 30 and return to 20 (10 days). Dump 1 at 35, return to 30 (1 day). Dump 4 at 40 and return to 30 (4 days). Dump 1 at 40 and return to 35. Pick up 1 and dump at 40 (1 day). Dump 2 at 50 and return to 40 (2 days). Dump 1 at 55 and return to 50 (1 day). Dump 1 at 60 and return to 55. Pick up 1 and dump at 60 (1 day). March to base (2 days). Total, 86 days.

78. THE BATH CHAIR

If the man leaving A goes 1⅔ miles at 5 miles per hour, he will take 20 minutes; and the return journey at 4 miles per hour will take them 25 minutes. He thus overtakes the invalid at 12:35, when the latter has gone ⅔ mile in 35 minutes, and his rate is 1⅐ miles per hour.

79. THE PEDESTRIAN PASSENGER

Assume that the train runs for an hour, and that it is itself of the absurd length of 3 miles. Then, as in the diagram, the train will have gone from B to C = 60 miles, but the passenger will have gone from A to C, or 63 miles. On the other hand, if he walks from the front to the rear of the train, the train will have gone from B to C (again 60 miles), while the passenger will have gone from B to D = 57 miles. So that in our first case the man would be travelling over the permanent way at the rate of 63 miles per hour, and in the second case, 57 miles per hour.

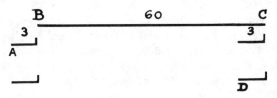

80. MEETING TRAINS

As the journey takes five hours, divide the route into five equal distances. Now, when the lady leaves Wurzletown there are four trains on the way and a fifth just starting. Each of these five she will meet. Also, when she has gone one-fifth of the distance, another will start; at two-fifths, another; at three-fifths, another; at four-fifths, another; and when she arrives at Mudville a train will be just on the point of starting. If we assume, as we must, that she does not meet this one "on the way," or meet the one that arrived at Wurzletown just as she left, she will have met altogether nine trains on the journey.

81. CARRYING BAGS

Let the boy continue to carry one bag for 1⅓ miles; then hand it to the gentleman, who will carry it to the station. Also let the man carry his bag 2⅔ miles and then deliver it to the boy, who will carry it for the remaining distance. Then each of the three persons will have carried one bag 2⅔ miles —an equal division of labor.

82. THE ESCALATOR

Let n equal the number of steps in staircase, and take as the unit of time the time taken by one step to disappear at bottom.

The second man takes 75 steps in $n - 75$ units of time, or (dividing by 25) 3 steps in $\dfrac{n-75}{25}$ units. Therefore first man takes 1 step in $\dfrac{n-75}{25}$ units. But first man also takes 50 steps in $n - 50$ units of time, or 1 step in $\dfrac{n-50}{50}$ units of time. Therefore $\dfrac{n-50}{50} = \dfrac{n-75}{25}$ and $n = 100$—the required answer.

83. THE FOUR CYCLISTS

A, B, C, D could ride one mile in ⅙, ⅑, ¹⁄₁₂, and ¹⁄₁₅ of an hour respectively. They could, therefore, ride once round in ¹⁄₁₈, ¹⁄₂₇, ¹⁄₃₆, and ¹⁄₄₅ of an hour, and consequently in ⅑ of an hour (that is, 6⅔ minutes) they would meet for the first time. Four times in 6⅔ minutes is 26⅔ minutes. So that they would complete their task in 26 minutes 40 seconds past noon.

84. THE DONKEY CART

The journey took 10⁵⁄₄₁ hours. Atkins walked 5³⁵⁄₄₁ miles at the end of his journey, Brown walked 13²⁷⁄₄₁ at the beginning, and Cranby's donkey went altogether 80⁴⁰⁄₄₁ miles. I hope the ass had a good rest after performing the feat.

85. THE THREE CARS

B would pass C in 6⅔ minutes.

86. THE FLY AND THE CARS

(1) The fly meets car B in 1 hour 48 minutes. (2) There is no necessity here to work out the distance that the fly travels—a difficult series for the novice. We simply find that the cars meet in exactly 2 hours. The fly really travels in miles:

$$\frac{270}{1} + \frac{270}{10} + \frac{270}{100} + \frac{270}{1,000} \cdots$$ to infinity, and the sum of this geometrical de-

creasing series is exactly 300 miles.

87. THE SUBWAY STAIRS

The least common multiple of 2, 3, 4, 5, 6, and 7 is 420. Deduct 1, and 419 is a possible number for the stairs, and every addition of 420 will also work. So the number of steps might be either 419, 839, 1,259, 1,679, etc., only we were told that there were fewer than 1,000, and that there was another stairway on the line with fewer steps that had the same peculiarity. Therefore there must have been 839 steps in the Curling Street stairway.

88. THE BUS RIDE

They can ride three times as fast as they can walk, therefore three-quarters of their time must have been spent in walking, and only a quarter in riding. Therefore they rode for 2 hours, going 18 miles, and walked back in 6 hours, thus exactly filling their 8 hours.

89. A QUESTION OF TRANSPORT

The car should take four men 12 miles, and drop them 8 miles from their destination; then return 8 miles and pick up four men from the eight who have walked to that point; then proceed 12 miles, and drop the second four 4 miles from destination; then return 8 miles and pick up the last four, who will be 8 miles from the starting point; then drive these 12 miles to their destination, where all will arrive at the same time. The car has thus gone 52 miles, which would take 2⅗ hours. The time of arrival was, therefore, 2:36 P.M.

90. HOW FAR WAS IT?

The distance must have been 300 miles.

91. OUT AND HOME

The distance must be 13⅛ miles, so that he walked into the town in 2⅝ hours and returned in 4⅜ hours, making 7 hours, as stated.

92. THE MEETING CARS

The distance from London to Bugleminster must be 72 miles.

93. A BICYCLE RACE

They will come together 12 minutes from the start.

94. A LITTLE TRAIN PUZZLE

There is no necessity for any algebraical working in the solution of this problem, nor need we know the distance between the two stations. Wherever they meet, just send the two trains back for an hour's journey at their respective rates. One will obviously go 60 miles and the other 40 miles, so they were 100 miles (60 added to 40) apart an hour before they met!

95. AN IRISH JAUNT

After travelling 20 minutes Pat said we had gone just half as far as the remaining distance to Pigtown, so it is clear that from Boghooley to Pigtown took one hour.

Five miles beyond Pigtown we were at a point half as far from Ballyfoyne as from Pigtown. Then we reached Ballyfoyne in an hour, from which we know that we took 3 hours from Pigtown to Ballyfoyne, and therefore the time of the complete journey was four hours. Now we find that the 5-mile run took 2 hours, so in the 4 hours we must have done 10 miles, which is the correct distance from Boghooley to Ballyfoyne.

96. A WALKING PROBLEM

The second man, on seeing his friend turn and walk towards him, walked backwards 200 yards. It was an eccentric thing to do, but he did it, and it is the only answer to the puzzle. They could thus have their faces towards each other and be going in a direct line.

97. THE FALSE SCALES

If the scales had been false on account of the pans being unequally weighted, then the true weight of the pudding would be 154 oz., and it would have weighed 130 oz. in one pan and 178 oz. the other. Half the sum of the apparent weights (the arithmetic mean) equals 154. But the illustration showed that the pans weighed evenly and that the error was in the unequal lengths of the arms of the balance. Therefore, the apparent weights were 121 oz. and 169 oz., and the real weight 143 oz. Multiply the apparent weights together and we get the square of 143—the geometric mean. The lengths of the arms were in the ratio 11 to 13.

If we call the true weight x in each case, then we get the equations:

$$\frac{\left(\frac{9}{11}x + 4\right) + \left(\frac{9}{11}x + 52\right)}{2} = x, \text{ and } x = 154.$$

$$\sqrt{\left(\frac{9}{11}x + 4\right) \times \left(\frac{9}{11}x + 52\right)} = x, \text{ and } x = 143.$$

98. WEIGHING THE GOODS

Since one canister weighs an ounce, the first illustration shows that in one pan eight packets equal 3 oz., and, therefore, one packet will weigh ⅜ oz. The second illustration shows that in the other pan one packet equals 6 oz. Multiply ⅜ by 6 and we get 9/4, the square root of which is 3/2, or 1½ oz. as the real weight of one packet. Therefore, eight packets weigh 12 oz., which is the correct answer.

99. WEIGHING THE BABY

It is important to notice that the man, baby, and dog weigh together 180 lb., as recorded on the dial in the illustration. Now, the difference between 180 and 162 is 18, which equals twice the weight of the dog, whose weight is 9 lb. Therefore the baby weighs 30 lb., since 30 less 70 per cent is 9.

100. FRESH FRUITS

Since the lower scales tell us that one apple and six plums equal in weight one pear, we can substitute one apple and six plums for the pear in the upper scales without disturbing the balance. Then we can remove six plums from each pan in the upper scales, and find that four apples equal four plums. Consequently, one apple equals one plum, and if we substitute a plum for the apple in the lower scales, as they originally stood, we see that seven plums equal one pear in weight. So the old book says Q.E.D. (quite easily done!).

101. WEIGHING THE TEA

(1) With the 5 lb. and 9 lb. weights in different pans weigh 4 lb. (2) With the 4 lb. weigh second 4 lb. (3) Weigh third 4 lb. (4) Weigh fourth 4 lb., and the remainder will also be 4 lb. (5), (6), (7), (8), (9) Divide each portion of 4 lb. in turn equally on the two sides of the scales.

102. AN EXCEPTIONAL NUMBER

1 3 4 5 2. The successive numbers are 1, 2, 3, 4, 5; 13 × 4 = 52. [For six other solutions see Joseph Madachy, *Journal of Recreational Mathematics,* Vol. 1, January 1968, page 41.–M. G.]

103. THE FIVE CARDS

The number is either 3 9 1 5 7 or 5 7 1 3 9. In either case the product of the two pairs 39 and 57, minus 1, results in 2 2 2 2.

104. SQUARES AND DIGITS

If a square number terminates in similar digits, those digits must be 4, as in the case of 144, the square of 12. But there cannot be more than three equal digits, and therefore the smallest answer is 1444, the square of 38.

105. THE TWO ADDITIONS

Arrange the figures in the following way:

$$
\begin{array}{cc}
173 & 85 \\
\underline{4} & \underline{92} \\
177 & 177
\end{array}
$$

and both sums add up alike.

106. THE REPEATED QUARTETTE

Multiply 273863 by 365 and the product is 99959995. Working the problem backwards, any number whatever consisting of eight figures with the first four repeated is divisible by 73 (and by 137) without remainder, and if it ends in 5 or 0 is divisible by 365 (or by 50005). Knowing this, the highest possible product can be written down at once.

107. EASY DIVISION

All we need do is to proceed as follows:

$$
7-\frac{71014492753623188840579}{1014492753623188405797}
$$

Divide 7 by 7, carry the 1 to the top line, divide again by 7 and carry the 0 to the top line, and so on until we come to a 7 in the bottom line without any remainder. Then stop, for the correct number is found. A solution may be found for any divisor and with any given figure at the beginning. A general examination of the question is very interesting.

If we take the divisor 2 we get the number 2–1 0–5 2–6–3 1 5 7 8–9 4–7 3 6–8–4–.

This is a complete circuit. The hyphens are at the places where there is no remainder when divided by 2. Note that the successive figures immediately following a hyphen are 1, 5, 6, 3, 9, 7, 8, 4, 2, so if I want my number to begin with an 8, I start 8 4 2 1 0 5, etc., taking the 8 that follows a hyphen. Where there is a complete circuit, as in this case, and in the case of the divisors 3, 6, and 11, the number of figures in the number will always be 10 times the divisor less 2. If you try the divisor 4, there are five broken circuits. Thus, 4–1 0 2 5 6– will give you numbers beginning with 4 or 1; or 2 0–5 1 2–8– with 2, 5, or 8; or 7 1 7 9 4 8– beginning with 7; or 3 0 7 6–9 2– with 9 or 3; or 6 1 5 3 8 4– for a number beginning with 6.

Some divisors, like 5 and 9, though producing broken circuits, require the same total of figures as if they were complete circuits. Our divisor 7 gives three broken circuits: the one shown above for the initial figures 7, 1, or 4, another for 5, 8, or 2, and a third for 6, 9, or 3.

108. A MISUNDERSTANDING

We may divide 8 5 7 1 4 2 by 3 by simply transferring the 2 from the end to the beginning. Or 4 2 8 5 7 1, by transferring the 1.

109. THE TWO FOURS

This is how 64 may be expressed by the use of only two fours with arithmetical signs:

The process of simplification shown should make everything quite clear.

$$\sqrt{\left(\sqrt{\sqrt{4}}\right)^{4!}} = \sqrt{(\sqrt{2})^{24}} = \sqrt{2^{12}} = \sqrt{4096} = 64$$

[Interest in the "Four Fours" problem has had periodic revivals since its first mention in the December 30, 1881, issue of *Knowledge,* a magazine of popular science edited by the astronomer Richard Proctor. For a recent discussion of the problem, see my *Scientific American* column for January 1964, and the answer section of the column for the following month. A table giving the integers from 1 to 100, each expressed with four fours, will be found in L. Harwood Clarke, *Fun With Figures* (William Heinemann Ltd., 1954), pp. 51–53, and Angela Dunn, *Mathematical Bafflers* (McGraw-Hill, 1964), pp. 5–8.

The number 64 is easily expressed with four fours: $(4 + 4)(4 + 4)$, and with three fours: $4 \times 4 \times 4$. In *Recreational Mathematics Magazine,* No. 14 (1964), M. Bicknell and V. E. Hoggatt show 64 ways of expressing 64 with four fours, and add a good list of references on the Four Fours problem.

D. E. Knuth, in his article "Representing Numbers Using Only One 4," *Mathematics Magazine,* Vol. 37, November–December, 1964, pp. 308–310, shows how to represent 64 by using only one four and three kinds of symbols: the square root sign, the factorial sign, and brackets. To express 64 by this method requires 57 square root signs, nine factorials, and 18 brackets. A computer program, Knuth reports, found that all positive integers less than 208 could be represented in a similar manner, and he conjectures that the method applies to all positive integers.

Dudeney is partially correct in his assertion about the number 113. So far as I know, no one has found a way to represent it without adopting highly unorthodox symbols or complicated procedures such as Knuth's.—M. G.]

110. THE TWO DIGITS

Of course it is entirely a matter of individual taste what arithmetical forms and signs are admissible, but I should personally draw the line at expressions introducing "log" and "antilog."

A few solutions are as follows:

$$25 = 5^2$$
$$36 = 6 \times 3!$$
$$64 = \sqrt{4^6} \text{ or } (\sqrt{4})^6$$
$$25 = 5 \div .2$$

111. DIGITAL COINCIDENCES

If we multiply 497 by 2 we get the product 994. If we add together 497 and 2 we get 499. The figures are the same in both cases. Also 263 multiplied by 2 and added to 2 will give 526 and 265 respectively.

[Harry Lindgren points out that by inserting 9's one obtains two answers with any desired number of digits: 4997 + 2 = 4999; 4997 × 2 = 9994; 2963 + 2 = 2965; 2963 × 2 = 5926; and similarly for 49997 + or × 2; 29963 + or × 2; and so on.—M. G.]

112. PALINDROMIC SQUARE NUMBERS

The square of 836 is 698896, which contains an even number of digits and reads backwards and forwards alike. There is no smaller square number containing an even number of figures that is a palindrome.

113. FACTORIZING

If the number of noughts enclosed by the two ones is 2 added to any multiple of 3, two factors can always be written down at once in this curious way. 1001 = 11 × 91; 1000001 = 101 × 9901; 1000000001 = 1001 × 999001; 1000000000001 = 10001 × 99990001. The last is our required answer, and 10001 = 73 × 137. The multiple of 3 in 11 is 3: therefore we insert 3 noughts in each factor and one more 9.

If our number contained 101 noughts, as I suggested, then the multiple of 3 is 33 and the factors will contain 33 noughts and 34 nines in the form shown. If the number of noughts in the number be even you can get two factors in this way: 1001 = 11 × 91; 100001 = 11 × 9091; 10000001 = 11 × 909091, and so on.

114. FIND THE FACTORS

The factors of 1234567890 are 2 × 3 × 3 × 5 × 3607 × 3803. If we multiply 3607 by 10 and 3803 by 9 we get two composite factors 36070 and 34227, which multiplied together produce 1234567890 and have the least possible difference between them.

115. DIVIDING BY ELEVEN

To be divisible by 11, four of the alternate digits must sum to 17 and the remaining five to 28, or four to 28 and five to 17. Thus, in the example I gave (4 8 2 5 3 9 7 6 1), 4, 2, 3, 7, 1 sum to 17, and 8, 5, 9, 6 to 28. Now four digits will sum to 17 in 9 different ways and five to 17 in 2 ways, making 11 together. In each of the 11 cases 4 may be permuted in 24 ways and 5 in 120 ways, or together in 2880 ways. So that $2880 \times 11 = 31,680$ ways. As the nine digits can be permuted in 362,880 ways, the chances are just 115 to 11 against a haphazard arrangement being divisible by 11.

116. DIVIDING BY 37

Write beneath the number successively, from right to left, the numbers 1, 10, 11, as follows:

4	9	1	2	9	3	0	8	2	1	3
10	1	11	10	1	11	10	1	11	10	1

Now, regarding the lower figures as multipliers, add together all the products of 1 and 10 and deduct all the products by 11. This is the same as adding 13, 08, 29, and 49 together (99) and deducting eleven times 2 plus 3 plus 1 (66). The difference, 33, will be the remainder when the large number is divided by 37.

Here is the key. If we divide 1, 10, 100, 1000, etc., by 37 we get successively the remainders 1, 10, 26, but for convenience we deduct the 26 from 37 and call it *minus* 11. If you try 49,629,708,213 you will find the minus or negative total 165, or in excess of the positive 99. The difference is 66. Deduct 37 and you get 29. But as the result is minus, deduct it from 37 and you have 8 as correct answer. You can now find the method for other prime divisors. The cases of 7 and 13 are easy. In the former case you write 1, 3, 2 (1, 3, 2), 1, 3, 2, etc., from right to left, the bracketed numbers being minus. In the latter case, 1 (3, 4, 1), 3, 4, 1 (3, 4, 1), etc.

117. ANOTHER 37 DIVISION

Call the required numbers ABCABCABC. If the sum of the A digits, the B digits, and the C digits respectively are:

A	B	C
18	19	8
15	15	15
12	11	22
19	8	18
22	12	11
8	18	19
11	22	12

then in the first three groups $11A - 10B = C$. In the next two groups $11A - 10B - C = 111$ (3×37); and in the last two groups $10B + C - 11A = 111$. It does not matter what the figures are, but if they comply with these conditions we can always divide by 37. Here is an example of the first case—

$$ABCABCABC,$$
$$984763251,$$

where the 3 A's sum to 18, the 3 B's to 19, and the 3 C's to 8.

You will find 22 cases with the first equation, 10 with the second, and 10 with the third, making 42 fundamental cases in all. But in every case the A figures may be permuted in 6 ways, and the B figures in 6 ways, and the C figures in 6 ways, making $6 \times 6 \times 6 = 216$, which multiplied by 42 gives the answer 9072 ways divisible by 37. As the 9 digits may be permuted in 362880 ways the chances are $\frac{9072}{362880}$ or $\frac{1}{40}$ or 39 to 1 against divisibility.

118. A DIGITAL DIFFICULTY

There are four solutions, as follows: 2,438,195,760; 3,785,942,160; 4,753,869,120; 4,876,391,520. The last figure must be zero. Any arrangement with an even figure next to the zero will be divisible by 2, 3, 4, 5, 6, 9, 10, 12, 15, and 18. We have therefore only to consider 7, 11, 13, 16, and 17. To be divisible by 11 the odd digits must sum to 28 and the even to 17, or vice versa. To be divisible by $7 \times 11 \times 13 = 1001$, if we ignore the zero, the numbers formed by the first three and the last three digits must sum to the middle three. (Note that the third case above is really 474—1386—912, with the 1 carried forward and added to the 4.) But, we cannot do better than take the lowest multiple (82) of the lowest common multiple of the divisors (12,252,240), which gives ten figures (this is 1,004,683,680), and keep on adding that lowest common multiple until all digits are different.

The 199th multiple will give us the first answer, 309 the second, 388 the third, and 398 the fourth. The work can be considerably shortened by leaping over groups where figures will obviously be repeated, and all the answers may be obtained in about twenty minutes by the use of a calculating machine.

119. THREES AND SEVENS

The smallest number possible is 3,333,377,733, which is divisible by 3 and by 7, and the sum of its digits (42) also divisible by 3 and by 7. There must be at fewest three 7's and seven 3's, and the 7's must be placed as far to the right as possible.

120. ROOT EXTRACTION

The only other numbers are 5832, 17,576, and 19,683, the cube roots of which may be correctly obtained by merely adding the digits, which come to 18, 26, and 27 respectively.

121. QUEER DIVISION

The smallest number that fulfills the conditions is 35,641,667,749. Other numbers that will serve may be obtained by adding 46,895,573,610 or any multiple of it.

122. THREE DIFFERENT DIGITS

The numbers are 162, 243, 324, 392, 405, 512, 605, 648, 810, and 972. These, we think, are all the cases that exist.

123. DIGITS AND CUBES

There are three solutions. They are 56,169 (the square of 237), where 56 + 69 = 125 (the cube of 5); 63,001 (the square of 251), where 63 + 01 =

64 (the cube of 4); 23,104 (the square of 152), where $23 + 04 = 27$ (the cube of 3).

124. REVERSING THE DIGITS

989,010,989 multiplied by 123,456,789 produces 122,100,120,987,654,321, where the last nine digits are in the reverse order.

125. DIGITAL PROGRESSION

The Professor's answer was:

297	564	831
291	564	837
237	564	891
231	564	897

where the common differences are respectively 267, 273, 327, and 333. He pointed out that the three digits in the central number may be arranged in any of the six possible ways, and a solution may be found.

[Victor Meally tells me that Victor Thébault, in *Parmi les Nombres Curieux*, page 140, shows that there are 760 such progressions. In addition to 456 and its permutations, the middle number may be any of the permutations of the following four sets of three digits: 258, 267, 348 and 357.—M. G.]

126. FORMING WHOLE NUMBERS

If you multiply 6,666 by the sum of the four given digits you will get the correct answer. As 1, 2, 3, 4 sum to 10, then 6,666 multiplied by 10 gives us 66,660 as our answer. Taking all possible selections of four different digits, the answer is 16,798,320, or $6,666 \times 2,520$.

127. SUMMING THE DIGITS

There are several ways of attacking this puzzle, and the answer is 201,599,999,798,400. The sum of the digits is 45 and

$$45 \times 8! = 1,814,400$$

Now write down—

18144
18144
18144
18144

to nine places, add up and put 00 at the end, and there is the answer.

128. SQUARING THE DIGITS

In four moves 7 3, 3 4, 4 8, 2 5, we can get 157,326,849, which is the square of 12,543. But the correct solution is 1 5, 8 4, 4 6, which gives us the number 523,814,769, the square of 22,887, which is in three moves only.

129. DIGITS AND SQUARES

(1) 1,026,753,849 (the square of 32,043); (2) 9,814,072,356 (the square of 99,066).

130. DIGITAL SQUARES

The only two solutions are 567, with its square, 321,489; and 854, with its square, 729,316. We need only examine cases where the digits in the root number sum to 9, 18, or 27; or 8, 17, or 26, and it can never be a lower sum than 317 to form the necessary six figures.

131. FINDING A SQUARE

Taking the six numbers in their order, the sums of their digits are:

46	31	42	34	25	34
1	4	6	7	7	7

Again adding, where necessary, the digits until we reach a single figure, we get the second row of numbers, which we call the digital roots. These may be combined in different triplets in eight different ways:

146	147	167	177	467	477	677	777
2	3	5	6	8	9	2	3

again giving the digital roots shown. Now, as shown in *Amusements in Mathematics,* the digital root of every square number must be either 1, 4, 7, or 9, so that the required numbers must have the roots 4, 7, 7, to be a square. The two 7's may be selected in three different ways. But if the fifth number is included, the total of the three will end in 189 or 389, which is impossible for a square, as the 89 must be preceded by an even figure or 0. Therefore the required numbers must be: 2,494,651 + 1,385,287 + 9,406,087 = 13,286,025, which is the square of 3,645.

As illustrating the value of this new method we may be allowed to quote from the late Professor W. W. Rouse Ball:

"This application is original on Mr. Dudeney's part. Digital properties are but little known to mathematicians, and we hope his example may serve to direct attention to the method. . . . In a certain class of arithmetical problems it is of great assistance."

132. JUGGLING WITH DIGITS

$$7 + 1 = 8; 9 - 6 = 3; 4 \times 5 = 20.$$

133. EQUAL FRACTIONS

The five answers are as follows:

$$\frac{2}{4} = \frac{3}{6} = \frac{79}{158}; \frac{3}{6} = \frac{7}{14} = \frac{29}{58}; \frac{3}{6} = \frac{9}{18} = \frac{27}{54}; \frac{2}{6} = \frac{3}{9} = \frac{58}{174}; \frac{2}{1} = \frac{.6}{3} = \frac{97}{485}.$$

134. DIGITS AND PRIMES

The 4, 6, and 8 must come in the tens place, as no prime number can end with one of these, and 2 and 5 can only appear in the units place if alone. When those facts are noted the rest is easy, as here shown:

$$
\begin{array}{r}
47 \\
61 \\
89 \\
2 \\
3 \\
\underline{5} \\
207
\end{array}
$$

135. A SQUARE OF DIGITS

In every one of the following eight sums all the nine digits are used once, and the difference between the successive totals is, throughout, 9:

243	341	154	317	216	215	318	235
675	586	782	628	738	748	654	746
918	927	936	945	954	963	972	981

136. THE NINE DIGITS

The number 94,857,312, multiplied by 6, gives the product 569,143,872, the nine digits being used once, and once only, in each case.

[There are 86 other solutions. All 87 are given by Joseph Madachy in *The Fibonacci Quarterly,* Vol. 6, February 1968, page 61.–M. G.]

137. EXPRESSING TWENTY-FOUR

The following is a simple solution (by G. P. E.) for three 7's:

$$\left(7 - \sqrt{\frac{7}{.7}}\right)!$$

From this we obtain the answer for three 1's by substituting 1 for 7 in every case, and putting plus instead of minus.

[Dudeney does not give solutions for the remaining digits, but Victor Meally has supplied them:

$$(4 + 4 - 4)!$$
$$\left(5 - \frac{5}{5}\right)!$$
$$\left(\frac{6}{.6} - 6\right)!$$
$$8 + 8 + 8$$
$$\left(\sqrt{9} + \frac{9}{9}\right)!$$

—M. G.]

138. THE NINE BARRELS

There are forty-two different arrangements. The positions of the 1 and 9 are fixed. Always place the 2 beneath the 1. Then, if the 3 be beneath the 2 there are five arrangements. If the 3 be to the right of the 1 there are five arrangements with 4 under the 2, five with 5 under the 2, four with 6 under 2, two with 7 under 2. We have thus twenty-one arrangements in all. But the 2 might have been always to the right of 1, instead of beneath, and then we get twenty-one reversed and reflected arrangements (practically similar), making forty-two in all. Either the 4, 5, or 6 must always be in the center.

139. THE EIGHT CARDS

You need only make the 8 and 9 change places, first turning the 9 round so as to change it to a 6. Then each column will add up 18.

140. FIND THE NUMBERS

The two numbers composed of 1's that sum and multiply alike are 11 and 1.1. In both cases the result is 12.1.

141. MULTIPLYING THE NINE DIGITS

Dora was not to be caught by George's question. She, of course, immediately gave the correct answer, 0.

142. CURIOUS MULTIPLICAND

The number is 142,857. This is, of course, the recurring decimal fraction of one-seventh.

143. ADDING THEIR CUBES

The required number is 153. The cubes of 1, 5, and 3 are respectively 1, 125, and 27, and these added together make 153.

[Dudeney overlooked a fourth number: 371. Aside from 1, these are the only four numbers that are the sums of the cubes of their digits. For the more general problem, of finding numbers that are the sums of the *n*th powers of their digits, see Joseph S. Madachy, *Mathematics on Vacation* (Scribner's, 1966, pp. 163–165.—M. G.]

144. THE SOLITARY SEVEN

The restored simple division sum is as follows:

```
124)12128316(97809
    1116
     968
     868
    1003
     992
    1116
    1116
```

[When Dudeney first published this in *The Strand Magazine,* a reader, Harold Revell, of Sussex, sent him a formal proof that the solution is indeed unique. Mr. Revell sent me a copy of his proof in 1964, but it is too lengthy to give here.—M. G.]

145. A COMPLETE SKELETON

```
625)631938(1011.1008
    625
    693
    625
    688
    625
    630
    625
    5000
    5000
```

The three 0's that must occur at the bottom show that the divisor is a sub-multiple of 1,000. The factors therefore can only be 5, 5, 5, 2, 2, 2, *x*, where *x* is less than 10. To form the three-figure divisor, one factor at least must be 5, and therefore the last figure must be 5 or 0. The subtraction from the single 0 near the bottom shows that it is a 5 and at once gives us the 5,000. The factor 2 being excluded from the divisor (or it could not end in a 5), the final figure in the quotient must be 8 ($2 \times 2 \times 2$), and the divisor 625, making x a fourth 5. The rest is quite easy.

146. SIMPLE MULTIPLICATION

Here is an answer:

$$\begin{array}{r} 4539281706 \\ 2 \\ \hline 9078563412 \end{array}$$

If you divide the first number into pairs—45, 39, etc.—these can be arranged in any order so long as the 06 is not at the beginning or the 45 at the end.

147. AN ABSOLUTE SKELETON

It can soon be discovered that the divisor must be 312, that 9 cannot be in the quotient because nine times the divisor contains a repeated figure. We therefore know that the quotient contains all the figures 1 to 8 once, and the rest is comparatively easy. We shall find that there are four cases to try, and that the only one that avoids repeated figures is the following:

312) 10,114,626,600 (32,418,675.

[Abraham S. Feigenbaum, Highland Park, New Jersey, has found an alternate answer: 310) 10,174,126,840 (32,819,764.–M. G.]

148. ODDS AND EVENS

249) 764,752,206 (3,071,294.
249) 767,242,206 (3,081,294.
245) 999,916,785 (4,081,293.
245) 997,466,785 (4,071,293.
248) 764,160,912 (3,081,294.
248) 761,680,912 (3,071,294.

If the reader will work out each of these little sums in simple division he will find that they fulfill all the conditions required by the asterisks and O's and E's.

149. SIMPLE DIVISION

Divide 4,971,636,104 by 124,972, and the quotient is 39,782. The reader can now work out the little sum for himself, and he will find that all the conditions are fulfilled. If we were allowed additional 7's in the dividend, an answer would be 7,471,076,104 divided by 124,972 equals 59,782.

[Abraham Feigenbaum, mentioned in the answer to Problem 147, has found three alternate solutions: 124,972)2,472,196,104(19,782; 124,974)-2,472,110,694(19,781; and 124,974)4,971,590,694(39,781.—M. G.]

150. A COMPLETE SKELETON

The first division sum is: 333)100,007,892(300,324 and the second: 29)300,324(10,356.

151. ALPHABETICAL SUMS

The answer is as follows:

$$
35\,)\,19775\,(\,565
$$
$$
\underline{175}
$$
$$
227
$$
$$
210
$$
$$
\underline{175}
$$
$$
175
$$

It is clear that R cannot be 1: it must therefore be either 5 or 6 to produce the R in the second line. Then D must be 0 to give the V in the fifth line. Also M must be 1, 2, 3, or 4, if R is 5, but may be 5 if R is 6. Again, S must be an even number if R is 5, to make D a 0, and if R is 6, then S must be 5. When we have discovered and noted these facts, only a little trial is necessary.

152. ALPHABETICAL ARITHMETIC

$$\begin{array}{r} 17 \\ \times\ 4 \\ \hline 68 \end{array} \qquad \begin{array}{r} 93 \\ -68 \\ \hline 25 \end{array}$$

153. FIGURES FOR LETTERS

$6,543 \times 98,271 = 642,987,153.$

154. THE SHOPKEEPER'S PUZZLE

The only word (not a jumble of letters) that will fit the conditions is REGULATION. Used in the way explained, the actual sum was:

$$\begin{array}{r} 36,407 \\ +98,521 \\ \hline 134,928 \end{array}$$

155. BEESWAX

The key is as follows:

1 2 3 4 5 6 7 8 9 0
A T Q B K X S W E P

from which we get

$$\begin{array}{r} 917947476 \\ -408857923 \\ \hline 509089553 \end{array}$$

and BEESWAX represents the number 4,997,816.

156. WRONG TO RIGHT

$$\begin{array}{r} 25938 \\ +25938 \\ \hline 51876 \end{array}$$

157. LETTER MULTIPLICATION

$$
\begin{array}{r}
4973 \\
\times \quad 8 \\
\hline
39784
\end{array}
$$

158. THE CONSPIRATORS' CODE

$$
\begin{array}{r}
598 \\
507 \\
8047 \\
\hline
9152
\end{array}
$$

159. LETTER-FIGURE PUZZLE

It is clear that A must be 1, and that B and C must be either 6 and 2 or 3 and 5, and that in the third equation they are shown to be 3 and 5, since D must be 7. Then E must be 8 in order that D $\times$ E should show C = 5. Then the rest is easy, and we find the answer as follows: A = 1, B = 3, C = 5, D = 7, E = 8, F = 9, H = 6, J = 4, K = 2, L = 0.

160. THE MILLER'S TOLL

There must have been one bushel and one-ninth, which after taking the one-tenth as toll, would leave exactly one bushel.

161. EGG LAYING

The answer is half a hen and a half hen; that is, one hen. If one and a half hens lay one and a half eggs in one and a half days, one hen will lay one egg in one and a half days. And a hen who lays better by half will lay one and a half eggs in one and a half days, or one egg per day. So she will lay ten and a half (half a score and a half) in ten and a half days (a week and a half).

162. THE FLOCKS OF SHEEP

Adam must have possessed 60 sheep, Ben 50, Claude 40, and Dan 30. If the distributions described had taken place, each brother would have then had 45 sheep.

163. SELLING EGGS

The smallest possible number of eggs is 103, and the woman sold 60 every day. Any multiple of these two numbers will work. Thus, she might have started with 206 eggs and sold 120 daily; or with 309 and sold 180 daily. But we required the smallest possible number.

164. PUSSY AND THE MOUSE

You have simply to divide the given number by 8. If there be no remainder, then it is the second barrel. If the remainder be 1, 2, 3, 4, or 5, then that re-mainder indicates the number of the barrel. If you get a remainder greater than 5, just deduct it from 10 and you have the required barrel. Now 500 divided by 8 leaves the remainder 4, so that the barrel marked 4 was the one that contained the mouse.

165. ARMY FIGURES

The five brigades contained respectively 5,670; 6,615; 3,240; 2,730; and 2,772 men. Represent all the fractions with the common denominator 12,012, and the numerators will be 4,004; 3,432; 7,007; 8,316; and 8,190. Combining all the *different* factors contained in these numbers, we get 7,567,560, which, divided by each number in turn, gives us 1,890; 2,205; 1,080; 910; and 924. To fulfill the condition that the division contained a "little over 20,000 men," we multiply these by 3 and have the correct total—21,027.

166. A CRITICAL VOTE

There must have been 207 voters in all. At first 115 voted for the motion and 92 against, the majority of 23 being just a quarter of 92. But when the 12 who could not sit down were transferred to the other side, 103 voted for the motion and 104 against. So it was defeated by 1 vote.

167. THE THREE BROTHERS

Arthur could do the work in $14\frac{34}{49}$ days, Benjamin in $17\frac{23}{41}$ days, and Charles in $23\frac{7}{31}$ days.

168. THE HOUSE NUMBERS

The numbers of the houses on each side will add up alike if the number of the house be 1 and there are no other houses; if the number be 6, with 8 houses in all; if 35, with 49 houses; if 204, with 288 houses; if 1,189, with 1,681 houses; and so on. But it was known that there were more than 50 and fewer than 500 houses, so we are limited to a single case, and the number of the house must have been 204.

Find the integral solutions of $\dfrac{x^2 + x}{2} = y^2$. Then we get the answers:

x = Number of houses. y = Number of particular house.

1	1
8	6
49	35
288	204
1,681	1,189

and so on.

169. A NEW STREET PUZZLE

Brown's number must have been 84, and there were 119 houses. The numbers from 1 to 84 sum to 3,570 and those from 1 to 119 to 7,140, which is just double, as stated.

Write out the successive solutions to the Pellian equation (explained on page 164 in my book *Amusements in Mathematics*) $2x^2 - 1 = y^2$, thus:

x	y
1	1
5	7
29	41
169	239
985	1,393

and so on. Then the integral half of any value of x will give you the house number and the integral half of y the total number of houses. Thus (ignoring the values 0–0) we get 2–3, 14–20, 84–119, 492–696, etc.

170. ANOTHER STREET PUZZLE

On the odd side of the street the house must have been No. 239, and there were 169 houses on that side. On the even side of the street the house must have been No. 408, and there were 288 houses.

In the first case, find integral solution of $2x^2 - 1 = y^2$. Then we get the answers:

x = Number of houses. y = Number of particular house.

1	1
5	7
29	41
169	239
985	1,393

and so on.

In the second case, find integral solution of $2(x^2 + x) = y^2$.

Then we get the answers:

x = Number of houses. y = Number of particular house.

1	2
8	12
49	70
288	408
1,681	2,378

and so on.

These two cases, and the two previous puzzles, all involve the well-known Pellian equation and are related.

171. CORRECTING AN ERROR

Hilda's blunder amounted to multiplying by 49, instead of by 409. Divide the error by the difference (328,320 by 360) and you will get the required number—912.

172. THE SEVENTEEN HORSES

The farmer's seventeen horses were to be divided in the *proportions* ½, ⅓, ⅑.

It was not stated that the sons were to receive those *fractions* of seventeen. The proportions are thus ⁹⁄₁₈, ⁶⁄₁₈, and ²⁄₁₈, so if the sons receive respectively 9, 6, and 2 horses each, the terms of the legacy will be exactly carried out. Therefore, the ridiculous old method described does happen to give a correct solution.

A correspondent suggested to me the ingenious solution:

$$\begin{array}{l}
\tfrac{1}{2}, \text{ i.e., 2 and 1 over} = 3 \\
\tfrac{1}{3}, \text{ i.e., 3 and 1 over} = 4 \\
\tfrac{1}{9}, \text{ i.e., 9 and 1 over} = \underline{10} \\
\phantom{\tfrac{1}{9}, \text{ i.e., 9 and 1 over} = } 17
\end{array}$$

173. EQUAL PERIMETERS

The six right-angled triangles having each the same, and the smallest possible, perimeter (720), are the following: 180, 240, 300; 120, 288, 312; 144, 270, 306; 72, 320, 328; 45, 336, 339; 80, 315, 325.

174. COUNTING THE WOUNDED

The three fractions are respectively ⁴⁰⁄₆₀, ⁴⁵⁄₆₀, and ⁴⁸⁄₆₀. Add together 40, 45, and 48, and deduct twice 60. The result is 13, as the minimum number for every 60 patients. Therefore as the minimum (who could have each lost an eye, an arm, and a leg) was 26, the number of patients must have been 120.

175. A COW'S PROGENY

Note the following series of numbers, first considered by Leonardo Fibonacci (born at Pisa in 1175), who practically introduced into Christian Europe our Arabic numerals:

$$0, 1, 1, 2, 3, 5, 8, 13, 21, 34, \ldots, 46{,}368.$$

Each successive number is the sum of the two preceding it. The sum of all numbers from the beginning will always equal 1 less than the next but one term. Twice any term, added to the preceding term, equals the next but one term. Now, there would be 0 calf in the first year, 1 in the second, 1 in the third, 2 in the fourth, and so on, as in the series. The twenty-fifth term is

46,368, and if we add all the twenty-five terms or years together we get the result, 121,392, as the correct answer. But we need not do that addition. When we have the twenty-fourth and twenty-fifth terms we simply say (46,368 multiplied by 2) plus 28,657 equals 121,393, from which we deduct 1.

176. SUM EQUALS PRODUCT

If you take any number in combination with 1 and a fraction whose numerator is 1 and its denominator 1 less than the given number, then the sum and product will always be the same. Thus, 3 and 1½, 4 and 1⅓, 5 and 1¼, and so on. Therefore, when I was given 987654321, I immediately wrote down $1\frac{1}{987654320}$ and their sum and product is $987654322\frac{1}{987654320}$.

Now, the reason why 2 and 2 are often regarded as an exceptional case is that the denominator is 1, thus 2 and 1⅟₁, which happens to make the second a whole number, 2. But it will be seen that it is really subject to the universal rule. A number may be fractional as well as whole, and I did not make it a condition that we must find a whole number, for that would be impossible except in the case of 2 and 2. Of course, decimal fractions may be used, such as 6 and 1.2, or 11 and 1.1, or 26 and 1.04.

In short, the general solution is n added to or multiplied by

$$\frac{n}{n-1} = (n+1) + \frac{1}{n-1}.$$

177. SQUARES AND CUBES

The solution in the smallest possible numbers appears to be this:

$$10^2 - 6^2 = 100 - 36 = 64 = 4^3.$$
$$10^3 - 6^3 = 1,000 - 216 = 784 = 28^2.$$

178. CONCERNING A CUBE

(1) 6 feet. (2) 1.57 feet nearly. (3) ⅟₃₆ foot.

179. A COMMON DIVISOR

Since the numbers have a common factor plus the same remainder, if the numbers are subtracted from one another in the manner shown below the results must contain the common factor without the remainder.

$$
\begin{array}{r}
508{,}811 \\
-\ 480{,}608 \\
\hline
28{,}203
\end{array}
\qquad
\begin{array}{r}
723{,}217 \\
-\ 508{,}811 \\
\hline
214{,}406
\end{array}
$$

Here the prime factors of 28,203 are 3, 7, 17, 79, and those of 214,406 are 2, 23, 59, 79. And the only factor common to both is 79. Therefore the required divisor is 79, and the common remainder will be found to be 51. Simple, is it not?

180. CURIOUS MULTIPLICATION

In the first column write in the successive remainders, which are 1 0 0 0 0 1 1, or reversed, 1 1 0 0 0 0 1. This is 97 in the binary scale of notation, or 1 plus 2^5 plus 2^6. In the second column (after rejecting the numbers opposite to the remainder 0) we add together 23×1, 23×2^5, 23×2^6, equals 2,231. The whole effect of the process is now obvious. It is merely an operation in the binary scale.

181. THE REJECTED GUN

The experts were right. The gun ought to have fired 60 shots in 59 minutes if it really fired a shot a minute. The time counts from the first shot, so that the second would be fired at the close of the first minute, the third at the close of the second minute, and so on. In the same way, if you put up 60 posts in a straight line, a yard apart, they will extend a length of 59 yards, not 60.

182. TWENTY QUESTIONS

There are various ways of solving this puzzle, but the simplest is, I think, the following. Suppose the six-figure number to be 843,712. (1) If you divide it by 2, is there any remainder? No. (2) If you divide the quotient by 2, is

there any remainder? No. (3) If you divide again by 2, is there any remainder?
No. Your twenty questions will be all the same, and writing from right to left,
you put down a zero for the answer "No," and 1 for the answer "Yes." The result will be that after the twentieth question you will get 11001101111111000000.
This is 843,712 written in the binary scale. Dropping the final 0 in the units
place, the first 1 is the sixth figure backwards. Add together the 6th, 7th, 8th,
9th, 10th, 11th, 12th, 14th, 15th, 18th, and 19th powers of 2 and you will get
843,712 in our denary scale.

If the number is a low one like 100,000, seventeen questions would be sufficient if only you knew that the 0 had been reached in the quotient, but the
three final questions will merely add three noughts to the left of your binary
number. But to prevent quibbles as to infinities, etc., it is best to state before
beginning your questions that zero divided by 2 is understood to mean zero
with no remainder.

183. A CARD TRICK

Every pile must contain 13 cards, less the value of the bottom card. Therefore, 13 times the number of piles less the sum of the bottom cards, and plus
the number of cards left over, must equal 52, the number in the pack. Thus
13 times the number of piles plus number of cards left over, less 52, must
equal sum of bottom cards. Or, which is the same thing, the number of piles
less 4, multiplied by 13, and plus the cards left over gives the answer as
stated. The algebraically inclined reader can easily express this in terms of his
familiar symbols.

184. THE QUARRELSOME CHILDREN

Each parent had three children when they married, and six were born
afterward.

185. SHARING THE APPLES

Ned Smith and his sister Jane took 3 and 3 respectively, Tom and Kate
Brown took 8 and 4 respectively, Bill and Anne Jones took 3 and 1 respectively, and Jack and Mary Robinson took 8 and 2 respectively. This accounts
for the 32 apples.

186. BUYING RIBBON

Mary's mother was Mrs. Jones. Now:

Daughters.

Hilda bought 4 yds. for $ .16
Gladys bought 6 yds. for .36
Nora bought 9 yds. for .81
Mary bought 10 yds. for 1.00

Mothers.

Mrs. Smith 8 yds. for $ .64
Mrs. Brown 12 yds. for 1.44
Mrs. White 18 yds. for 3.24
Mrs. Jones 20 yds. for 4.00

187. SQUARE AND TRIANGULARS

To find numbers that are both square and triangular, one has to solve the Pellian equation, 8 times a square plus 1 equals another square. The successive numbers for the first square are 1, 6, 35, etc., and for the relative second squares 3, 17, 99, etc. Our answer is therefore 1,225 (35^2), which is both a square and a triangular number.

188. PERFECT SQUARES

Several answers can, of course, be found for this problem, but we think the smallest numbers that satisfy the conditions are:

$a = 10,430, b = 3,970, c = 2,114, d = 386.$
$a + b = 10,430 + 3,970 = 14,400 = 120^2.$
$a + c = 10,430 + 2,114 = 12,544 = 112^2.$
$a + d = 10,430 + 386 = 10,816 = 104^2.$
$b + c = 3,970 + 2,114 = 6,084 = 78^2.$
$b + d = 3,970 + 386 = 4,356 = 66^2.$
$c + d = 2,114 + 386 = 2,500 = 50^2.$
$a + b + c + d = 10,430 + 3,970 + 2,114 + 386 = 16,900 = 130^2.$

The general solution depends on the fact that every prime number of the form $4m + 1$ is the sum of two squares. Readers will probably like to work out the solution in full.

189. ELEMENTARY ARITHMETIC

The answer must be 2⅔. It is merely a sum in simple proportion: If 5 be 4, then 3⅓ will be 2⅔.

190. TRANSFERRING THE FIGURES

The required number is:

2,173,913,043,478,260,869,565,

which may be multiplied by 4 and the product divided by 5 by simply moving the 2 from the beginning to the end.

191. A QUEER ADDITION

Write the following four numbers, composed of five odd figures, in the form of an addition sum, 11, 1, 1, 1, and they will add up to 14.

192. SIX SIMPLE QUESTIONS

(1) 8,111½; (2) 18⅔; (3) 7 and 1; (4) 1⅕; (5) 8¼; (6) 6/9.

193. THE THREE DROVERS

Jack had 11 animals, Jim 7, and Dan 21 animals, making 39 animals in all.

194. PROPORTIONAL REPRESENTATION

The number of different ways in which the ballot may be marked is 9,864,100.

195. A QUESTION OF CUBES

The cubes of 14, 15, up to 25 inclusive (twelve in all) add up to 97,344, which is the square of 312. The next lowest answer is the five cubes of 25, 26, 27, 28, and 29, which together equal 315².

196. TWO CUBES

The cube of 7 is 343, and the cube of 8 is 512; the difference, 169, is the square of 13.

197. CUBE DIFFERENCES

The cube of 642 is 264,609,288, and the cube of 641 is 263,374,721, the difference being 1,234,567, as required.

198. ACCOMMODATING SQUARES

The number is 225,625 (the squares of 15 and 25), making the square of 475.

199. MAKING SQUARES

An answer is as follows: 482, 3,362, 6,242, which have a common difference of 2,880. The first and second numbers sum to 62², the first and third to 82², and the second and third to 98².

200. FIND THE SQUARES

If you add 125 to 100 and also to 164, you get two square numbers, 225 and 289, the squares of 15 and 17 respectively.

201. FORMING SQUARES

The officer must have had 1,975 men. When he formed a square 44 × 44 he would have 39 men over, and when he attempted to form a square 45 × 45 he would be 50 men short.

202. SQUARES AND CUBES

If we make one number $625m^6$, and the other number double the first, we can get any number of solutions of a particular series. Thus, if we make $m = 1$, we get the answer $625^2 + 1,250^2 = 125^3$, and $625^3 + 1,250^3 = 46,875^2$.

203. MILK AND CREAM

Half a pint of skimmed milk must be added.

204. FEEDING THE MONKEYS

The smallest number of nuts is 2,179. The best way of solving this is to deal first with the first two cases, and find that 34 (or 34 added to 143 or any multiple of it) will satisfy the case for 11 and 13 monkeys. You then have to find the lowest number of this form that will satisfy the condition for the 17 monkeys.

205. SHARING THE APPLES

The ratio is clearly 6, 4, and 3, which sum to 13. Therefore the boys receive $\frac{6}{13}$, $\frac{4}{13}$, and $\frac{3}{13}$, or 78, 52, and 39 apples.

206. SAWING AND SPLITTING

The men must saw $3\frac{1}{13}$ cords of wood.

207. THE BAG OF NUTS

The five bags contained respectively 27, 25, 18, 16, 14 nuts. Each bag can be found by subtracting the other two pairs together from 100. Thus, $100 - (52 + 30) = 18$, the third bag.

208. DISTRIBUTING NUTS

There were originally 1,021 nuts. Tommy received 256; Bessie, 192; Bob, 144; and Jessie, 108. Thus the girls received 300 and the boys 400, or 100 more, and Aunt Martha retained 321.

209. JUVENILE HIGHWAYMEN

The woman must have had 40 apples in her basket. Tom left her 30, Bob left 22, and Jim left 12.

210. BUYING DOG BISCUITS

The salesman supplied four boxes of 17 lbs. each, and two boxes of 16 lbs. each, which would make exactly the 100 lbs. required.

211. THE THREE WORKMEN

Alec could do the work in $14^{34}/_{49}$ days; Bill in $17^{23}/_{41}$ days; and Casey in $23^{7}/_{31}$ days.

212. WORKING ALONE

Sixty days and forty days.

213. THE FIRST "BOOMERANG" PUZZLE

When you are given the remainder after dividing by 3 multiply it by 70, the remainder by 5 multiply by 21, and the remainder by 7 multiply by 15. Add these results together and they will give you either the number thought of, or that number increased by some multiple of 105. Thus, if the number thought of was 79, then the remainder 1 multiplied by 70, the remainder 4 multiplied by 21, and the remainder 2 multiplied by 15, added together makes 184. Deduct 105, and you get 79—the number thought of.

214. LONGFELLOW'S BEES

The number of bees must have been 15.

215. LILIVATI, 1150 A.D.

The answer is 28. The trick lies in reversing the whole process—multiplying 2×10, deducting 8, squaring the result, and so on. Remember, for example, that to increase by three-fourths of the product is to take seven-fourths. And in the reverse process, at this step, you take four-sevenths.

216. BIBLICAL ARITHMETIC

There were seven in the Sunday School class. The successive numbers required by the questions in their order are as follows: 12, 7, 6, 10, 7, 50, 30, 5, 15, 4, 8.

217. THE PRINTER'S PROBLEM

The printer must have purchased the following twenty-seven types:

AABCDEEEFGHIJLMNOOPRRSTUUVY

218. THE SWARM OF BEES

There were seventy-two bees.

219. BLINDNESS IN BATS

The fewest possible would be 7, and this might happen in either of three ways:

(1) 2 with perfect sight, 1 blind only in the right eye, and 4 totally blind.

(2) 1 with perfect sight, 1 blind in the left eye only, 2 blind in the right eye only, and 3 totally blind.

(3) 2 blind in the left eye only, 3 blind in the right eye only, and 2 totally blind.

220. THE MENAGERIE

As the menagerie contained two monstrosities—the four-footed bird and the six-legged calf—there must have been 24 birds and 12 beasts in all.

221. SHEEP STEALING

The number of sheep in the flock must have been 1,025. It will be found that no mutilation of any sheep was necessary.

222. SHEEP SHARING

The share of Charles is 3,456 sheep. Probably some readers will first have found Alfred's share, and then subtracted 25 per cent, but this will, of course, be wrong.

223. THE ARITHMETICAL CABBY

The driver's number must have been 121.

224. THE LENGTH OF A LEASE

The number of years of the lease that had expired was 54.

225. MARCHING AN ARMY

There must have been 4,550 men. At first they were placed with 65 in front and 70 in depth; afterwards 910 in front and 5 in depth.

226. THE YEAR 1927

$$2^{11} - 11^2 = 1927.$$

227. BOXES OF CORDITE

The dump officer should give boxes of 18 until the remainder is a multiple of 5. Then, unless this is 5, 10, or 25, he gives this remainder in 15's and 20's. The biggest number for which this system breaks down is 72 plus 25, or 97. Of course, in the case of higher numbers, such as 133, where 108, in six boxes of 18, leaves 25, he would give only one box of 18, leaving 115, which he would deliver in one box of 15 and five boxes of 20. But in the case of 97, 72 is the first and only case leaving a multiple of 5—that is, 25.

228. THE ORCHARD PROBLEM

At first he had 7,890 trees, which formed a square 88 × 88, and left 146 trees over; but the additional 31 trees made it possible to plant a square 89 × 89, or a total of 7,921 trees.

229. BLOCKS AND SQUARES

The smallest number of blocks in each box appears to be 1,344. Surrounding the hollow square 34^2, the first girl makes her square 50^2, the second girl 62^2, and the third girl 72^2, with her four blocks left over for the corners.

230. FIND THE TRIANGLE

The sides of the triangle are 13, 14, and 15, making 14 the base, the height 12, and the area 84. There is an infinite number of rational triangles composed of three consecutive numbers, like 3, 4, and 5, and 13, 14, and 15, but there is no other case in which the height will comply with our conditions.

The triangles having three consecutive numbers for their sides, and having an integral area, are:

3	4	5
13	14	15
51	52	53
193	194	195
723	724	725, etc.

They are found very simply:

$$52 = 4 \times 14 - 4$$
$$194 = 4 \times 52 - 14$$
$$724 = 4 \times 194 - 52,$$

or generally $U_n = 4 U_{n-1} - U_{n-2}$, or the general mathematical formula: Find x, so that $3(x^2 - 1) = $ a perfect square, where $2x$, $2x + 1$, $2x - 1$ are the sides of the triangle.

231. COW, GOAT, AND GOOSE

As cow and goat eat $\frac{1}{45}$ in a day, cow and goose $\frac{1}{60}$ in a day, and goat and goose $\frac{1}{90}$ in a day, we soon find that the cow eats $\frac{5}{360}$ in a day, the goat $\frac{3}{360}$ in a day, and the goose $\frac{1}{360}$ in a day. Therefore, together they will eat $\frac{9}{360}$ in a day, or $\frac{1}{40}$. So they will eat all the grass in the field in 40 days, since there is no growth of grass in the meantime.

232. THE POSTAGE STAMPS PUZZLE

The number of postage stamps in the album must have been 2,519.

233. MENTAL ARITHMETIC

There are two solutions with numbers less than ten: 3 and 5, and 7 and 8.
The general solution to this problem is as follows:
Calling the numbers *a* and *b*, we have:

$$a^2 + b^2 + ab = \square = /a - mb/^2 = a^2 - 2amb + b^2m^2.$$
$$\therefore b + a = -2am + bm^2,$$
$$\therefore b = \frac{a(2m + 1)}{m^2 - 1}$$

in which *m* may be any whole number greater than 1, and *a* is chosen
to make *b* rational. The general values are $a = m^2 - 1$ and $b = 2m + 1$.

234. SHOOTING BLACKBIRDS

Twice 4 added to 20 is 28. Four of these (a seventh part) were killed, and
these were those that remained, for the others flew away.

235. THE SIX ZEROS

$$
\begin{array}{r}
100 \\
330 \\
505 \\
077 \\
099 \\
\hline
1,111
\end{array}
$$

236. MULTIPLICATION DATES

There are 215 different dates in this century complying with the conditions,
if we include such cases as 25/4/00. The most fruitful year was 1924, when we

get the seven cases: 24/1/24, 12/2/24, 2/12/24, 8/3/24, 3/8/24, 6/4/24, 4/6/24. One has only to seek the years containing as many factors as possible.

237. SHORT CUTS

To multiply 993 by 879, proceed as follows: Transfer 7 from 879 to 993, and we get 872 and 1,000, which, multiplied together, produce 872,000. And 993 less 872 is 121, which, multiplied by the 7, will produce 847. Add the two results together, and we get 872,847, the correct answer.

238. MORE CURIOUS MULTIPLICATION

The number is 987,654,321, which, when multiplied by 18, gives 17,777,777,778, with 1 and 8 at the beginning and end. And so on with the other multipliers, except 90, where the product is 88,888,888,890, with 90 at the end.

[Dudeney overlooked such numbers as 1,001; 10,101; and 100,101 (made up of 1's and 0's, with 1's at the ends and no two consecutive 1's), all of which provide other answers.—M. G.]

239. CROSS-NUMBER PUZZLE

The difficulty is to know where to start, and one method may be suggested here. In reading the clues across, the most promising seems to be 18 across. The three similar figures may be 111, 222, 333, and so on. 26 down is the square of 18 across, and therefore 18 across must be either 111 or 222, as the squares of 333, 444, etc., have all more than five figures. From 34 across we learn that the middle figure of 26 down is 3, and this gives us 26 down as the square of 111, *i.e.,* 12321.

We now have 18 across, and this gives us 14 down and 14 across. Next we find 7 down. It is a four-figure cube number ending in 61, and this is sufficient to determine it. Next consider 31 across. It is a triangular number—that is, a number obtained by summing 1, 2, 3, 4, 5, etc. 210 is the only triangular number that has one as its middle figure. This settles 31 across, 18 down, 21 down, and 23 across. We can now get 29 across, and this gives us 30 down.

From 29 down we can obtain the first two figures of 15 across, and can complete 15 across and 29 down. The remainder can now be worked out.

240. COUNTING THE LOSS

The number killed was 472. If the reader checks the figures for himself he will find that there were 72 men in each of the four gangs set to work in the end. The general solution of this is obtained from the indeterminate equation

$$\frac{35x - 48}{768}$$

which must be an integer, where x = number of survivors. Solving in the usual way, we get $x = 528$. Therefore, the number killed is $1{,}000 - 528 = 472$.

241. THE TOWER OF PISA

The ball would come to rest after travelling 218 ft. 9⅓ in.

242. A MATCHBOARDING ORDER

The answer is: 8 pieces of 20 ft., 1 piece of 18 ft., and 7 pieces of 17 ft. Thus there are 16 pieces in all, measuring together 297 ft., in accordance with the conditions.

243. GEOMETRICAL PROGRESSION

$$1 + 3 + 9 + 27 + 81 = 121 = 11^2,$$
and
$$1 + 7 + 49 + 343 = 400 = 20^2.$$

244. A PAVEMENT PUZZLE

One floor was 38 ft. (1,444 stones) and the other 26 ft. square (676 stones).

245. THE MUDBURY WAR MEMORIAL

The number of posts in hand must have been 180, and the length of the enclosing line 330 ft. Then, at a foot apart, they would require 150 more, but at a yard apart 110 would suffice, and they would have 70 too many.

246. MONKEY AND PULLEY

We find the age of the monkey works out at 1½ years, and the age of the mother 2½ years, the monkey therefore weighing 2½ lb., and the weight the same. Then we soon discover that the rope weighed 1¼ lb., or 20 oz.; and, as a foot weighed 4 oz., the length of the rope was 5 ft.

247. UNLUCKY BREAKDOWNS

There must have been 900 persons in all. One hundred wagons started off with 9 persons in each wagon. After 10 wagons had broken down, there would be 10 persons in every wagon—"one more." As 15 more wagons had to be withdrawn on the home journey, each of the remaining 75 wagons would carry 12 persons—"three more than when they started out in the morning."

248. PAT IN AFRICA

Pat said, "Begorra, one number's as good as another and a little better, so, as there are ten of us and myself, sure I'll take eleven, and it's myself that I'll begin the count at." Of course, the first count fell on himself. Eleven, starting at No. 1, is thus the smallest number to count out all the Britons. He was, in fact, told to count twenty-nine and begin at No. 9. This would have counted out all the natives. These are the smallest numbers.

249. BLENDING THE TEAS

The grocer must mix 70 lb. of the 32¢ tea with 30 lb. of the 40¢ tea.

250. THE WEIGHT OF THE FISH

The fish must have weighed 72 oz. or 4½ lb. The tail weighed 9 oz., the body 36 oz., and the head 27 oz.

251. CATS AND MICE

It is clear that 999,919 cannot be a prime number, and that if there is to be only one answer it can have only two factors. As a matter of fact these are 991 and 1,009, both of which are primes, and as each cat killed more mice than there were cats, the correct answer is clearly that 991 cats each killed 1,009 mice.

252. THE EGG CABINET

Say the number of drawers is n. Then there will be $2n - 1$ strips one way and $2n - 3$ strips the other, resulting in $4n^2 - 4n$ cells and $4n - 4$ strips. Thus, in the twelfth drawer we shall get 23 and 21 strips (44 together), and 528 cells. This applies to all drawers except the second, where we may have any number of strips one way, and a single one the other. So 1 and 1 will here serve (a single strip is not admissible, because "intersecting" was stipulated). There are thus only 262 strips in all, and 2,284 cells (not 264 and 2,288).

253. THE IRON CHAIN

The inner width of a link, multiplied by the number of links, and added to twice the thickness of the iron, gives the exact length. Every link put on the chain loses a length equal to twice the thickness of the iron. The inner width must have been 2⅓ in. This, multiplied by 9 and added to 1 makes 22 in., and multiplied by 15 and added to 1 makes 36 in. The two pieces of chain, therefore, contained 9 and 15 links respectively.

254. LOCATING THE COINS

If his answer be "even," then the dime is in the right pocket and the nickel in the left; if it be "odd," then the dime is in the left pocket and the nickel in the right.

255. THE THREE SUGAR BASINS

The number in each basin was originally 36 lumps, and after each cup had received 2 (⅟₁₈) every cup would then hold 6, and every basin 18—a difference of 12.

256. A RAIL PROBLEM

There must have been 51 divisions and 23 whole rails in every division. There were thus 1,173 whole rails, and 50 pairs of halves, making together 1,223 rails as stated.

257. MAKING A PENTAGON

Let AB be the required 1 inch in length. Make BC perpendicular to AB and equal to half AB. Draw AC, which produce until CD equals CB. Then join BD, and BD is the radius of the circumscribing circle. If you draw the circle the sides of the pen-tagon can be marked off—1 inch in length.

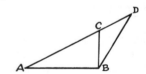

258. WITH COMPASSES ONLY

In order to mark off the four corners of a square, using the compasses only, first describe a circle, as in the diagram. Then, with the compasses open at the

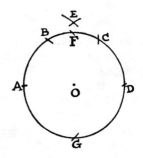

same distance, and starting from any point, A, in the circumference, mark off the points B, C, D. Now, with the centers A and D and the distance AC, describe arcs at E, and the distance EO is the side of the square sought. If, therefore, we mark off F and G from A with this distance, the points A, F, D, G will be the four corners of a perfect square.

259. LINES AND SQUARES

If you draw 15 lines in the manner shown in the diagram, you will have formed exactly 100 squares. There are 40 with sides of the length AB, 28 of the length AC, 18 of the length AD, 10 of the length AE, and 4 squares with sides of the length AF, making 100 in all. It is possible with 15 straight lines to form 112 squares, but we were restricted to 100. With 14 straight lines you cannot form more than 91 squares.

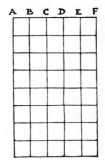

The general formula is that with n straight lines we can form as many as $\dfrac{(n-3)(n-1)(n+1)}{24}$ squares if n be odd, and $\dfrac{(n-2)n(n-1)}{24}$ if n be even.

If there are m straight lines at right angles to n straight lines, m being less than n, then $\dfrac{m(m-1)(3n-m-1)}{6}$ = number of squares.

260. MR. GRINDLE'S GARDEN

The rule is this. When the four sides are in arithmetical progression the greatest area is equal to the square root of their continual product. The square root of $7 \times 8 \times 9 \times 10$ is 70.99, or very nearly 71 square rods. This is the correct answer.

261. THE GARDEN PATH

The area of the path is exactly 66⅔ square yards, which is clearly seen if you imagine the little triangular piece cut off at the bottom and removed to the top right-hand corner. Here is the proof. The area of the garden path is 55 × 40 = 2,200. And (53⅓ × 40) + 66⅔ also equals 2,200. Finally, the sum of the squares of 53⅓ and 40 must equal the square of 66⅔, as it does.

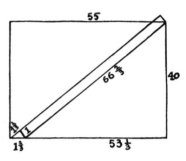

The general solution is as follows: Call breadth of rectangle B, length of rectangle L, width of path C, and length of path x.

Then
$$x = \frac{\pm\, B\sqrt{(B^2 - C^2)(B^2 + L^2)} + C^2L^2 - BCL}{B^2 - C^2}$$

In the case given above x = 66⅔, from which we find the length, 53⅓.

262. THE GARDEN BED

Bisect the three sides in A, B, and E. If you join AB and drop the perpendiculars AD and BC, then ABCD will be the largest possible rectangle and exactly half the area of the triangle. The two other solutions, FEAG and KEBH, would also serve (all these rectangles being of the same area) except for the fact that they would enclose the tree. This applies to any triangle with acute angles, but in the case of a right-angled triangle there are only two equal ways of proceeding.

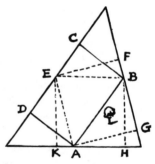

263. A PROBLEM FOR SURVEYORS

A rectilinear figure of any number of sides can be reduced to a triangle of equal area, and as AGF happens to be a right-angle the thing is quite easy in this way. Continue the line GA. Now lay a parallel ruler from A to C, run it up to B and mark the point 1. Then lay the ruler from 1 to D and run it down to C, marking point 2. Then lay it from 2 to E, run it up to D and mark point 3.

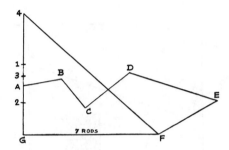

Then lay it from 3 to F, run it up to E and mark point 4. If you now draw the line 4 to F the triangle G4F is equal in area to the irregular field. As our scale map shows GF to be 7 inches (rods), and we find the length G4 in this case to be exactly 6 inches (rods), we know that the area of the field is half of 7 times 6, or 21 square rods. The simple and valuable rule I have shown should be known by everybody—but is not.

264. A FENCE PROBLEM

The diagram gives all the measurements. Generally a solution involves a biquadratic equation, but as I said the answer was in *"exact feet,"* the square of 91 is found to be the sum of two squares in only one way—the

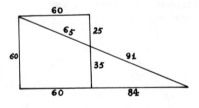

squares of 84 and 35. Insert these numbers as shown and the rest is easy and proves itself. The required distance is 35 feet.

265. THE FOUR CHECKERS

Draw a line from A to D. Then draw CE perpendicular to AD, and equal in length to AD. Then E will be the center of another square. Draw a line from

E to B and extend it on both sides. Also draw a line FG through C and parallel to EB and the lines through A and D perpendicular to EB and FG. Now, as H is the center of a corner square, we can mark off the length HE all round the square and we find the board is 10 × 10.

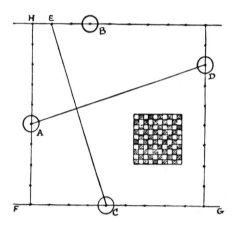

If the size of the men were not given we might subdivide into more squares, but the men would be too large for the squares. As the distance between the centers of squares is the same as the width of the squares, we can now complete the board with ease, as shown in the diagram inset.

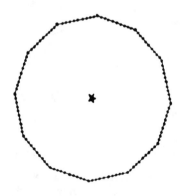

266. A MILITARY PUZZLE

The illustration shows the supremely easy way of solving this puzzle. The central star is the officer, and the dots are the men.

267. THE HIDDEN STAR

The illustration shows the symmetrical star in its exact position in the silk patchwork cloth. All the other pieces contributed are omitted for the sake of clearness, and it can be at once located on reference to the illustration given

with the puzzle. It is surprising how bewildering it is to find the star until you have been once shown it or have found it, and then it will appear pretty obvious.

268. A GARDEN PUZZLE

The trapezium will be inscribable in a circle. Half the sum of the sides is 29. From this deduct the sides in turn, and we get 9, 13, 17, 19, which, multiplied together, make 37,791. The square root of this, 194.4 square rods, will be the area.

269. A TRIANGLE PUZZLE

If you extend the table on the following page you may get as many rational triangles, with consecutive numbers, as you like.

P	Q	Height	Area
2	4	3	6
8	14	12	84
30	52	45	1,170
112	194	168	16,296
418	724	627	226,974
1,560	2,702	2,340	3,161,340

Here three times the square of P, added to 4, will make the square of Q. Every value of P is four times the last number less the previous one, and Q is found in the same way after the first step. The height is half as much again as P, and the area is the height multiplied by half of Q. The middle number of our three sides will always be found as Q. The last line will give us the first case where the area is divisible by 20. The triangle is 2,701, 2,702, 2,703, with height 2,340.

270. THE DONJON KEEP WINDOW

The illustration will show how the square window may be divided into eight lights "whose sides are all equal." Every side of the pane is of the same length.

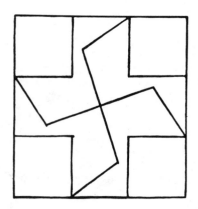

It was understood (though not actually stated) that the lights should be all of the same area, but the four irregular lights are each one-quarter larger than the square lights. And neither the shape nor the number of sides of the lights are equal. Yet the solution strictly complies with the conditions as given. If you shut out all these tricks and quibbles in a puzzle you spoil it by overloading the conditions. It is better (except in the case of competitions) to leave certain things to be understood.

271. THE SQUARE WINDOW

The diagram shows the original window, a yard square. After he had blocked out the four triangles indicated by the dotted lines, he still had a square window, as seen, measuring a yard in height and a yard in breadth.

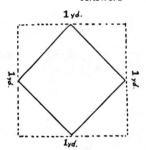

272. DIVIDING THE BOARD

The distance from end B at which the cut must be made is $5\sqrt{10} - 10 = 5.811+$.

273. A RUNNING PUZZLE

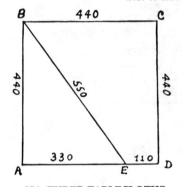

Each side of the field is 440 yards; BAE is a right-angled triangle, AE being 330 yards and BE 550 yards. Now, if Brown could run 550 yards while Adams ran 360 (330 + 30), then Brown can run the remaining 110 yards while Adams runs 72 yards. But 30 + 72 = 102 yards leaves Adams just 8 yards behind. Brown won by 8 yards.

274. THREE TABLECLOTHS

The three tablecloths, each 4 ft. by 4 ft., will cover a table 5 ft. 1 in. by 5 ft. 1 in. if laid in the manner here shown. ABCD is the table top, and 1, 2, and 3 are the three square cloths. Portions of 2 and 3, of course, fall over the edge of the table.

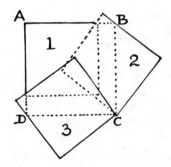

275. AN ARTIST'S PUZZLE

The canvas must be 10 in. in width and 20 in. in height; the picture itself 6 in. wide and 12 in. high. The margin will then be as required.

276. IN A GARDEN

The garden bed must have been 14 ft. long and 10 ft. in width.

277. COUNTING THE TRIANGLES

There are various ways of making the count, and the answer is 35.

278. A HURDLES PUZZLE

The old answer is that you can arrange them as in A, and then, by adding one more hurdle at each end, as in B, you double the area. No particular form

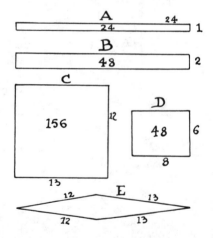

was stated. But even if you admit that the original pen was 24 × 1 the answer fails, for if you arrange the 50 as in Figure C, the area is increased from 24 square hurdles to 156, with accommodation for 650 sheep with no extra hurdles. Or you can double the area, as in D, with 28 hurdles only. If all the hurdles must be used you might construct it as in Figure E.

279. THE ROSE GARDEN

Make AD a quarter of the distance AB, and measure DE and AF each a quarter of BC. Now, if we make G the same distance from E that D is from F, then AG is the correct width of the path. If the garden is, for example, 12 ft. by 5 ft., the path will be 1 ft. wide, yet it cannot always be

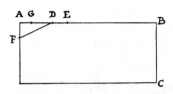

given in exact figures, though correct in measurement.

280. CORRECTING A BLUNDER

The correctness of the diagram can be easily proved, since the squares of 15 and 20 equal the square of 25; the squares of 15 and 36 equal the square of 39; and the squares of 15 and 8 equal the square of 17. Also, 20 + 8 = 28. If a right-angled triangle had been allowed, the one on the left, 15, 25, 20, would itself give the solution, since the height on the base 25 would be 12, and the median line 12½.

Perhaps our readers would like to try their hand at constructing the general solution to triangles of this class.

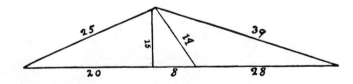

[Victor Meally has found a second solution to this problem: an obtuse triangle with base 66, sides of 41 and 85, and altitude of 40. The line bisecting the base is 58. In this case the altitude is exterior to the triangle, meeting the extended base line to form a right triangle with a base of 9, and sides of 40 and 41.—M. G.]

281. THE RUSSIAN MOTORCYCLISTS

The two distances given were 15 miles and 6 miles. Now, all you need do is to divide 15 by 6 and add 2, which gives us 4½. Now divide 15 by 4½, and the result (3⅓ miles) is the required distance between the two points. This pretty little rule applies to all such cases where the road forms a right-angled triangle. A simple solution by algebra will show why that constant 2 is added.

We can prove the answer in this way. The three sides of the triangle are 15 miles, 9⅓ miles (6 plus 3⅓ miles) and 17⅔ miles (to make it 21 miles each way). Multiply by 3 to get rid of the fractions, and we have 45, 28, and 53. Now, if the square of 45 (2,025) added to the square of 28 (784) equal the square of 53 (2,809) then it is correct—and it will be found that they do so.

282. THOSE RUSSIAN CYCLISTS AGAIN

The diagram gives all the correct distances. All the General had to do was to square Pipipoff's 60 miles (3,600) and divide by twice the sum of that 60 and Sliponsky's 12 miles—that is, by 144. Doing it in his head, he, of course, saw that this is the same as dividing 300 by 12, which at once gave him the correct answer, 25 miles, as the distance from A to B. I need not show how all the other distances are now easily obtained, if we want them.

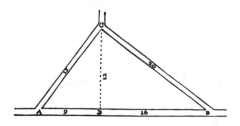

283. THE PRICE OF A GARDEN

The measurements given are absurd, and will not form a triangle. To do so the two shorter sides must together be greater than the third. The Professor gave it to his pupils just to test their alertness.

284. CHOOSING A SITE

This was another little jest. He may build wherever he pleases, for if perpendiculars are drawn to the sides of an equilateral triangle from *any* point in the triangle, their united length will be equal to the altitude of the triangle.

285. THE COUNTER CROSS

There are 19 different squares to be indicated. Of these, nine will be of the size shown by the four A's in the diagram, four of the size shown by the B's, four of the size shown by the C's, and two of the size shown by the D's. If you now remove the six coins marked "E," not one of these squares can be formed from the counters that remain.

[Actually, there are 21 squares. Can the reader find the two that Dudeney missed? The answer to the second part of the puzzle continues, however, to be correct.—M. G.]

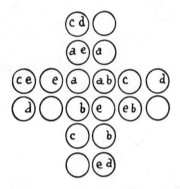

286. THE TRIANGULAR PLANTATION

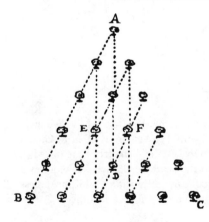

The number of ways in which 3 trees may be selected from 21 is

$$\frac{21}{1} \times \frac{20}{2} \times \frac{19}{3}, \text{ or } 1,330;$$

and a triangle may be formed with any one of these selections that does not happen to be three in a straight line. Let us enumerate these cases of three in a line. Three trees may be selected from the dotted line, AB, in 20 ways; from the next line of 5 trees parallel with it, in 10 ways; from the next line of 4, in 4 ways; and from the next parallel of 3 trees, in 1 way—making, in all, 35 ways in that direction. Similarly BC and the lines parallel with it will give 35 ways, and AC and the lines parallel with it, 35 ways. Then AD and the two lines parallel with it will give 3 ways, and similarly BF and CE, with their parallels, will give 3 ways each. Hence 3 trees in a straight line may be selected in 35 + 35 + 35 + 3 + 3 + 3 = 114 different ways. Therefore 1,330 − 114 = 1,216 must be the required number of ways of selecting three trees that will form the points of a triangle.

287. THE CIRCLE AND DISCS

In our diagram the dotted lines represent the circumference of the red circle and an inscribed pentagon. The center of both is C. Find D, a point equidis-

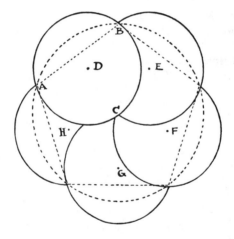

tant from A, B, and C, and with radius AD draw the circle ABC. Five discs of this size will cover the circle if placed with their centers at D, E, F, G, and H. If the diameter of the large circle is 6 inches, the diameter of the discs is a little less than 4 inches, or 4 inches "to the nearest half-inch." It requires a little care and practice correctly to place the five discs without shifting, unless you make some secret markings that would not be noticed by others.

If readers require a closer approximation or further information as to the manner of solving this puzzle, I cannot do better than refer them to a paper, on "Solutions of Numerical Functional Equations, illustrated by an account of a Popular Puzzle and its Solution," by Mr. Eric H. Neville, in the *Proceedings of London Mathematical Society,* Series II, Vol. 14, Part 4. I will just add that covering is possible if the ratio of the two diameters exceeds .6094185, and impossible if the ratio is less than .6094180. In my case above, where all five discs touch the center, the ratio is .6180340.

288. THE THREE FENCES

To divide a circular field into four equal parts by three fences of equal length, first divide the diameter of circle in four parts and then describe semicircles on each side of the line in the manner shown in the diagram. The curved lines will be the required fences.

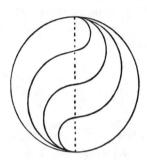

289. SQUARING THE CIRCLE

If you make a rectangle with one side equal to the diameter, and the other three times the diameter, then the diagonal will be something near correct. In

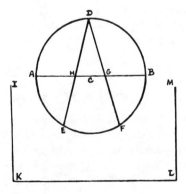

fact, it would be 1 to $1/\sqrt{10}$, or 1 to 3.1622+. The method we recommend is the following:

In the diagram, AB is the diameter. Bisect the semicircle in D. Now, with the radius AC mark off the points E and F from A and B, and draw the lines DE and DF. The distance DG, added to the distance GH, gives a quarter of the length of the circumference (IK), correct within a five-thousandth part. IKLM is the length of complete straight line.

There is another way, correct to a seventeen-thousandth part, but it is a little more difficult. [See W. W. Rouse Ball, *Mathematical Recreations and Essays,* revised 11th edition, Macmillan, 1960, p. 348.—M. G.]

290. THE CIRCLING CAR

Since the outside wheels go twice as fast as the inside ones, the circle they describe is twice the length of the inner circle. Therefore, one circle is twice the diameter of the other, and, since the wheels are 5 ft. apart, the diameter of the larger circle is 20 ft. Multiply 20 ft. by 3.1416 (the familiar approximate value for "pi") to get 62.832 ft. as the length of the circumference of the larger circle.

291. SHARING A GRINDSTONE

The first man should use the stone until he has reduced the radius by 1.754 in. The second man will then reduce it by an additional 2.246 in., leaving the last man 4 in. and the aperture. This is a very close approximation.

292. THE WHEELS OF THE CAR

The circumference of the front wheel and the rear wheel respectively must have been 15 ft. and 18 ft. Thus 15 ft. goes 24 times in 360 ft., and 18 ft. 20 times—a difference of four revolutions. But if we reduced the circumference by 3 ft., then 12 goes 30 times, and 15 goes 24 times—a difference of 6 revolutions.

293. A WHEEL FALLACY

The inner circle has half the diameter of the whole wheel, and therefore has half the circumference. If it merely ran along the imaginary line CD it would require two revolutions: after the first, the point D would be at E. But

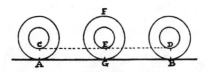

the point B would be at F, instead of at G, which is absurd. The fact is the inner circle makes only one revolution, but in passing from one position to the other it progresses partly by its own revolution and partly by carriage on the wheel. The point A gets to B entirely by its own revolution, but if you imagine a point at the very center of the wheel (a point has no dimensions and therefore no circumference), it goes the same distance entirely by what I have called carriage. The curve described by the passage of the point A to B is a common cycloid, but the point C in going to D describes a trochoid.

We have seen that if a bicycle wheel makes one complete revolution, so that the point A touches the ground again at B, the distance AB is the exact length of the circumference, though we cannot, if we are given the length of the diameter, state it in exact figures. Now that point A travels in the direction of the curved line shown in our illustration. This curve is called, as I have said, a "common cycloid." Now, if the diameter of the wheel is 28 inches, we can give the exact length of that curve. This is remarkable—that we cannot give exactly the length from A to B in a straight line, but can state exactly the length of the curve. What is that length? I will give the answer at once. The length of the cycloid is exactly four times that of the diameter.

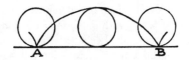

Therefore, four times 28 gives us 112 inches as its length. And the area of the space enclosed by the curve and the straight line AB is exactly three times the area of the circle. Therefore, the enclosed space on either side of the circle is equal in area to the circle.

294. A FAMOUS PARADOX

Of course, every part of the wheel revolves round the axle at a uniform speed, and, therefore, in the case of a *fixed* wheel, such as a grindstone, the answer is in the negative. But in the case of a bicycle wheel in *motion* along a road it is an undoubted fact that what is the upper part for the time being always moves faster *through space* than the lower part. If it did not do so, no progress would be made and the cyclist would have to remain as stationary as the grindstone.

Look at our diagram and you will see the wheel in four different positions that occur during one complete revolution from A_1 to A_4. I have earlier explained the peculiar curve, called a common cycloid, that is described by a point on the edge of the tire. The curve is shown here for two points at A_1

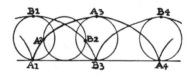

and B_1. Note that in a half-revolution A_1 goes to A_3 and B_1 to B_3, equal distances. But neither point moves *throughout* at a uniform speed. This is at once seen if we examine the quarter-revolution, where A_1 has only moved as far as A_2, while B_1 has gone all the way to B_2. We thus see that a point on the rim moves slowest through space when at the bottom, and fastest when near the top.

And here is a simple practical way of demonstrating it to your unbelieving friends without the aid of my diagrams. Draw a straight line on a sheet of paper and lay down a penny with the base of Lincoln's head on the line. Now make the penny run along the line a very short distance to the right and then to the left. That the base hardly leaves the original point on the line, while Lincoln's head travels a considerable distance, ought to be at once obvious to everybody. It should be quite convincing that the part of the wheel that is for the time being at the top moves faster through space than the part at the bottom.

295. ANOTHER WHEEL PARADOX

I have already shown that, if you mark a spot on the circumference of a bicycle wheel, that spot, when the wheel is progressing, will describe in space a curve known as a common cycloid. If, however, you mark the edge of the flange of a locomotive or railroad-car wheel, the spot will describe a trochoid curve, terminating in nodes or loops, as shown in the diagram. I have shown a wheel, with flanges below the railway line, in three positions—the start, a half-revolution, and a complete revolution. The spot marked A_1, has gone to A_2 and A_3. As the wheel is supposed to move from left to right, trace with your pencil the curve in that direction. You will then find that at the lower part of the loop you are actually going from right to left.

The fact is that "at any given moment" certain points at the bottom of the loop must be moving in the opposite direction to the train. As there is an in-

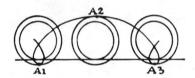

finite number of such points on the flange's circumference, there must be an infinite number of these loops being described while the train is in motion. In fact, certain points on the flanges are always moving in a direction opposite to that in which the train is going.

296. A MECHANICAL PARADOX

The machine shown in our illustration on page 302 consists of two pieces of thin wood, B, C, made into a frame by being joined at the corners. This frame, by means of the handle, n, may be turned round an axle, a, which pierces the frame and is fixed in a stationary board or table, A, and carries within the frame

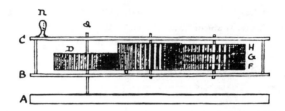

an immovable wheel. This first wheel, D, when the frame revolves, turns a second and thick wheel, E, which, like the remaining three wheels, F, G, and H, moves freely on its axis. The thin wheels, F, G, and H, are driven by the wheel E in such a manner that when the frame revolves H turns the same way as E does, G turns the contrary way, and F remains stationary. The secret lies in the fact that though the wheels may be all of the same diameter, and D, E, and F may (D and F *must*) have an equal number of teeth, yet G must have at least one tooth fewer, and H at least one tooth more, than D. Readers will find a full account of this paradox and its inventor in a little book, *Remarkable Men,* published by the Society for the Promotion of Christian Knowledge.

297. THE FOUR HOUSEHOLDERS

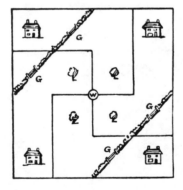

The simplest, though not the only solution, is that shown in our illustration.

298. THE FIVE FENCES

The illustration explains itself.

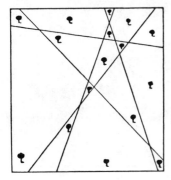

299. THE FARMER'S SONS

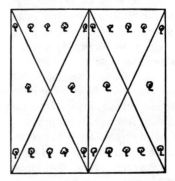

The illustration shows the simple solution to this puzzle. The land is divided into eight equal parts, each containing three trees.

300. AVOIDING THE MINES

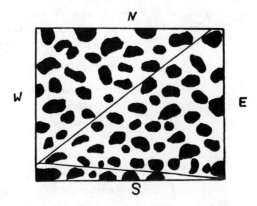

The illustration shows the passage through the mines in two straight courses.

301. SIX STRAIGHT FENCES

The six straight fences are so drawn that every one of the twenty trees is in a separate enclosure. We stated that twenty-two trees might be so enclosed in the square by six straight fences if their positions were more accommodating. We will here state that in such a case every line must cross every other line without any two crossings coinciding. As there are in our puzzle only twenty trees, this is not necessary, and it will be seen that four of the fences cross only four others instead of five.

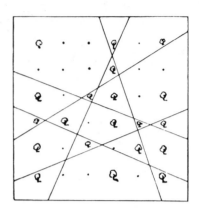

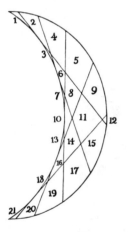

302. DISSECTING THE MOON

The illustration shows that the five cuts can be so cunningly made as to produce as many as twenty-one pieces.

Calling the number of cuts n, then in the case of a circle the maximum number of pieces will be $\dfrac{n^2 + n}{2} + 1$, but in the case of the crescent it will be $\dfrac{n^2 + 3n}{2} + 1$.

303. DRAWING A STRAIGHT LINE

Take pieces of thick cardboard (they need not have straight edges!) and join them with shoemakers' eyelets, as in the illustration. The two long pieces are of equal length from center of eyelet to eyelet, and the four pieces at the bot-

tom forming a diamond are all of
equal length. Nails or pins at A and B
fasten the instrument to the table, B
being so fixed that the distance from
A to B is the same as from B to C.
Then the pencil at D (if all is accu-
rately made and adjusted) will draw
the straight line shown.

[For other linkages that do the job,
see A. B. Kempe, *How to Draw a
Straight Line* (1877), reprinted by
Chelsea, 1953.—M. G.]

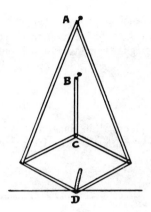

304. DRAWING AN ELLIPSE

Draw the two lines CD and EF at right angles (CD being equal to the required length, 12 inches, and EF to the required breadth, 8 inches), intersect-

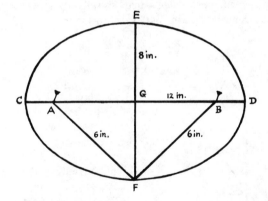

ing midway. Find the points A and B, so that AF and FB each equals half the
length CD, that is 6 inches, and place your pins at A and B, making the length
of your loop of string equal to ABFA. Say the distance CA = x. Then, when

the pencil is at F the length of string is $12 + (12 - 2x) = 24 - 2x$, and when the pencil is at C the length of string is $2(12 - x) = 24 - 2x$ also, proving the correctness of the solution.

305. THE BRICKLAYER'S TASK

A glance at the illustration will show that if you could cut off the portion of wall marked 1 and place it in the position indicated by 2, you would have

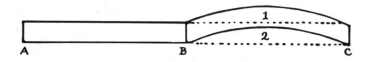

a piece of straight wall, BC, enclosed by the dotted lines, exactly similar to the wall AB. Therefore, both men were wrong, and the price should be the same for the portion of wall that went over the hill as for the part on the level. Of course, the reader will see at a glance that this will only apply within a certain limitation. But an actual drawing of the wall was given.

306. MEASURING THE RIVER

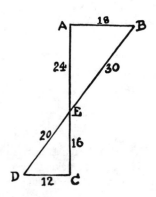

Measure any convenient distance along the bank from A to C, say 40 yards. Then measure any distance perpendicularly to D, say 12 yards. Now sight along DB and find the point E. You can then measure the distance from A to E, which will here be 24 yards, and from E to C, which will be 16 yards. Now AB:DC = AE:EC, from which it is evident that AB, the width of the river, must be 18 yards.

307. PAT AND HIS PIG

The pig will run and be caught at 66⅔ yards, and Pat will run 133⅓ yards. The curve of Pat's line is one of those curves the length of which may be exactly measured. It is $\dfrac{an^2}{n^2 - 1}$, where the pig's speed is assumed to be 1, and Pat runs n times as fast, and a is the initial distance between Pat and the pig.

308. THE LADDER

The distance from the top of the ladder to the ground was ⅘ of the length of the ladder. Multiply the distance from the wall—4 yards—by the denominator of this fraction—5—and you get 20. Now deduct the square of the numerator from the square of the denominator of ⅘, and you have 9, which is the square of 3. Finally, divide 20 by 3, and there is the answer 6⅔ yards.

309. A MAYPOLE PUZZLE

The height of the pole above ground must have been 50 ft. In the first case it was broken at a distance of 29 ft. from the top, and in the second case 34 ft. from the top.

310. THE BELL ROPE

The bell rope must have been 32 ft. 1½ in. in length from ceiling to floor.

311. THE DISPATCH RIDER IN FLANDERS

Of course, a straight line from A to C would not be the quickest route. It would be quicker to ride from A to E and then direct to C. The quickest possible route of all is that shown in the diagram on the following page by the dotted line from A to G (exactly 1 mile from E) and then direct to C.

It is necessary that the sine of the angle FGC shall be double the sine of AGH. In the first case the sine is 6 divided by the square root of $6^2 + 3^2$, which is 6 divided by the square root of 45, or the same as 2 divided by the square root of 5. In the second case the sine is 1 divided by the square root of $1^2 + 2^2$, which is 1 divided by the square root of 5. Thus the first is exactly double the second.

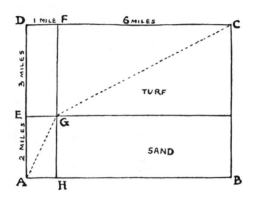

312. THE SIX SUBMARINES

It will be seen from the illustration that this puzzle is absurdly easy—when you know how to do it! And yet I have not the slightest doubt that

many readers found it a hard nut to crack. It will be seen that every match undoubtedly touches every other match.

[The number of matches can be increased to seven and still meet the puzzle's conditions. See my *Scientific American Book of Mathematical Puzzles & Diversions* (Simon & Schuster, 1959), p. 115.—M. G.]

313. ECONOMY IN STRING

The total length of string that passes along the length, breadth, or depth must in every case be the same to allow of the maximum dimensions—that is, 4 feet. When the reader is told this, or has found it for himself (and I think the point will be found interesting), the rest is exceedingly easy. For the string passes 2 times along length, 4 times along breadth, and 6 times along depth. Therefore 4 feet divided by 2, 4, and 6 will give us 2 feet, 1 foot, and ⅔ foot respectively for the length, breadth, and depth of the largest possible parcel. The following general solution is by Mr. Alexander Fraser. Let the string pass a times along length x, b times along breadth y, and c times along depth z, and let length of string be m.

Then $ax + by + cz = m$. Find maximum value of xyz.

First find maximum area of xy.

Put $ax + by = n$, $x = \dfrac{n - by}{a}$, $xy = \dfrac{n}{a}y - \dfrac{b}{a}y^2$, $\dfrac{dxy}{dy} = \dfrac{n}{a} - \dfrac{2b}{a}y = 0$,

$\therefore y = \dfrac{n}{2b}$, or $by = \dfrac{n}{2}$.

$\therefore ax$ also $= \dfrac{n}{2}$, and $ax = by$.

Similarly, $ax = by = cz = \dfrac{m}{3}$.

$\therefore x = \dfrac{m}{3a}, y = \dfrac{m}{3b}, z = \dfrac{m}{3c}$, and $xyz = \dfrac{m^3}{27abc}$.

In the case of the puzzle, $a = 2, b = 4, c = 6, m = 12$.

$\therefore x = 2, y = 1, z = ⅔$.

$xyz = 1⅓$.

314. THE STONE PEDESTAL

The cube of a square number is always a square. Thus:—

The cube of 1 is 1, the square of 1.
The cube of 4 is 64, the square of 8.
The cube of 9 is 729, the square of 27.
The cube of 16 is 4,096, the square of 64.

And so on.

We were told to look at the illustration. If there were one block in pedestal and one in base, the base would be entirely covered, which it was not. If 64 in pedestal and base, the side of the former would measure 4 feet, and the side of square 8 feet. A glance will show that this is wrong. But 729 blocks in each case is quite in agreement with the illustration, for the width of the pedestal

(9 feet) would be one-third of the width of the square (27 feet). In all the successive higher cases the square will be increasingly too large for the pedestal to be in agreement with the illustration.

315. A CUBE PARADOX

It is a curious fact that a cube can be passed through another cube of smaller dimensions. Suppose a cube to be raised so that its diagonal AB is perpendicular to the plane on which it rests, as in Figure 1. Then the resulting projection will be a regular hexagon, as shown. In Figure 2 the square hole is cut for the passage of a cube of the same dimensions. But it will be seen that there is room for cutting a hole that would pass a cube of even larger dimensions. Therefore, the one through which I cut a hole was not, as the reader may have hastily supposed, the larger one, but the smaller! Consequently, the larger cube would obviously remain the heavier. This could not happen if the smaller were passed through the larger.

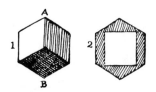

316. THE CARDBOARD BOX

There are eleven different shapes in all, if turning over is allowed, and they are as shown. If the outside of the box is blue and the inside white, and every

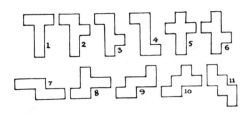

possible shape has to be laid out with white uppermost, then there are twenty different ways, for all except Nos. 1 and 5 can be reversed to be different.

317. THE AUSTRIAN PRETZEL

The pretzel may be divided into as many as ten pieces by one straight cut of the knife in the direction indicated in the illustration.

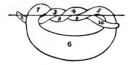

318. CUTTING THE CHEESE

Mark the mid-points in BC, CH, HE, EF, FG, and GB. Then insert the knife at the top and follow the direction indicated by the dotted plane. Then

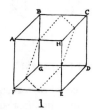 

the two surfaces will each be a perfect hexagon, and the piece on the right will, in perspective, resemble Figure 2.

319. THE FLY'S JOURNEY

A clever fly would select the route shown by the line in the illustration, which will take him 2.236 minutes. He will not go in the direction indicated by the dotted line that will probably have suggested itself to the reader. This is longer, and would take more time.

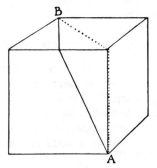

320. THE TANK PUZZLE

(1) The water rises 1.8 inches, and (2) rises an additional 2.2 inches.

321. THE NOUGAT PUZZLE

First cut off the piece marked A from the end, 1 in. thick. The remainder can then be cut in the manner shown, into twenty-four pieces of the required size, 5 × 3 × 2½ in. All but four of the pieces are visible—two under B and two under C.

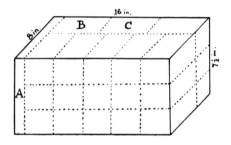

322. AN EASTER EGG PROBLEM

The volumes of similar solids are as the cubes of corresponding lengths. The simplest answer, to be exact as required, is that the three small eggs were 1½ in., 2 in., and 2½ in. respectively in length. The cubes of these numbers are 2⅞, 8, and 12⅝, the sum of which is exactly 27—the cube of 3. The next easiest answer is 2⅔ in., 2 in., and ⅓ in. But there is an infinite number of answers.

323. THE PEDESTAL PUZZLE

The man made a box 3 × 1 × 1 ft. inside, and into this he placed the pedestal. Then he filled the box with fine dry sand, shaking it down and levelling the top. Then he took out the pedestal, and the sand was shaken down and levelled, when the surface was found to be exactly 2 ft. from the top of the box. It was, therefore, obvious that the pedestal, when completed, contained 2 cubic ft. of wood, and that 1 cubic ft. had been removed.

324. THE SQUIRREL'S CLIMB

The squirrel climbs 5 ft. in ascending 4 ft. of the pole. Therefore he travels 20 ft. in a 16-ft. climb.

325. THE FLY AND THE HONEY

The drop of honey is represented by H, the fly by F. The fly clearly has to go over the edge to the other side. Now, imagine we are dealing with a cylinder of cardboard. If we cut it we can lay it out flat. If we then extend the line of the side 1 inch to B, the line FB will cut the edge at A, which will be the point at which the fly must go over. The shortest distance is thus the hypotenuse of a right-angled triangle, whose height is 4 and base 3. This we know is 5, so that the fly has to go exactly 5 inches.

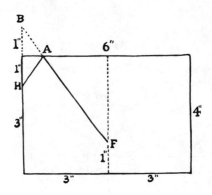

326. PACKING CIGARETTES

Say the diameter of a cigarette is 2 units and that 8 rows of 20 each, as in Figure A (that is, 160 cigarettes) exactly fit the box. The inside length of the box

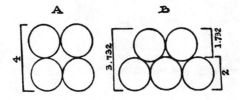

is therefore 40 and the depth 16. Now, if we place 20 in the bottom row, and, instead of placing 20 in the next row, we drop 19 into the position shown in Figure B, we save .268 (i.e., $2 - \sqrt{3}$) in height. This second row, and every additional row of 20 and 19 alternately, will increase the height by 1.732. Therefore, we shall have 9 rows reaching to a height of $2 + 8 \times 1.732$ or 15.856, which is less than our depth of 16. We shall thus increase the number of cigarettes by 20 (through the additional row), and reduce it by 4 (1 in each row of 19), making a net increase of 16 cigarettes.

327. A NEW CUTTING-OUT PUZZLE

Make the cuts as shown in the illustration and fit the pieces into the places enclosed by the dotted lines.

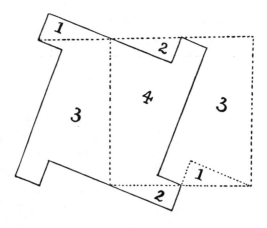

[The cuts can be shifted to make a more symmetrical solution. See Harry Lindgren, *Geometric Dissections*, (D. Van Nostrand, 1964), p. 40, Figure 9.2. —M. G.]

328. THE SQUARE TABLE TOP

The illustration shows the simplest, and I think the prettiest, solution in six pieces. Move piece A up a step on B and you have the original piece 12 × 12. Move C up a step on D and the two pieces will join E and form the square 15 × 15. The piece 16 × 16 is not cut.

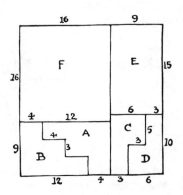

329. THE SQUARES OF VENEER

The sides of the two squares must be 24 in. and 7 in., respectively. Make the cuts as in the first diagram and the pieces A, B, and C will form a perfect square as in the second diagram. The square D is cut out intact.

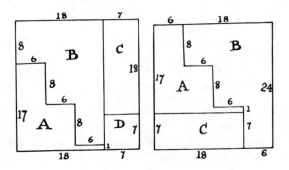

330. DISSECTING THE LETTER E

The first illustration shows how to cut the letter into five pieces that will fit together to form a perfect square, without turning over any pieces.

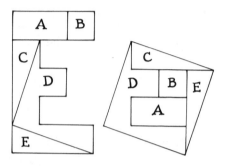

If pieces may be turned over, the dissection can be accomplished with four pieces, as shown in the second illustration.

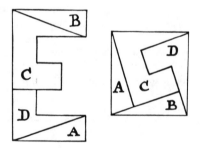

331. HEXAGON TO SQUARE

Cut your hexagon in half and place the two parts together to form the figure ABCD. Continue the line DC to E, making CE equal to the height CF. Then, with the point of your compasses at G, describe the semicircle DHE, and draw the line CH perpendicular to DE. Now CH is the mean pro-

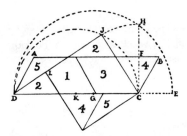

portional between DC and CE, and therefore the side of the required square. From C describe the arc HJ, and with the point of your compasses at K describe the semicircle DJC. Draw CJ and DJ. Make JL equal to JC, and complete the square. The rest requires no explanation.

This solution was first published by me in the *Weekly Dispatch,* in August, 1901.

[Victor Meally informs me that Dudeney's solution had earlier been discovered by Paul Busschop. It appeared in *Nouvelle Correspondance Mathématique,* Brussels, 1875, Vol. II, p. 83.—M. G.]

332. SQUARING A STAR

I give the very neat solution by Mr. E. B. Escott, of Oak Park, Illinois. The five pieces of the star form a perfect square. Find side of equal square (a mean proportional between AB and BC) and make BD equal to such side. Drop perpendicular from A on BD at E and AE will equal BD. The rest is obvious.

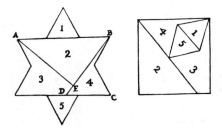

[Edward B. Escott, a mathematics teacher and insurance company actuary, was a number-theory expert who contributed to many mathematical journals until his death in 1946. See also Puzzle No. 348. For other five-piece solutions of the star to square, see Lindgren, *Geometric Dissections,* p. 18, Figures 3.3 and 3.4.—M. G.]

333. THE MUTILATED CROSS

The illustration shows clearly how to cut the mutilated cross into four pieces to form a square. Just continue each side of the square until you strike a corner, and there you are!

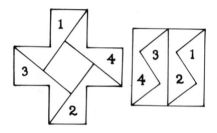

334. THE VICTORIA CROSS

The illustration will show how to cut the cross into seven pieces to form a square.

This solution was sent to me by Mr. A. E. Hill.

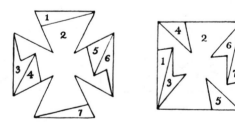

[I have been unable to identify Mr. Hill, who discovered this truly remarkable dissection, and do not even know if he lived in England or somewhere else.—M. G.]

335. SQUARING THE SWASTIKA

The illustration shows how the swastika should be cut into four parts and placed together to form a square. The direction of the nearly horizontal cut is obvious, the other is at right angles to it.

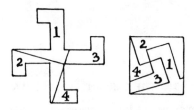

[See Lindgren, *Geometric Dissections,* p. 43, Figures 9.15 and 9.16, for more symmetrical four-part solutions.—M. G.]

336. THE MALTESE CROSS

Cut the star in four pieces across the center, and place them in the four corners of the frame. Then you have a perfect Maltese Cross in white, as indicated.

337. THE PIRATES' FLAG

The illustration will show that the flag need only be cut in two pieces—along the zigzag line. If the lower piece is then moved up one step we shall get a flag with the required ten stripes.

338. THE CARPENTER'S PUZZLE

In order that it may be cut in two pieces, on the step principle, to form a square, take any rectangular board whose sides are the squares of two consecutive whole numbers. Thus, in the following table, the square of 1 (1) and the square of 2 (4); or 2 (4) and 3 (9); or 3 (9) and 4 (16);—and so on. The table may be extended to any length desired.

Sides	No. of Steps	Side of Square
1 × 4	1	2
4 × 9	2	6
9 × 16	3	12
16 × 25	4	20
25 × 36	5	30

In Figure I is shown the simple case of a board 1 × 4, in Figure II the case of 4 × 9, and Figure III shows the case of 16 × 25. It will be seen that the number of steps increases regularly as we advance, but with the table they are easily found. Thus, for the case 16 × 25, as the side of the square will be 20, the steps will be 20 − 16 = 4 in height and 25 − 20 = 5 in breadth.

As the sides are square numbers, and two square numbers multiplied together always make another square, the area will always be a perfect square. But we must not conclude from this that a board, say, 9 × 25 would work just because its area is a square with side 15. Figure IV shows the best that can be done in that case, but there are three pieces instead of two as required. This is because 9 is not a multiple of the added height, 6, nor 25 a multiple of the reduced length, 10. Consequently, the steps cannot be formed.

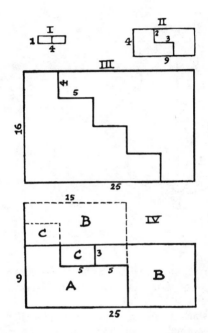

Of course, any multiple of the sides will work. Thus, a board 8 × 18 is solved exactly like 4 × 9, in two steps, by just doubling all the measurements. Similarly, a board 4 × 6¼ will work, for it is the same ratio as 16 × 25, the steps being 1 in height and 1¼ in breadth. In the former case we should reduce it like a fraction, and in the second case multiply it by 4 to get rid of the fraction. Then we should see that 4 × 9 and 16 × 25 were, in each case, squares of consecutive numbers and know that a solution is possible.

339. THE CRESCENT AND THE STAR

Though we cannot square a circle, certain portions of a circle may be squared, as Hippocrates first discovered. If we draw the circle in the diagram and then, with the point of the compasses at E, draw the arc BA, the area of

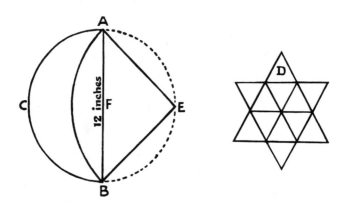

the lune or crescent is exactly the same as the area of the triangle ABE. As we know the line AB to be 12 in., the area of the triangle (and therefore of the crescent) is obviously 36 sq. in. Also, as the triangle D is known to contain 3 sq. in., the star, which is built up of twelve such triangles, contains 36 sq. in. Therefore the areas of the crescent and the star were exactly the same.

340. THE PATCHWORK QUILT

Except for my warning the reader might have supposed that the dark zig-zag line from A to B would solve the puzzle. But it will not, because the pieces are not of the same size and shape. It would be all right if we could go along the dotted line D instead of C, but that would mean cutting a piece. We must cut out all the shaded portion in one piece, which will exactly match the other.

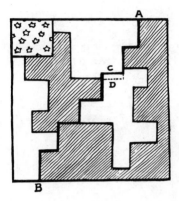

One portion of the patchwork is drawn in just to guide the eye when comparing with the original.

341. THE IMPROVISED CHECKERBOARD

The illustration shows how to cut into two pieces, A and B, that will fit together and form the square board.

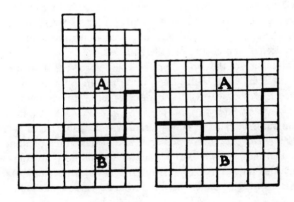

342. TESSELLATED PAVEMENTS

The illustration shows how the square space may be covered with twenty-nine square tiles by laying down seventeen whole and cutting each of the re-

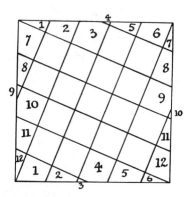

maining twelve tiles in two parts. Two parts having a similar number form a whole tile.

343. SQUARE OF SQUARES

There is, we believe, only one solution to this puzzle, here shown. The fewest pieces must be 11, the portions must be of the sizes given, the three largest pieces must be arranged as shown, and the remaining group of eight squares may be "reflected" but cannot be differently arranged.

[For a discussion of the general problem, still unsolved, of dividing a square lattice of any size, along lattice lines, into the minimum number of smaller squares, see J. H. Conway, "Mrs. Perkins's Quilt," *Proceedings of the Cambridge Philosophical Society,* Vol. 60, 1964, pp. 363–368; G. B. Trustrum's paper of the same title, in the same journal, Vol. 61, 1965, pages 7–11; and my *Scientific American* column for September 1966. The corresponding problem on a triangular lattice has not, to my knowledge, yet been investigated.

Although this puzzle also appears in Dudeney's earlier book, *Amusements in Mathematics* (1917), under the title "Mrs. Perkins's Quilt" (Problem 173,

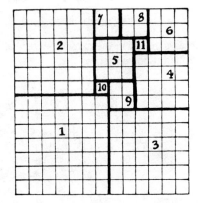

on p. 47), I have allowed it to remain in this volume because of current interest in the problem. Sam Loyd gave the same problem in the first issue of *Our Puzzle Magazine,* which he edited in 1907, the pages of which later became the pages of his posthumously published *Cyclopedia of Puzzles* (1914). This is the earliest appearance of the problem I have been able to trace. If Loyd took it from Dudeney, then Dudeney must have published it in a magazine or newspaper before 1907.—M. G.]

344. STARS AND CROSSES

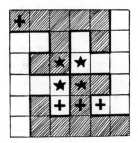

The illustration shows how the square may be cut into four pieces, each of the same size and shape, so that each part shall contain a star and a cross.

345. GREEK CROSS PUZZLE

Place the four pieces together in the manner shown, and the symmetrical Greek cross will be found in the center.

346. SQUARE AND CROSS

If we cut the smaller Greek cross in the manner shown in Figure 1, the four pieces A, B, C, and D will fit together and form a perfect square, as shown in Figure 2.

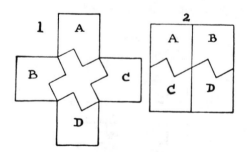

347. THREE GREEK CROSSES FROM ONE

Cut off the upper and lower arms of your large cross and place them in the positions A and B, so as to form the rectangle in Figure I. Now cut the larger

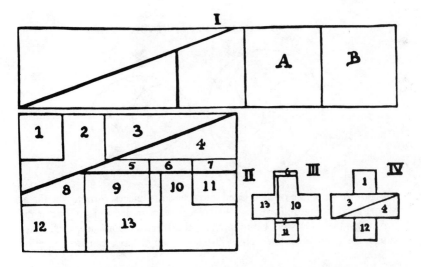

piece, as shown, into three pieces so that the five will form the rectangle in Figure II. This figure may be said to be built up of fifteen equal squares, five of which will be required for each new cross. Cutting is then not difficult, and 2, 5, 8, 9 clearly form one cross; 13, 6, 10, 7, and 11 will form the second cross, as in Figure III; and 1, 3, 4, 12 will form the third cross, as in Figure IV. The smaller arms are one-third of the area of the larger arms. It is shown on page 232 of *The Canterbury Puzzles* how to find the side of the smaller squares. The rest is now easy.

[Lindgren, in *Geometric Dissections,* pp. 55–56, shows how the number of pieces can be reduced to twelve.—M. G.]

348. MAKING A SQUARE

The diagram will make it clear how the figure should be cut into four pieces of the same size and shape that will fit together and form a perfect square.

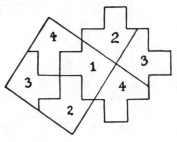

349. TABLE TOP AND STOOLS

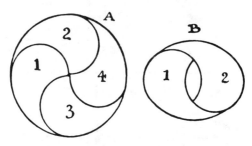

Figure A shows the circle divided into four equal pieces, forming the Great Monad, and in Figure B we have two pieces reassembled to form one of the two stools, the other stool being similarly constructed from 3 and 4. Unfortunately the hand holes are across instead of lengthways, but no condition is broken.

350. TRIANGLE AND SQUARE

Cut one triangle in half, and place the pieces together as in Figure 1. Now cut in the direction of the dotted lines, making *ab* and *cd* each equal to the side of the required square. Then fit together the six pieces as in Figure 2,

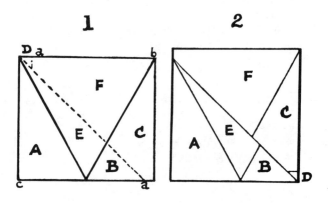

sliding the pieces F and C upwards to the left, and bringing down the little piece D from one corner to the other.

[Lindgren has found a way to accomplish this result in as few as five pieces. See his *Geometric Dissections,* p. 9.—M. G.]

351. CHANGING THE SUIT

The diagram shows how the spade may be cut into three parts that will fit together and form a heart.

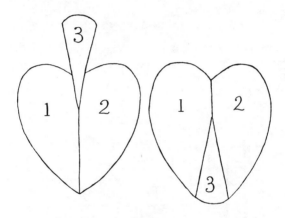

352. PROBLEM OF THE EXTRA CELL

The fallacy lies in the fact that the oblique edges of the pieces do not coincide in direction. If you carefully lay out the pieces so that the outer edges

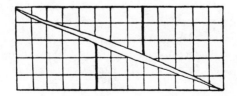

form a true rectangle, then there is a long diamond-shaped space in the middle uncovered, as in the diagram. This space is exactly equal in area to one of the little square cells. Therefore we must deduct one from 65 to get 64 as the actual area covered. The size of the diamond-shaped piece has been exaggerated to make it quite clear to the eye of the reader.

[For a discussion of many new and closely related paradoxes of this type, see the two chapters on "Geometrical Vanishes" in my *Mathematics, Magic, and Mystery* (Dover, 1956, pp. 114–155).—M. G.]

353. PROBLEM OF THE MISSING CELL

The diagram shows how the four pieces may be put together in a different way, so that, on first sight, it may appear that we have lost a cell, there now

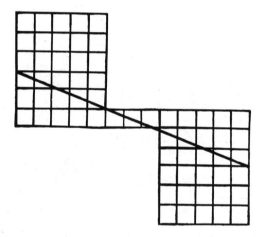

being only sixty-three of these. The explanation, as in the case of the preceding fallacy, lies in the fact that the lines formed by the slanting cuts do not coincide in direction. In the case of the fallacy shown in the puzzle here, if the pieces are so replaced that the outside edges form a true rectangle, there will be a long diamond-shaped space not covered, exactly equal in area to the supposed extra cell. In this case the pieces, if truly laid, will overlap, and the area of the overlapping is exactly equal to the supposed missing cell. This is the simple explanation in a nutshell.

354. A HORSESHOE PUZZLE

First make cut AB. Then so place the three pieces together that with one clip of the scissors you can make the cut CD together with EF and GH.

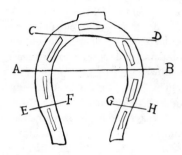

355. SQUARE TABLE TOP

The eight pieces of veneer may be fitted together, as in the illustration, to form a perfect square, and the arrangement is symmetrical and pleasing.

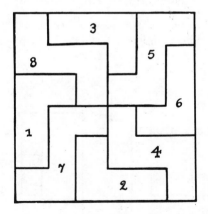

356. TWO SQUARES IN ONE

Place the two squares together, so that AB and CD are straight lines. Then find the center of the larger square, and draw through it the line EF parallel to AD. If you now make GH (also through the center) perpendicular to EF, you can cut out the four pieces and form the lower square, as shown.

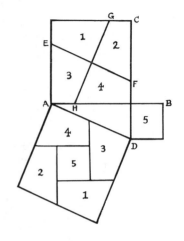

[This dissection was discovered about 1830 by Henry Perigal, a British stockbroker and amateur mathematician, and first published by him in 1873. It is one of the best of many ways to demonstrate the Pythagorean theorem by cutting. See the chapter on "Paper Cutting" in my *New Mathematical Diversions from Scientific American* (Simon & Schuster, 1966). —M. G.]

357. CUTTING THE VENEER

The illustration will show clearly how the veneer may be cut. Squares A and B are cut out entire, as in Figure 1, and the four pieces C, D, E, F will fit together, as in Figure 2, to form a third square.

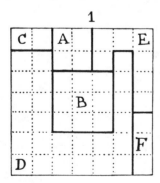

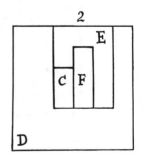

[Victor Meally found many ways to solve this problem with as few as five pieces. Can the reader discover a five-piece pattern on which the total length of the cuts is as low as 16 units?—M. G.]

358. IMPROVISED CHESSBOARD

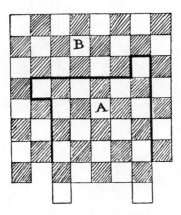

Cut out the piece A, and inset it again after having given it a quarter turn in a clockwise direction, and the chessboard will be formed.

359. THE PATCHWORK CUSHION

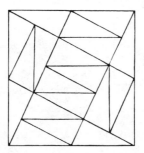

The illustration shows how the twenty pieces will form a perfect square.

360. THE DAMAGED RUG

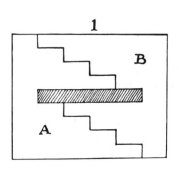
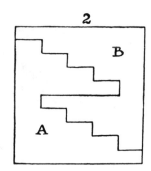

If we cut as in Figure 1, the two pieces will fit together, as in Figure 2, and form a square. The steps are 2 ft. wide and 1 ft. in height.

361. FOLDING A HEXAGON

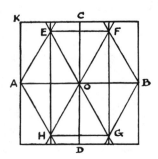

Fold through the midpoints of the opposite sides and get the lines AOB and COD. Also fold EH and FG, bisecting AO and OB. Turn over AK so that K lies on the line EH, at the point E, and then fold AE and EOG. Similarly find H and fold AH and HOF. Now fold BF, BG, EF and HG, and EFBGHAE is the regular hexagon required.

362. FOLDING A PENTAGON

Fold AB on itself and find the mid-point E. Fold through EC. Lay EB on EC and fold so as to get EF and FG. Make CH equal to CG. Find K, the mid-point on BH, and make CL equal to BK. BC is said to be divided in medial section, and we have found KL, the side of the pentagon. Now (see

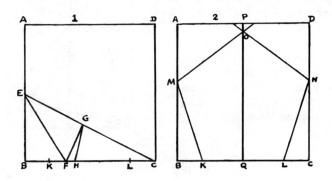

second diagram) lay KM and LN equal to KL, so that M and N may lie on BA and CD respectively. Fold PQ and lay MO and NO equal to KM and LN. Then KMONL is the pentagon required. For this solution I am indebted to a little book, *Geometrical Exercises in Paper Folding*, by T. Sundara Row (Madras, 1893).*

363. FOLDING AN OCTAGON

By folding the edge CD over AB we can crease the middle points E and G. In a similar way we can find the points F and H, and then crease the square EHGF. Now fold CH on EH and EC on EH, and the point where the creases cross will be I. Proceed in the same way at the other three corners, and the regular octagon, as shown, will be marked out by the creases and may be at once cut out.

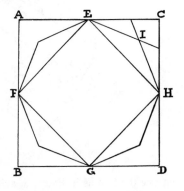

[* Currently available in a Dover paperback reprint.—M. G.]

364. SQUARE AND TRIANGLE

Fold the square in half and make the crease FE. Fold the side AB so that the point B lies on FE, and you will get the points G and H from which you can fold HGJ. While B is on G, fold AB back on AH, and you will have the line AK. You can now fold the triangle AJK, which is the largest possible equilateral triangle obtainable.

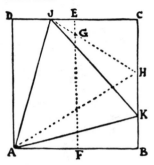

365. STRIP TO PENTAGON

By folding A over, find C, so that BC equals AB. Then fold as in Figure 1, across the point A, and this will give you the point D. Now fold as in Figure 2, making the edge of the ribbon lie along AB, and you will have the point E.

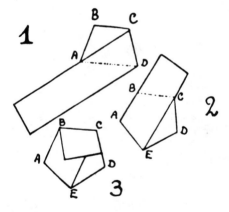

Continue the fold as in Figure 3, and so on, until all the ribbon lies on the pentagon. This, as we have said, is simple, but it is interesting and instructive.

366. A CREASE PROBLEM

Bisect AB in C and draw the line CG, parallel to BH. Then bisect AC in D and draw the semicircle DB, cutting the line CG in E. Now the line DEF gives the direction of the shortest possible crease under the conditions.

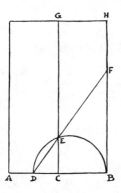

367. FOLDING POSTAGE STAMPS

Number the stamps as in the diagram shown previously—that is, 1 2 3 4 in the first row and 5 6 7 8 in the second row. To get the order 1 5 6 4 8 7 3 2 (with No. 1 face upwards, only visible), start this way, with all faces downwards:

5 6 7 8
1 2 3 4

Fold 7 over 6. Lay 4 flat on 8 and tuck them both in between 7 and 6 so that these four are in the order 7 8 4 6. Now bring 5 and 1 under 6, and it is done.

The order 1 3 7 5 6 8 4 2 is more difficult and might well have been overlooked, if one had not been convinced that, according to law, it must be possible. First fold so that 5 6 7 8 only are visible with their faces uppermost. Then fold 5 on 6. Now, between 1 and 5 you have to tuck in 7 and 8, so that 7 lies on the top of 5, and 8 bends round under 6. Then the order will be as required.

368. COUNTER SOLITAIRE

Play in the following manner and all the counters except one will be removed in seven moves, and the final leap will be made by number 1, as required: 2–10, 4–12, 6–5, 3–6, 7–15 (8–16, 8–7, 8–14, 8–3), (1–9, 1–2, 1–11, 1–8, 1–13, 1–4).

369. A NEW LEAP-FROG PUZZLE

Play 9 over 13, 14, 6, 4, 3, 1, 2, 7, 15, 17, 16, 11. Play 12 over 8. Play 10 over 5 and 12. Play 9 over 10.

370. TRANSFERRING THE COUNTERS

Make a pile of five counters (1 to 5) on B in 9 moves. Make a pile of four (6 to 9) on C in 7 moves. Make a pile of three (10 to 12) on D in 5 moves. Make a pile of two (13 and 14) on E in 3 moves. Place one (15) on F in 1 move. Replace 13 and 14 on F in 3, 10 to 12 on F in 5, 6 to 9 in 7, and 1 to 5 in 9 moves. Forty-nine moves in all.

371. MAGIC FIFTEEN PUZZLE

Move the counters in the following order: 12, 8, 4, 3, 2, 6, 10, 9, 13, 15, 14, 12, 8, 4, 7, 10, 9, 14, 12, 8, 4, 7, 10, 9, 6, 2, 3, 10, 9, 6, 5, 1, 2, 3, 6, 5, 3, 2, 1, 13, 14, 3, 2, 1, 13, 14, 3, 12, 15, 3—fifty moves in all.
[If the 14 and 15 counters are in correct serial order at the start, a magic square can be achieved in 37 moves: 15, 14, 10, 6, 7, 3, 2, 7, 6, 11, 3, 2, 7, 6, 11, 10, 14, 3, 2, 11, 10, 9, 5, 1, 6, 10, 9, 5, 1, 6, 10, 9, 5, 2, 12, 15, 3.—M. G.]

372. TRANSFERRING THE COUNTERS

The two additional counters should be placed one on the fourth square in the second row from the top and the other in the second square in the fourth row. The puzzle is then quite possible, and so easy that it is quite unnecessary to give all the moves.

373. ODDS AND EVENS

The fewest possible moves are 24. Play as follows. (It is only necessary to give, by the letters, the circles from which and to which the counters are moved. Only a single counter can be moved at a time.) E to A, E to B, E to C, E to D, B to D, E to B, C to B, A to B, E to C, E to A, B to A, C to E, B to C, A to C, B to A, C to B, C to A, B to A, E to C, E to B, C to B, D to E, D to B, E to B—24 moves.

374. RAILWAY SHUNTING

Make a rough sketch like our diagram and use five counters marked X, L, R, A, and B. The engines are L and R, and the two cars on the right A and B. The three cars on the left are never separated, so we call them X. The side-track is marked S. Now, play as follows: R to left, R to S, XL to right, R to left, XLA to left, L takes A to S, L to left, XL to right, R to A, RA to left,

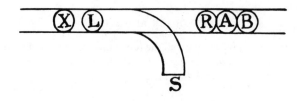

XLB to left, L takes B to S, L to left, LX right away, RA to B, RAB right away. Fourteen moves, because the first and third moves (R to left and XL to right) do not involve a change of direction. It cannot be done in fewer moves.

375. ADJUSTING THE COUNTERS

Make the exchanges of pairs as follows: (1–7, 7–20, 20–16, 16–11, 11–2, 2–24), (3–10, 10–23, 23–14, 14–18, 18–5), (14–19, 19–9, 9–22), (6–12, 12–15, 15–13, 13–25), (17–21). The counters are now all correctly arranged in 19 exchanges. The numbers within a pair of brackets represent a complete cycle, all being put in their proper places. Write out the numbers in their original order, and beneath them in their required order, thus:

7	24	10	19	3	12	20	8	22, etc.
1	2	3	4	5	6	7	8	9, etc.

The construction of the cycles is obvious, for 1 in the bottom row is exchanged with the 7 above it, then this 7 with the 20 above it, and so on until the cycle completes itself, when we come to 24 under 1.

376. NINE MEN IN A TRENCH

Let the men move in the following order: 2–1, 3–2, 4–3, 5–11, 6–4, 7–5, 8–6, 9–7, 1–13, 9–10, 8–9, 1–12, 7–13, 6–8, 5–7, 1–11, 4–12, 3–6, 2–5, 1–1, 2–2, 3–3, 4–4, 5–5, 6–6, 7–7, 8–8, 9–9, and the sergeant is in his place in 28 moves.

The first number in a move is that of a man, and the second number that of his new position, the places being numbered 1 to 10 in the row, and the recesses 11 to 13 above.

377. BLACK AND WHITE

In the first case move the pairs in the following order: 6 7 before the 1, then 3 4, 7 1, and 4 8 to the vacant spaces, leaving the order 6 4 8 2 7 1 5 3.

In the second case move 3 4 and replace them as 4 3 before the 1. Then remove and reverse 6 7 (as 7 6), 6 5 (as 5 6), 3 1 (as 1 3), and 6 8 (as 8 6), leaving the order 4 8 6 2 7 1 3 5—five moves in this case.

378. THE ANGELICA PUZZLE

Though we start with the A's in correct positions, the puzzle can only be solved by making them change places. Represent the A in the bottom row with a capital letter, and the A in the top corner with a small letter. Then here is a solution in 36 moves: A N L E G   A N G C I   A N G C I   A N G C L   E a   A N G   I L C I L   a E C a L   I (36 moves).

[Dudeney's solution is not minimal. Can the reader find a way to solve it in 30 moves?—M. G.]

379. THE FLANDERS WHEEL

Move the counters in the following order: A N D A F L N D A F D N L D R S D L N A F R S E R S L N A L—30 moves in all.

[The solution can be reduced to 28 moves, the lowest possible. Readers may have noticed that the problem is isomorphic with a square, eight-counter sliding puzzle like the preceding one. For a general discussion of eight-counter sliding puzzles of this type, see my *Scientific American* columns for March and June 1965.—M. G.]

380. CATCHING THE PRISONERS

It is impossible for W 1 (warder) to catch P 2 (prisoner), or for W 2 to catch P 1. In the example we gave it was therefore hopeless, for each warder

1	2	3	4	5	6	7	8
9	10	11	12	13	14	15	16
ⓟ17 ₂	18	Ⓦ19 ₁	20	21	Ⓦ22 ₂	23	24 ⓟ₁
25	26	27	28	29	30	31	32
33	34	35	36	37	38	39	40

would not be chasing "his prisoner," but the other fellow's prisoner. It is a case of what we call in chess "gaining the opposition." Between W 1 and P 2 there is only one square (an odd number), but between W 1 and P 1 (as also between W 2 and P 2) there are four squares (an even number). In the second

case the warders have the opposition, and can win. We will give a specimen
game. The warders' moves are above the line, the prisoners' below:

$$\frac{19\text{–}20}{17\text{–}18} \frac{22\text{–}14}{24\text{–}23}\text{'} \frac{20\text{–}21}{18\text{–}26} \frac{14\text{–}13}{23\text{–}31}\text{'} \frac{21\text{–}22}{26\text{–}27} \frac{13\text{–}12}{31\text{–}32}\text{'} \frac{22\text{–}23}{27\text{–}26} \frac{12\text{–}20}{32\text{–}40}\text{'} \frac{23\text{–}31}{40\text{–}32} \frac{20\text{–}19}{26\text{–}34}\text{'}$$

$$\frac{31\text{–}32 \text{ Capture, } 19\text{–}27}{34\text{–}33} \frac{27\text{–}26}{33\text{–}25}\text{'} \frac{26\text{–}25 \text{ Capture.}}{}$$

There is no possible escape for the prisoners if each warder pursues his
proper man.

381. GRASSHOPPERS' QUADRILLE

If we regard only the central column containing three white and three black
pieces, these can be made to change places in fifteen moves. Number the seven
squares downwards 1 to 7. Now play 3 to 4, 5 to 3, 6 to 5, 4 to 6, 2 to 4, 1 to
2, 3 to 1, 5 to 3, 7 to 5, 6 to 7, 4 to 6, 2 to 4, 3 to 2, 5 to 3, 4 to 5. Six of these
moves are simple moves, and nine are leaps.

There are seven horizontal rows of three white and three black pieces, if we
exclude that central column. Each of these rows may be similarly interchanged
in fifteen moves, and because there is some opportunity of doing this in
every case while we are manipulating the column—that is to say, there is
always, at some time or other, a vacant space in the center of every row—it
should be obvious that all the pieces may be interchanged in $8 \times 15 = 120$
moves.

382. THE FOUR PENNIES

First place the four pennies together as in the first diagram; then remove
number 1 to the new position shown in the second diagram; and finally,

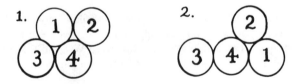

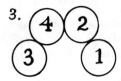

3.

carefully withdraw number 4 downwards and replace it above against numbers 2 and 3. Then they will be in the position shown in the third diagram, and the fifth penny may be added so that it will exactly touch all four.

A glance at the last diagram will show how difficult it is to judge by the eye alone the correct distance from number 1 to number 3. One is almost certain to place them too near together.

383. THE SIX PENNIES

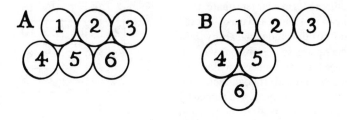

First arrange the pennies as in Figure A. Then carefully shift 6 and get position B. Next place 5 against 2 and 3 to get the position C. Number 3 can now be placed in the position indicated by the dotted circle.

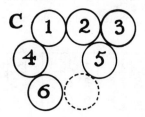

384. AN IRREGULAR MAGIC SQUARE

If for the 2 and 15 you substitute 7 and 10, repeated, the square can be formed as shown. Any sixteen num-

1	10	9	14
13	10	5	6
8	3	16	7
12	11	4	7

bers can be arranged to form a magic square if they can be written in this way, so that all the horizontal differences are alike and all the vertical differences also alike. The differences here are 3 and 2:

```
1    4    7    10
3    6    9    12
5    8    11   14
7    10   13   16
```

385. A MAGIC SQUARE DELUSION

If you make nine squares precisely similar to this one and then place them together to form a larger square, then you can pick out a square of 25 cells in any position and it will always be a magic square, so it is obvious you can arrange for any number you like to be in the central cell. It is, in fact, what is called a Nasik square (so named by the late Mr. Frost after the place in India where he resided), and it is only perfect squares of this character that

9	11	18	5	22
3	25	7	14	16
12	19	1	23	10
21	8	15	17	4
20	2	24	6	13

can be treated in the manner described.

386. DIFFERENCE SQUARES

The three examples I give are, I believe, the only cases possible. The difference throughout is 5.

2	1	4
3	5	7
6	9	8

8	1	4
3	5	7
6	9	2

2	1	6
3	5	7
4	9	8

387. SWASTIKA MAGIC SQUARE

It will be seen that the square is perfectly "magic" and that all the prime numbers are placed within the swastika.

17	5	13	21	9
4	12	25	8	16
11	24	7	20	3
10	18	1	14	22
23	6	19	2	15

388. IS IT VERY EASY?

All that is necessary is to push up the second figure in every cell and so form powers of 2, as in the first square. Then the numbers become those in the second square, where all the eight rows give the same product—4,096. Of course, every arithmetician knows that 2^0 equals 1.

2^7	2^0	2^5
2^2	2^4	2^6
2^3	2^8	2^1

128	1	32
4	16	64
8	256	2

389. MAGIC SQUARE TRICK

Though the figures in each cell must be different in every case, it is not required that the *numbers* shall be different. In our smaller square the rows of cells add to 15 in ten different directions, for in addition to the rows, columns, and two long diagonals, two of the short diagonals also add to 15. This is the greatest number of directions possible. Now, all we have to do is to express each number with a different figure by repeating it with arithmetical signs. The

$7\frac{1}{2}$	5	$2\frac{1}{2}$
0	5	10
$7\frac{1}{2}$	5	$2\frac{1}{2}$

$\dfrac{(8\times 8)-8}{8} + \dfrac{8}{8+8}$	$1+1+1+1+1$	$\dfrac{6+6}{6} + \dfrac{6}{6+6+6}$
$3-3$	5	$\dfrac{(7\times 7)+7+7+7}{7}$
$\dfrac{(4\times 4)+4+4+4}{4} + \dfrac{4}{4+4}$	$\dfrac{9+9+9+9+9}{9}$	$2+\dfrac{2}{2}+2$

larger square shows how this may be done. All the conditions of the puzzle are thus complied with, and the maximum ten directions obtained.

[The squares using 4, 7 and 8 are needlessly complex. Victor Meally suggests:

$$4 + 4 - \frac{4}{4+4} = 7\frac{1}{2}$$

$$7 + \frac{7+7+7}{7} = 10$$

$$8 - \frac{8}{8+8} = 7\frac{1}{2}.$$

—M. G.]

390. A FOUR-FIGURE MAGIC SQUARE

The solution explains itself. The columns, rows, and two diagonals all add up alike to 6,726, and nine of each of the figures 1, 2, 3, 4 have been employed.

2243	1341	3142
3141	2242	1343
1342	3143	2241

391. PROGRESSIVE SQUARES

Fill in the following numbers in the order given, beginning at the cell in the top right-hand corner and proceeding downwards and "round the square": 13, 81, 78, 6, 75, 8, 15, 16, 77, 70, 19, 79, 21, 9, 23, 2, 69, 66, 67, 74, 7, 76, 4, 1, 5, 80, 59, 73, 61, 3, 63, 12. It is obvious that opposite numbers in the border must sum to 82 in all cases, but a correct adjustment of them is not very easy. Of course there are other solutions.

18	22	1	10	14
24	3	7	11	20
5	9	13	17	21
6	15	19	23	2
12	16	25	4	8

392. CONDITIONAL MAGIC SQUARE

The example here shown is a solution, with the odd numbers and even numbers placed in the positions desired.

393. THE FIVE-POINTED STAR

Referring to Figure I, on page 348, we will call A, B, C, D, E the "pentagon," and F, G, H, J, K the "points." Write in the numbers 1, 2, 3, 4, 5 in the pentagon in the order shown in Figure II, where you go round in a clockwise direction, starting with 1 and jumping over a disc to the place for 2, jumping over another for 3, and so on. Now to complete the star for the constant summation of 24, as required, use this simple rule. To find H subtract the sum of B and C from half the constant plus E. That is, subtract 6 from 15. We thus get 9 as the required number for H. Now you are able to write in successively 10 at F (to make 24), 6 at J, 12 at G, and 8 at K. There is your solution.

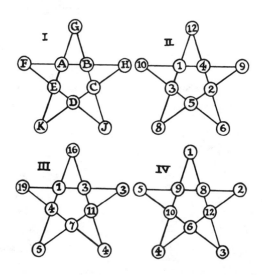

You can write any five numbers you like in the pentagon, in any order, and with any constant summation that you wish, and you will always get, by the rule shown, the only possible solution for that pentagon and constant. But that solution may require the use of repeated numbers and even negative numbers. Suppose, for example, I make the pentagon 1, 3, 11, 7, 4, and the constant 26, as in Figure III, then I shall find the 3 is repeated, and the repeated 4 is negative and must be deducted instead of added. You will also find that if we had written our pentagon numbers in Figure II in any other order we should always get repeated numbers.

Let us confine our attention to solutions with ten different positive whole numbers. Then 24 is the smallest possible constant. A solution for any higher constant can be derived from it. Thus, if we want 26, add 1 at each of the points; if we want 28, add 2 at every point or 1 at every place in both points and pentagon. Odd constants are impossible unless we use fractions. Every solution can be "turned inside out." Thus, Figure IV is simply a different arrangement of Figure II. Also the four numbers in G, K, D, J may always be changed, if repetitions do not occur. For example, in Figure II substitute 13, 7, 6, 5 for 12, 8, 5, 6 respectively. Finally, in any solution the constant will be two-fifths of the sum of all the ten numbers. So, if we are given a particular set of numbers we at once know the constant, and for any constant we can determine the sum of the numbers to be used.

394. THE SIX-POINTED STAR

I have insufficient space to explain fully the solution to this interesting problem, but I will give the reader the main points.

(1) In every solution the sum of the numbers in the triangle ABC (Figure I)

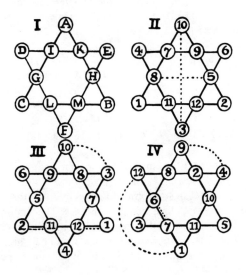

must equal the sum of the triangle DEF. This sum may be anything from 12 to 27 inclusive, except 14 and 25, which are impossible. We need only obtain solutions for 12, 13, 15, 16, 17, 18, and 19, because from these all the complementaries, 27, 26, 24, 23, 22, 21, and 20, may be derived by substituting for every number in the star its difference from 13.

(2) Every arrangement is composed of three independent diamonds, AGHF, DKBL, and EMCI, each of which must always sum to 26.

(3) The sum of the numbers in opposite external triangles will always be equal. Thus AIK equals LMF.

(4) If the difference between 26 and the triangle sum ABC be added to any number at a point, say A, it will give the sum of the two numbers in the relative positions of L and M. Thus (in Figure II) 10 + 13 = 11 + 12, and 6 + 13 = 8 + 11.

(5) There are six pairs summing to 13; they are 12 + 1, 11 + 2, 10 + 3, 9 + 4, 8 + 5, 7 + 6, and one pair or two pairs may occur among the numbers at the points, but never three. The relative positions of these pairs determine the type of solution. In the regular type, as in Figure II, A and F and also G and H, as indicated by the dotted lines, always sum to 13, though I subdivide this class. Figures III and IV are examples of the two irregular types. There are 37 solutions in all (or 74, if we count the complementaries described in my first paragraph), of which 32 are regular and 5 irregular.

Of the 37 solutions, 6 have their points summing to 26. They are as follows:

10	6	2	3	1	4	7	9	5	12	11	8
9	7	1	4	3	2	6	11	5	10	12	8
5	4	6	8	2	1	9	12	3	11	7	10
5	2	7	8	1	3	11	10	4	12	6	9
10	3	1	4	2	6	9	8	7	12	11	5
8	5	3	1	2	7	10	4	11	9	12	6

The first is our Figure II, and the last but one our Figure III, so a reference to those diagrams will show how to write the numbers in the star. The reader should write them all out in star form and remember that the 6 are increased to 12 if you also write out their complementaries. The first four are of the regular type and the last two of the irregular. If the reader should be tempted to find all the 37 (or 74) solutions to the puzzle it will help him to know that, where the six points sum to 24, 26, 30, 32, 34, 36, 38, the respective number of solutions is 3, 6, 2, 4, 7, 6, 9, making 37 in all.

395. THE SEVEN-POINTED STAR

Place 5 at the top point, as indicated in diagram. Then let the four numbers in the horizontal line (7, 11, 9, 3) be such that the two outside numbers shall sum to 10 and the inner numbers to 20, and that the difference between the two outer numbers shall be twice the difference between the two inner numbers. Then their complementaries to 15 are placed in the relative positions shown by the dotted lines. The remaining four numbers (13, 2, 14, 1) are easily adjusted. From this fundamental arrangement we can get three others. (1) Change the 13 with the 1 and the 14 with the 2. (2 and 3) Substitute for every number in the two arrangements already found its difference from 15. Thus, 10 for 5, 8 for 7, 4 for 11, and so on. Now, the reader should be able to construct a second group of four solutions for himself, by following the rules.

The general solution is too lengthy to be given here in full, but there are, in all, 56 different arrangements, counting complementaries. I divide them into three classes. Class I includes all cases like the above example, where the pairs in the positions of 7–8, 13–2, 3–12, 14–1 all sum to 15, and there are 20 such cases. Class II includes cases where the pairs in the positions of 7–2, 8–13, 3–1, 12–14 all sum to 15. There are, again, 20 such cases. Class III includes cases where

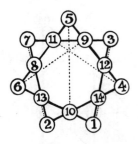

the pairs in the positions of 7–8, 13–2, 3–1, 12–14 all sum to 15. There are 16 such cases. Thus we get 56 in all.

[Dudeney erred in his enumeration of solutions for both the seven-pointed and the six-pointed stars. When I published his results in a column on magic stars (*Scientific American,* December 1965), two readers—E. J. Ulrich, Enid, Oklahoma, and A. Domergue, Paris—independently confirmed that there are 80 patterns for the six-pointed star, or 6 more than listed by Dudeney. That the seven-pointed star has 72 distinct solutions (as against Dudeney's figure of 56) was first reported to me by Mrs. Peter W. Montgomery, North Saint Paul, Minn. This was confirmed by the independent work of Ulrich and Domergue. In 1966 Alan Moldon, Toronto, using a computer at the University of Waterloo, also obtained 72 solutions for the seven-pointed star, so there seems little doubt that this is correct.—M. G.]

396. TWO EIGHT-POINTED STARS

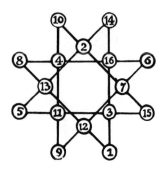

The illustration is the required solution. Every line of four numbers adds up 34. If you now find any solution to one of the stars, you can immediately transfer it to the other by noting the relative positions in the case given.

I have not succeeded in enumerating the stars of this order. The task is, I think, a particularly difficult one. Perhaps readers may like to attempt the solution.

[Domergue (see preceding note), in his 1963 analysis of the six-, seven-, and eight-pointed stars, found 112 different solutions for the eight-pointed star. He estimated that the nine-point star has more than 2,000 distinct patterns.—M. G.]

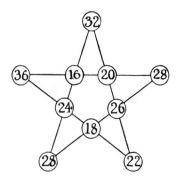

397. FORT GARRISONS

The illustration shows one way of arranging the men so that the numbers in every straight line of four forts add up to one hundred.

398. THE CARD PENTAGON

Deal the cards 1, 2, 3, 4, 5 in the manner indicated by the dotted lines (that is, drop one at every alternate angle in a clockwise direction round the pentagon), and then deal the 6, 7, 8, 9, 10 in the opposite direction, as shown, taking care to start with the 6 on the correct side of the 5. The pips on every side add to 14. If you deal the 6, 7, 8, 9, 10 in the first manner and the 1, 2, 3, 4, 5 in the second manner, you will get another solution, adding up to 19. Now work with the two sets of numbers 1, 3, 5, 7, 9 and 2, 4, 6, 8, 10 in the same way and you will get two more solutions, adding, respectively, to 16 and 17.

There are six different solutions in all. The last two are peculiar. Write in, in the same order, 1, 4, 7, 10, 13 and

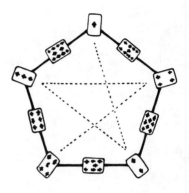

6, 9, 12, 15, 18; also write in 8, 11, 14, 17, 20 and 3, 6, 9, 12, 15. Then deduct 10 from every number greater than 10.

399. A HEPTAGON PUZZLE

The diagram shows the solution. Starting at the highest point, write in the numbers 1 to 7 in a clockwise direction at alternate points. Then, starting just above the 7, write 8 to 14 successively in the opposite direction, taking every vacant circle in turn. If instead you write in 1, 3, 5, 7, 9, 11, 13, and then 2, 4, 6, 8, 10, 12, 14, you will get a solution with the sides adding to 22 instead of 19. If you substitute for every number in these solutions its difference from 15 you will get the complementary solutions, adding re-

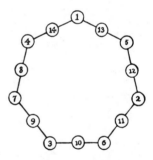

spectively to 26 and 23 (the difference of 19 and 22 from 45).

400. ROSES, SHAMROCKS, AND THISTLES

It is clear that the sum obtained in the different ways must be 26. Here is one of many arrangements that solve the puzzle.

401. THE MAGIC HEXAGON

Our illustration shows the only correct answer.

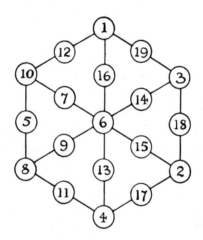

402. THE WHEEL PUZZLE

All you have to do is to place 10 in the center and write in their proper order round the circle 1, 2, 3, 4, 5, 6, 7, 8, 9, 19, 18, 17, 16, 15, 14, 13, 12, 11.

403. AT THE BROOK

A					B			
15	16				15	16		
0	16*	15	5*		*15	0	0	11
15	1*	0	5		0	15	15	11
0	1	5	0		15	15	*10	16
1	0	5	16		*14	16	10	0
1	16	15	6*		14	0	0	10
15	2*	0	6		0	14	15	10
0	2	6	0		15	14	*9	16
2	0	6	16		*13	16	9	0
2	16	15	7*		13	0	0	9
15	3*	0	7		0	13	15	9
0	3	7	0		15	13	*8	16
3	0	7	16		*12	16		
3	16	15	8*		12	0		
15	4*	0	8		0	12		
0	4	8	0		15	12		
4	0	8	16		*11	16		
4	16				11	0		

Every line shows a transaction. Thus, in column A, we first fill the 16 measure; then fill the 15 from the 16, leaving 1, if we want it; then empty the 15; then transfer the 1 from 16 to 15; and so on. The asterisks show how to measure successively 1, 2, 3, 4, etc. Or we can start, as in column B, by first filling the 15 and so measure in turn, 14, 13, 12, 11, etc. If we continue A we get B read upwards, or vice versa. It will thus be seen that to measure from 1 up to 7 inclusive in the fewest transactions we must use the method A, but to get from 8 to 14 we must use method B. To measure 8 in the A direction will take 30 transactions, but in the B manner only 28, which is the correct answer.

It is a surprising fact that with any two measures that are prime to each other (that have no common divisor, like 15 and 16) we can measure any whole number from 1 up to the largest measure. With measures 4 and 6 (each divisible by 2) we can only measure 2, 4, and 6. With 3 and 9 we could only measure 3, 6, and 9. In our tables the quantities measured come in regular numerical ures 9 and 16, under A we should get the order 7, 14, 5, 12, 3, etc., a cyclical difference of 7 (since $16 - 9 = 7$). After adding 7 to 14 we must deduct 16 to get 5, and after adding 7 to 12 we must deduct 16 to get 3, and so on.

[For a clever method of solving liquid pouring puzzles of this type by graphing the problem on isometric paper see my *Scientific American* column, September 1963, and the fuller discussion of the method in T. H. O'Beirne, *Puzzles and Paradoxes* (Oxford University Press, 1965), Chapter 4.—M. G.]

404. A PROHIBITION POSER

First fill and empty the 7-quart measure 14 times and you will have thrown away 98 and leave 22 quarts in the barrel in 28 transactions. (Filling and emptying are 2 transactions.) Then, fill 7-qt.; fill 5-qt. from 7-qt., leaving 2 in 7-qt.; empty 5-qt.; transfer 2 from 7-qt. to 5-qt.; fill 7-qt.; fill up 5-qt. from 7-qt., leaving 4 in 7-qt.; empty 5-qt.; transfer 4 to 5-qt.; fill 7-qt.; fill up 5-qt. from 7-qt., leaving 6 in 7-qt.; empty 5-qt.; fill 5-qt. from 7-qt., leaving 1 in 7-qt.; empty 5-qt., leaving 1 in 7-qt.; draw off remaining 1-qt. from barrel into 5-qt., and the thing is done in 14 more transactions, making, with the 28 above, 42 transactions. Or you can start by wasting 104 and leaving 16 in barrel. These 16 can be dealt with in 10 transactions, and the 104 require 32 in the emptying (12 times 7 and 4 times 5 is the quickest way).

405. PROHIBITION AGAIN

Fill 7-qt.; fill 5-qt.; empty 108 quarts from barrel; empty 5-qt. into barrel; fill 5-qt. from 7-qt.; empty 5-qt. into barrel; pour 2 quarts from 7-qt. into 5-qt.; fill 7-qt. from barrel; fill up 5-qt. from 7-qt.; empty 5-qt. into barrel; pour 4 quarts from 7-qt. into 5-qt.; fill 7-qt. from barrel; fill up 5-qt. from 7-qt.; throw away contents of 5-qt.; fill 5-qt. from barrel; throw away 5 quarts from 5-qt.; empty 1 quart from barrel into 5-qt. The feat is thus performed in 17 transactions—the fewest possible.

406. THE KEG OF WINE

The capacity of the jug must have been a little less than 3 gallons. To be more exact, it was 2.93 gallons.

407. WATER MEASUREMENT

Two pints may be measured in fourteen transactions as below, where the vessels above the line are empty and every other row shows a transaction.

7	11
7	0
0	7
7	7
3	11
3	0
0	3
7	3
0	10
7	10
6	11
6	0
0	6
7	6
2	11

The contents of the vessels, after each transaction, will make everything clear.

408. MIXING THE WINE

The mixture will contain ⁷⁄₂₄ wine, and ¹⁷⁄₂₄ water.

409. THE STOLEN BALSAM

One of several solutions is as follows:

	OZ.	OZ.	OZ.	OZ.
The vessels can hold	24	13	11	5
Their contents at the start	24	0	0	0
Make their contents.....	0	8	11	5
Then..................	16	8	0	0
Then..................	16	0	8	0
Then..................	3	13	8	0
Then..................	3	8	8	5
Finally	8	8	8	0

[Victor Meally has found a better solution that requires only five transactions:

$$
\begin{array}{cccc}
8 & 0 & 11 & 5 \\
8 & 11 & 0 & 5 \\
8 & 13 & 3 & 0 \\
8 & 8 & 3 & 5 \\
8 & 8 & 8 & 0 \\
\end{array}
$$

—M. G.]

410. DELIVERING THE MILK

The simplest way of showing the solution is as follows: At the top we have four vessels, in the second line their contents at the start, and in every subsequent line the contents after a transaction:

80-pt. can	80-pt. can	5-pt. jug	4-pt. jug
80	80	0	0
75	80	5	0
75	80	1	4
79	80	1	0
79	80	0	1
74	80	5	1
74	80	2	4
78	80	2	0
78	76	2	4
80	76	2	2

Thus we first fill the 5-pint jug from one of the cans, then fill the 4-pint jug from the 5-pint, then empty the 4-pint back into the can, and so on. It can be followed quite easily this way. Note the ingenuity of the last two transactions—filling the 4-pint jug from the second can and then filling up the first can to the brim.

411. THE WAY TO TIPPERARY

The thick line in the illustration shows a route from London to Tipperary in eighteen moves. It is absolutely necessary to include the stage marked "Irish Sea" in order to perform the journey in an even number of stages.

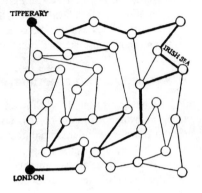

412. MARKING A TENNIS COURT

The ten points lettered in the illustration are all "odd nodes," that is points from which you can go in an odd number of directions—three. Therefore we know that five lines (one-half of 10) will be required to draw the figure. The

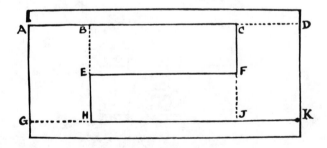

dotted lines will be the four shortest possible between nodes. Note that you cannot here use a node twice or it would be an improvement to make

EH and CF dotted lines instead of CD and GH. Having fixed our four shortest lines, the remainder may all be drawn in one continuous line from A to K, as shown. When you get to D you must run up to C and back to D, from G go to H and back, and so on. Or you can wait until you get to C and go to D and back, etc. The dotted lines will thus be gone over twice and the method shown gives us the minimum distance that must be thus repeated.

413. WATER, GAS, AND ELECTRICITY

This puzzle can only be solved by a trick. If one householder will allow one pipe for a neighbor to pass through his house there is no difficulty, and the conditions did not prohibit this not very unreasonable arrangement. Look at Figure 1, and you will see that the water pipe for supplying house C passes through house A, but no pipe anywhere crosses another pipe. I am, however, often asked to *prove* that there is no solution without any trick, and I will now give such a proof for the first time in a book.

Assume that only two houses, A and B, are to be supplied. The relative positions of the various buildings clearly make no difference whatever. I give two positions for the two houses in Figures 2 and 3. Wherever you build those houses the effect will be the same—one of the supply stations will be cut off. In the examples it will be seen that if you build a third house on the

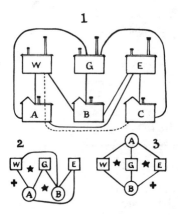

outside (say in the position indicated by one of the black crosses) the gas can never reach you without crossing a pipe. Whereas if you put the house inside one of the enclosures (as indicated by the stars), then you must be cut off either from the water or the electricity—one or the other. But the house must be either inside or outside. Therefore a position is impossible in which it can be supplied from all three stations without one pipe crossing another. I hope that is thoroughly convincing. Build your two houses wherever you like and you will find that those conditions that I have described will always obtain.

[In modern graph theory this is called the "utilities problem," and the nonplanar graph that supplies the desired connections is known as a Thomsen graph. The graph cannot be drawn on the plane without one line crossing another; can it be drawn, without such a crossing, on the surface of a doughnut?—M. G.]

414. CROSSING THE LINES

Let us suppose that we cross the lines by bridges, represented in Figure 1 by the little parallels. Now, in Figure 2, I transform the diagram, reducing the

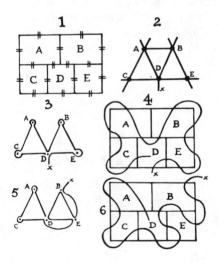

spaces A, B, C, D, E to mere points, and representing the bridges that connect these spaces by lines or roads. This transformation does not affect the conditions, for there are 16 bridges or roads in one case, and 16 roads or lines in the other, and they connect with A, B, C, D, E in precisely the same way. It will be seen that 9 bridges or roads connect with the outside. Obviously we are free to join these up in pairs in any way we choose, provided the roads do not cross one another. The simplest way is shown in Figure 3, where on coming out from A, B, C, or E, we immediately return to the same point by the adjacent bridge, leaving one point, X, necessarily in the open. In Figure 2 there are 4 odd nodes, A, B, D, and X (if we decide on the exits and entrances, as in Figure 3), so, as I have already explained, we require 2 strokes (half of 4) to go over all the roads, proving a perfect solution to be impossible.

Now, let us cancel the line AB. Then A and B become even nodes, but we must begin and end at the odd nodes, D and X. Follow the line in Figure 3, and you will see that this can be done, omitting the line from A to B. This route the reader will easily transform into Figure 4 if he says to himself, "Go from X to D, from D to E, from E to the outside and return into E," and so on. The route can be varied by linking up those outside bridges differently, by making X an outside bridge to A or B, instead of D, and by taking the cancelled line either at AB, AD, BD, XA, XB, or XD. In Figure 5 I make X lead to B. We still omit AB, but we must start and end at D and X. Transformed in Figure 6, this will be seen to be the precise example that I gave in stating the problem. The reader can now write out as many routes as he likes for himself, but he will always find it necessary to omit one line or crossing. It is thus seen how easily sometimes a little cunning, like that of the transformation shown, will settle a perplexing question of this kind.

415. THE NINE BRIDGES

Transform the map as follows. Reduce the four islands, A, B, C, and D, to mere points and extend the bridges into lines, as in Figure 1, and the conditions are unchanged. If you link A and B for outside communication, and also C and D, the conditions are as in Figure 2; if you link A and D, and also B and C, you get Figure 3; if you link A and C, and also B and D, you get Figure 4. In each case B and D are "odd nodes" (points from which you can proceed in an odd number of ways, three), so in every route you

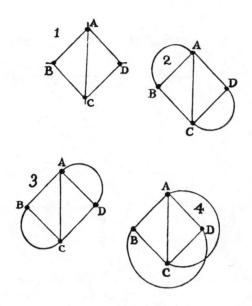

must start and finish at B or D, to go over every line once, and once only. Therefore, Tompkins must live at B or D: we will say B, and place Johnson at D. There are 44 routes by scheme 2, 44 by scheme 3, and 44 by scheme 4, making 132 in all, not counting reverse routes as different. Taking Figure 2, and calling the outside curved lines O, if you start BOAB, BOAC, BAOB, or BAC, there are 6 ways of continuing in each case. If you start BOAD, BAD, BCOD, BCA, or BCD, there are always 4 ways of continuing. In the case of Figure 3, BOCA, BOCB, BCA, or BCOB give 6 ways. BOCD, BAOD, BAC, BAD, or BCD give 4 ways each. Similarly, in the case of Figure 4.

416. SINKING THE FISHING-BOATS

The diagram shows how the warship sinks all the forty-nine boats in twelve straight courses, ending at the point from which she sets out. Follow every line to its end before changing your direction.

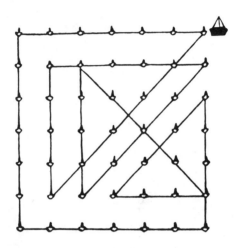

[M. S. Klamkin, in *American Mathematical Monthly,* February 1955, p. 124, proved that a continuous path of as few as $2n - 2$ straight line segments could be drawn through all the dots in a square array of n dots on the side, provided n is greater than 2. The case of $n = 3$ is a well-known puzzle which most people fail to solve in four moves because they do not think of extending line segments beyond the square's borders. The 5 × 5 is the smallest square that can be solved in $2n - 2$ segments without going outside the borders.

S. W. Golomb has shown that a path of $2n - 2$ segments is also sufficient for a *closed* path (one that ends, as in the above problem, at the starting point) on all squares with sides greater than 3. The 7 × 7 is the smallest odd-sided square with a closed path of $2n - 2$ segments that lies entirely within its border. (The smallest even-sided square on which such a path can be drawn is the 6 × 6.) The solution given here by Dudeney also appears in Sam Loyd's *Cyclopedia of Puzzles* as the solution to his Presidential Puzzle on page 293. Loyd says he first gave the puzzle in 1908, and describes the solution as "a wonderfully difficult trick." Whether Loyd copied the puzzle from Dudeney, or vice versa, has not yet been determined.

Note that this solution for the 7 × 7 array also provides a solution to the problem of making a closed "queen's tour" on a 7 × 7 chessboard in $2n - 2$ moves. Closed queen's tours in $2n - 2$ moves are also possible on all boards with sides greater than 7. The closed 14-move queen's tour on the standard 8 × 8 board was first solved by Sam Loyd, who considered it one of his best puzzles. (See Alain C. White, *Sam Loyd and His Chess Problems*, 1913, reprinted by Dover in 1962, pp. 42–43.)

A proof that $2n - 2$ segments are also necessary for any square array was given by John L. Selfridge in *American Mathematical Monthly*, Vol. 62, 1955, p. 443.—M. G.]

417. GOING TO CHURCH

Starting from the house, H, there is only one way of getting to each of the points in a northerly direction, and also going direct east, so I write in the

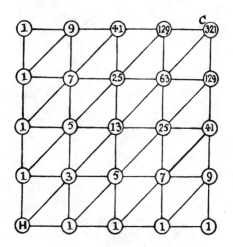

figure 1, as shown. Now take the second column, and you will find that there are three ways of going to the second point from the bottom, five ways to the next above, seven to the next, and so on, continually adding two. The same applies to the second row from the bottom. Write in these numbers. Then the central point of all can be reached in thirteen ways, because we can enter it either from the point below that can be reached in five ways, from the point to the left that can also be reached in five ways, or from the diagonal point below that can be reached in three ways, making together thirteen. So all we have to do is to write in turn at every point the sum of those three numbers from which it can be immediately reached. We thus find that the total number of different routes from H to C is 321.

418. THE SUBMARINE NET

The illustration will show the best way of cutting the net. It will be seen that eight cuts are made from A to B, dividing the net into two parts.

419. THE TWENTY-TWO BRIDGES

It will be found that every department has an even number (2, 4, or 6) of bridges leading from it, except C and L, which can each be approached by three bridges—an odd number. Therefore to go over every bridge once, and only once, it is necessary to begin and end at C and L, which are the two departments in which the houses stand. Thus, starting from C, we may take the following route: C, G, F, C, B, A, D, H, E, I, H, J, K, L, M, G, I, F, B, E, F, I, L.

420. FOOTPRINTS IN THE SNOW

The illustration explains itself.

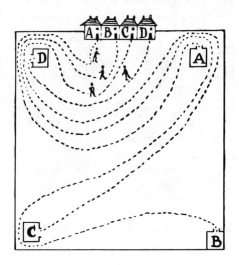

421. A MONMOUTH TOMBSTONE

The number of different ways in which "HERE LIES JOHN RENIE" can be read is 45,760; or, if diagonal readings are allowed, 91,520, because on reaching one of the corner I's we have the option of ending in the extreme corner or going backwards to an E diagonally. There is not space to give the solution in detail. The only other information on the stone is "who died May 31, 1832, aged 32 years."

422. THE FLY'S TOUR

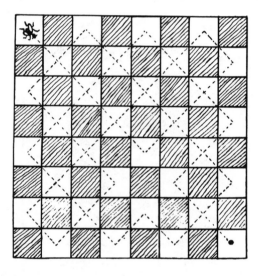

The line here shows the fly's route under the condition.

423. INSPECTING THE ROADS

The shortest possible route is as follows: ABCHCDEIEFGBHDIHGIFAG. Thus he has gone 211 miles, and passed along the two short roads CH and EI twice.

424. RAILWAY ROUTES

There are 2,501 ways of going from B to D, as follows:

1-line journey	1 route	2 variations	2
2-line journey	1 route	9 variations	9
3-line journey	2 routes	12 variations	24
4-line journey	5 routes	18 variations	90
5-line journey	4 routes	72 variations	288
6-line journey	14 routes	36 variations	504
8-line journey	22 routes	72 variations	1,584
			2,501

We have only to consider the routes from B to D. The 1-line route is direct to D. The 2-line route is CD. The two 3-line routes are CBD and DCD. The five 4-line routes are DBCD, DCBD, CBCD, CDCD, and CDBD. Each of these routes is subject to a number of variations in the actual lines used, and for a journey of a given number of lines there is always the same number of variations, whatever the actual route. A 7-line journey is not possible.

425. A CAR TOUR

The number of different routes is 264. It is quite a difficult puzzle, and consideration of space does not admit of my showing the best method of making the count.

426. MRS. SIMPER'S HOLIDAY TOUR

There are sixty different routes by which Mrs. Simper, starting from H, might visit every one of the towns once, and once only, by the roads shown, and return to H, counting reversals of routes as different. But if the lady is to avoid going through the tunnels between N and O, and S and R, it will be found that she is restricted to eight different routes.

If the reader is sufficiently interested he may wish to discover these eight routes for himself. If he does so, he will find that the route that complies with the conditions, avoids the two tunnels, and delays her visit to D as long as possible, is as follows: HISTLKBCMNUQRGFPODEAH. This is, therefore, undoubtedly her best route.

427. SIXTEEN STRAIGHT RUNS

The illustration shows how the traveller could have driven his car 76 miles in sixteen straight runs and left only three towns unvisited. This is not an easy puzzle, and the solution is only to be found after considerable trial.

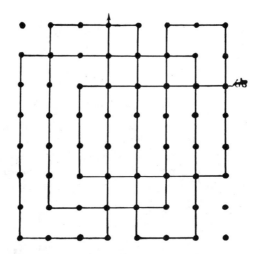

[Victor Meally improved this answer by finding a 76-mile, 16-segment path that leaves only *one* town unvisited. It is believed to be the best possible solution. The reader may enjoy searching for it.—M. G.]

428. PLANNING TOURS

In our illustration, in which the roads not used are omitted for the sake of clearness, every man's route is shown. It will be seen that no two drivers ever go along the same road, and that no man ever crosses the track of another. Although no hard-and-fast rules can be laid down for the solution of puzzles in this particular class, a little careful thought will generally overcome our difficulties. For example, we showed in the puzzle that if A goes direct to A in a straight line, we shall hopelessly cut off C, D, and E. It soon becomes evident that A must go to the left of the upper D, and having done so, must

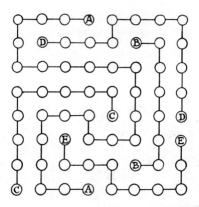

then get to the right of C. Also the route from D to D then becomes evident, as does that from B to B, and the rest is easy.

429. A MADAM PROBLEM

Every reading must begin with an M, and as there are only four M's there can only be four starting-points. It will be found that there are 20 different ways of reading MADAM, always starting from the same M, therefore the correct answer is that there are 80 ways in all.

430. THE ENCIRCLED TRIANGLES

This puzzle may be solved in the astonishingly small number of fourteen

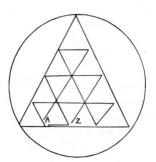

strokes, starting from A and ending at Z. Places in the figure are purposely not joined up, in order to make the route perfectly clear.

431. THE SIAMESE SERPENT

The drawing cannot be executed under the conditions in fewer than thirteen lines. We have therefore to find the longest of these thirteen lines. In the illustration we start at A and end at B, or the reverse. The dotted lines represent the lines omitted. It requires a little thought. Thus, the unbroken line from D to C is longer than the dotted line, therefore we take the former. Again, we can get in a little more of the drawing by taking the tongue rather than the mouth, but

the part of the tongue that ends in a straight line has to be omitted.

432. A BUNCH OF GRAPES

There are various routes possible, and our illustration shows one of them. But it is absolutely necessary that you begin at A and end at B, or the reverse. At any other point in the drawing a departure can be made in two or four ways (even numbers), but at A and B there are three ways of going (an odd number), therefore the rule is that you must begin and end at A and B.

433. A HOPSCOTCH PUZZLE

The hopscotch puzzle may be drawn in one continuous line without taking the pencil off the paper, or going over the same line twice. But it is necessary to begin at the point A and end at B, or begin at B and end at A. It cannot otherwise be done.

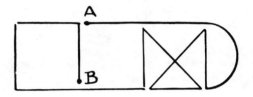

434. A WILY PUZZLE

In the diagram it will be seen that the prisoner's course is undoubtedly all right until we get to B. If we had been the prisoner, when we got to that point we should have placed one foot at C, in the neighboring cell, and have said, "As one foot has been in cell C we have undoubtedly entered it, and yet when we withdraw that foot into B we do not *enter* B a second time, for the simple reason that we have never left it since we first went in!"

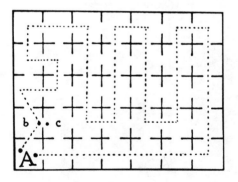

435. A TREE PLANTING PUZZLE

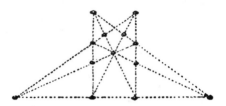

The illustration shows the graceful manner of planting the trees so as to get nine rows with four trees in every row.

436. THE TWENTY PENNIES

Arrange the sixteen pennies in the form of a square 4 by 4. Then place one penny on top of the first one in the first row; one on the third in the second row; one on the fourth in the third row; and one on the second in the fourth row.

437. TRANSPLANTING THE TREES

The illustration explains itself. Only six trees have been transplanted, and they now form twenty rows with four trees in every row.

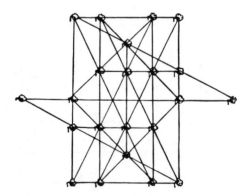

438. A PEG PUZZLE

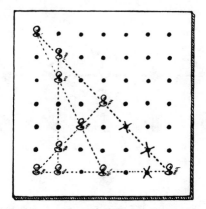

The diagram shows how to place the pegs. The three removed from the holes bearing a cross are replaced in the top left-hand corner. The ten pegs now form five rows with four pegs in every row. If you reflect the diagram in a mirror you will get the only other solution.

439. FIVE LINES OF FOUR

The illustration shows the solution to this puzzle. The ten counters form five rows with four counters in every row.

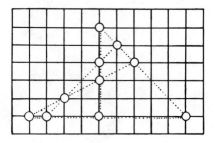

440. DEPLOYING BATTLESHIPS

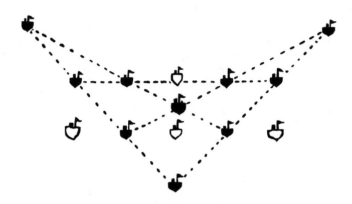

The illustration shows that the ships form five lines with four in every line, and the white phantom ships indicate the positions from which four of them have been removed.

441. CONSTELLATION PUZZLE

Here is a symmetrical solution in which the 21 stars form 11 straight lines, with 5 stars in every line.

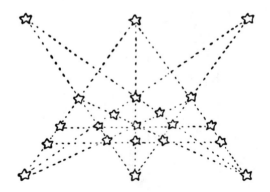

442. THE FOUR-COLOR MAP THEOREM

With two or more contiguous countries, two colors at least are obviously necessary (Figure 1). If three countries are contiguous each with each, three colors are necessary (Figure 2). With four countries, three will be required if the fourth (Y) is contiguous with each of two that are already contiguous (Figure 3). (For, as in Figure 4, G may be contiguous with two countries not

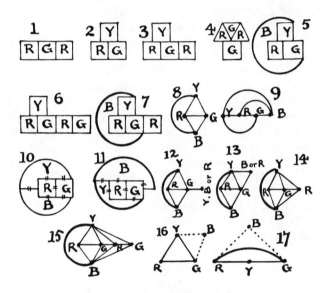

contiguous with one another, when only two colors are needed.) And four colors will be necessary if the fourth country is contiguous with each of three already contiguous each with each (Figure 5).

With five contiguous countries, three will be required if one country is contiguous with two already contiguous (Figure 6). And four will be necessary if the fifth country is contiguous with each of three countries that are contiguous each with each (Figure 7). Yet five colors would be needed if a fifth country were contiguous with each of four that are contiguous each with each. If such a map is possible, the theorem breaks down.

First, let us consider four countries contiguous each with each. We will use a simple transformation and suppose every two contiguous countries to be connected by a bridge across the boundary line. The bridge may be as long as we like, and the countries may be reduced to mere points, without affecting the conditions. In Figures 8 and 9 I show four countries (points) connected by bridges (lines), each with each. The relative positions of these points is quite immaterial, and it will be found in every possible case that one country (point) must be unapproachable from the outside.

The proof of this is easy. If three points are connected each with each by straight lines these points must either form a triangle or lie in a straight line. First suppose they form a triangle, YRG, as in Figure 16. Then a fourth contiguous country, B, must lie either within or without the triangle. If within, it is obviously enclosed. Place it outside and make it contiguous with Y and G, as shown: then B cannot be made contiguous with R without enclosing either Y or G. Make B contiguous with Y and R: then B cannot be made contiguous with G without enclosing either Y or R. Make B contiguous with R and G: then B cannot be made contiguous with Y without enclosing either R or G.

Take the second case, where RYG lie in a straight line, as in Figure 17. If B lies within the figure it is enclosed. Place B outside and make it contiguous with R and G, as shown: then B cannot be made contiguous with Y without enclosing either R or G. Make B contiguous with R and Y: then B cannot be made contiguous with G without enclosing either R or Y. Make B contiguous with Y and G: then B cannot be made contiguous with R without enclosing either Y or G.

We have thus taken every possible case and found that if three countries are contiguous each with each a fourth country cannot be made contiguous with all three without enclosing one country.

Figure 10 is Figure 8 before the transformation, and Figure 11 is the same as Figure 9, and it will be seen at once that you cannot possibly reach R from the outside. Therefore four countries cannot possibly be drawn so that a fifth may be contiguous with every one of them, and consequently the fifth country may certainly repeat the color R. And if you cannot draw five countries, it is quite obvious that you cannot draw any greater number contiguous each with each.

It is now clear that, at each successive addition of a new country, all the countries previously drawn must be contiguous each with each to prevent the employment of a *repeated* color. We can draw four countries under this condition, only one country must always be enclosed. Now, we can make the fifth country contiguous with only one country (as in Figure 12), with two countries (as in Figure 13), or with three countries (as in Figure 14). In the first case the new country can be Y or B or R, in the second case B or R, and in the third case R only. We take the last case (Figure 14) and "bring out," or repeat, R. But in doing so we have been compelled to enclose G. In drawing a sixth country the best we can do (in trying to up-set the theorem) is to "bring out" G (as in Figure 15), and the result is that we must enclose R. And so on into infinity. We can never avoid enclosing a color at every successive step, and thus making the color available for the next step. If you cannot artificially *construct* a map that will require a fifth color, such a map cannot possibly *occur*. Therefore a fifth color can never be necessary, and the truth of the theorem is proved.

[Dudeney correctly shows that no more than four regions can be drawn so that each borders all the others, but his proof fails to show that four colors are sufficient for all maps. It is true that if any four regions of a map are considered in isolation, no fifth color is necessary for any fifth region. What is required, however, is a proof that on a map with a large number of regions, these various sets of five will never conflict with each other in such a way that five colors are demanded.

The difficulty is best seen by actually constructing a complicated map, using the step by step procedure proposed by Dudeney. If each new region is drawn so as to border three others, its color is determined automatically and four-color maps can indeed be extended to infinity. But if many new regions are added that touch only one, two, or no other previously drawn regions, the choice of colors for these regions becomes arbitrary. As the map grows in size and complexity, one suddenly discovers that it is possible to construct a new region that will require a fifth color. By backtracking and altering previous colors, it appears that it is always possible to rectify the mistake and take care of the new region without going to a fifth color. But *is* it always possible? *This* is the conjecture that remains unproved. For a discussion of the problem, and a list of recent references, see the chapter on the four-color map theorem in my *New Mathematical Diversions from Scientific American.*—M. G.]

443. A SWASTIKLAND MAP

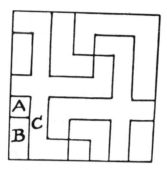

Three different colors are necessary. The bottom right-hand corner of the map is here reproduced. The Lord High Keeper of the Maps had introduced that little line dividing A and B by mistake, and this was his undoing. A, B, and C must be different colors. Except for this slip, two colors would have been sufficient.

444. COLORING THE MAP

Two! The map requires four colors. If the boy had three pigments (red, blue, and yellow) in his box, he could have obtained green, orange, or purple by mixing any two. But he cannot obtain four colors from fewer than three; consequently, there must have been only two ("not enough colors by one") in his box. "Color" refers to red, orange, yellow, green, blue and purple. Variant shades, such as bluish-green and yellowish-green, are not to be considered.

445. PICTURE PRESENTATION

Multiply together as many 2's as there are pictures and deduct 1. Thus 2 raised to the tenth power is 1,024, and deducting 1 we get 1,023 as the correct answer. Suppose there had been only three pictures. Then one can be selected in 3 ways, two in 3 ways, and three in 1 way, making together 7 ways, which is the same as the cube of 2 less 1.

446. A GENERAL ELECTION

The answer is 39,147,416 different ways. Add 3 to the number of members (making 618) and deduct 1 from the number of parties (making 3). Then the answer will be the number of ways in which 3 things may be selected from 618. That is:

$$\frac{618 \times 617 \times 616}{1 \times 2 \times 3} = 39,147,416 \text{ ways.}$$

The general solution is as follows. Let p = parties and m = members. The number of ways the parliament can be elected is equal to the number of combinations in which $p - 1$ objects may be selected from $m + p - 1$ objects.

447. THE MAGISTERIAL BENCH

Apart from any conditions, ten men can be arranged in line in 10! ways = 3,628,800. Now how many of these cases are barred? Regard two of a nationality in brackets as one item.

(1) Then (EE) (SS) (WW) FISA can be permuted in 7! $\times 2^3$ ways = 40,320. Remember the two E's can change places within their bracket wherever placed, and so with the S's and the W's. Hence the 2^3.

(2) But we may get (EE) (SS) WWFISA, where the W's are not bracketed, but free. This gives 8! $\times 2^2$ cases, but we must deduct result (1) or these will be included a second time. Result, 120,960.

(3) Deal similarly with the two S's unbracketed. Result, 120,960.

(4) Deal again, with the E's unbracketed. Result, 120,960.

(5) But we may have (EE) SSWWFISA, where both S and W are unbracketed. This gives 9! $\times 2$ cases, but we must deduct results (1), (2), and (3) for reasons that will now be obvious. Result, 443,520.

(6) When only S is bracketed, deducting (1), (2), and (4). Result, 443,520.

(7) When only W is bracketed, deducting (1), (3), and (4). Result, 443,520.

Add these seven results together and you get 1,733,760, which deducted from the number first given above leaves 1,895,040 as the number of ways in which the ten men may sit.

448. CROSSING THE FERRY

The puzzle can be solved in as few as nine crossings, as follows: (1) Mr. and Mrs. Webster cross. (2) Mrs. Webster returns. (3) Mother and daughter-in-law cross. (4) Mr. Webster returns. (5) Father-in-law and son cross. (6) Daughter-in-law returns. (7) Mr. Webster and daughter-in-law cross. (8) Mr. Webster returns. (9) Mr. and Mrs. Webster cross.

449. MISSIONARIES AND CANNIBALS

Call the three missionaries M m m, and the three cannibals C c c, the capitals denoting the missionary and the cannibal who can row the boat. Then C c row across; C returns with the boat; C c row across; C returns; M m row across; M c return; M C row across; M c return; M m row across; C returns; C c row across; C returns; C c row across; and all have crossed the river within the conditions stated.

[River crossing problems of this and the preceding type lend themselves to solution by a simple graph technique. See Robert Fraley, Kenneth L. Cooke, and Peter Detrick, "Graphical Solution of Difficult Crossing Puzzles," in *Mathematics Magazine,* Vol. 39, May 1966, pp. 151–157. See also the first chapter, "One More River to Cross," in Thomas H. O'Beirne, *Puzzles and Paradoxes* (Oxford University Press, 1965).—M. G.]

450. CROSSING THE RIVER

The two children row to the opposite shore. One gets out and the other brings the boat back. One soldier rows across; soldier gets out, and boy returns with boat. Thus it takes four crossings to get one man across and the boat brought back. Hence it takes four times 358, or 1,432 journeys, to get the officer and his 357 men across the river and the children left in joint possession of their boat.

451. A GOLF COMPETITION PUZZLE

The players may be paired and arranged as follows:

ROUNDS					
	1	**2**	**3**	**4**	**5**
1ST LINKS	BC	BF	EF	CE	AD
2ND LINKS	FA	CD	CA	DF	BE
3RD LINKS	DE	EA	DB	AB	CF

452. FOOTBALL RESULTS

We see at once from the table that England beat Ireland and drew with Wales. As E. scored 2 goals to 0 in these games, they must have won 2–0 and drew 0–0. This disposes of E. and leaves three games, W. *v.* I., S. *v.* I., and S. *v.* W., to be determined. Now, S. had only 1 goal scored against them—by W. or I. I. scored only 1 goal, and that must have been against W. or S. Assume it was against S. In that case W. did not score against S. But W. scored 3 goals altogether; therefore these must have been scored against I. We find I. had 6 goals against them: 2 scored by E., as shown, 3 by W. (if we assume that I. scored *v.* S.), and the remaining goal was scored by S. But, as we have just assumed I. scored 1 goal against S., the match would have been drawn. It was won by S., and therefore I. could not have scored against S. Thus the goal against S. must have been scored by W. And as W. scored 3 goals, the other two must have been *v.* I., who must have scored their only goal against W. Thus S. beat W. by 2–1 and I. by 2–0, while W. won by 2–1 *v.* I.

453. THE DAMAGED MEASURE

Let the eight graduation marks divide the 33-inch measure into the following nine sections: 1, 3, 1, 9, 2, 7, 2, 6, 2, and any length can be measured from 1 inch up to 33 inches. Of course, the marks themselves will be at 1, 4, 5, 14,

16, 23, 25, and 31 inches from one end. Another solution is 1, 1, 1, 1, 6, 6, 6, 6, 5. This puzzle may be solved in, at fewest, sixteen different ways. I have sought a rule for determining the fewest possible marks for any number of inches, and for at once writing out a solution, but a general law governing all the multiplicity of answers has still to be found.

[Although no general rule has yet been found for the ruler problem, considerable progress has been made since it was proposed by Dudeney. The reader is referred to John Leech's paper, "On the Representation of 1, 2, . . . , n by Differences," in the *Journal of the London Mathematical Society,* Vol. 31, 1956, pp. 160–169. Leech discovered that eight marks are also sufficient for marking a 36-inch yardstick so that all integral values from 1 to 36 can be measured. The reader may like to search for this pattern. Had Dudeney known it, he would have surely found it preferable to his broken yardstick of 33 inches.—M. G.]

454. THE SIX COTTAGES

If the distances between the cottages are as follows, in the order given, any distance from one mile up to twenty-six inclusive may be found as from one cottage to another: 1, 1, 4, 4, 3, 14 miles round the circular road.

[This problem is, of course, a circular version of the preceding one. As before, Dudeney could have increased the length of the "measuring stick" (in this case, the road) without altering the other aspects of his puzzle. It turns out that six cottages can be placed on a circular road of 31 miles so that all integral distances from 1 to 30 are represented by a distance, on the circle, between a pair of houses. It is not hard to see that for n houses the maximum number of different ways to measure a length between houses is $n(n-1)$. For $n = 6$, the formula gives 30, so in this case it is possible to place the 6 houses on the 31-mile road so that no distance between any pair of houses duplicates any other distance. Similar optimum solutions can be found when $n = 1, 2, 3, 4,$ or 5. See Michael Goldberg's solution to Problem E176 in *American Mathematical Monthly,* September 1965, p. 786.—M. G.]

455. FOUR IN LINE

There are nine fundamentally different arrangements, as shown in the illustration, the first, A, being the arrangement given as an example. Of these, D, E, and I each give eight solutions, counting reversals and reflections as explained, and the others give only four solutions each. There are, therefore, in all, forty-eight different ways in which the four counters may be placed on the board, so that every square shall be in line with at least one counter.

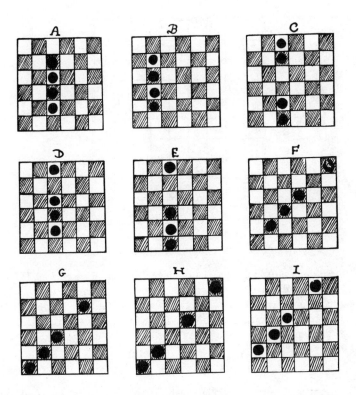

It may interest the reader to know that on a chessboard, 8 × 8, five counters may be placed in line under precisely the same conditions in four fundamental different ways, producing twenty different solutions in all. The arrangements are given in the solution to Number 311, "The Five Dogs Puzzle," in the book *Amusements in Mathematics*.

456. FLIES ON WINDOW PANES

The three lively flies have taken up new positions, as indicated by the arrows, and still no two flies are in a straight line.

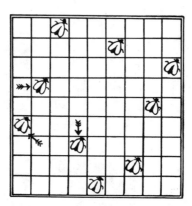

457. CITY LUNCHEONS

If the Pilkins staff had been 11 in number, and the Radson staff 12, they could have sat down differently in 165 and 495 ways respectively, which would have solved the question. Only we were told that there happened to be the same number of men in each staff. Therefore the answer is 15 in threes for 455 days, and 15 in fours for 1,365 days.

458. THE NECKLACE PROBLEM

The number of different necklaces with eight beads under the conditions is 30.

A general solution for any number of beads is difficult, if not impossible. But with as few as eight beads the reader will have no difficulty in finding the correct answer by mere trial.

[For a discussion of the general problem, with a recursive formula that gives the number of different necklaces with *n* beads of *m* different colors, see the chapter on "The Calculus of Finite Differences" in my book *New Mathematical Diversions from Scientific American.*—M. G.]

459. AN EFFERVESCENT PUZZLE

The answer to the first case is 88,200 ways. There is an easy way of getting the answer, but it would require too much space to explain it in detail. In the second case the answer is reduced to 6,300 ways.

460. TESSELLATED TILES

Discard the first tile in each of the four horizontal rows. Then the remaining sixteen may be arranged as shown in the illustration, in accordance with the conditions.

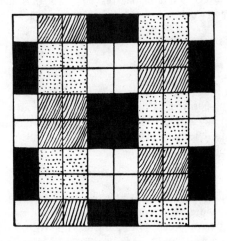

461. THE THIRTY-SIX LETTER PUZZLE

If you have tried, as most people do, first to place all six of one letter, then all six of another letter, and so on, you will find, after you have placed four different kinds of letters six times each, it is impossible to place more than two letters each of the last two letters, and you will get our arrangement number 1. The secret is to place six of each of two letters, and five of each of the remaining four, when we get our second diagram, with only four blanks.

A	B	C	D	E	F
D	F	E	B	A	C
E	C			D	B
B	D		c	E	
C		B	E		D
	E	D	C	B	

A	B	C	D	E	F
D	E	A	F	B	C
F	C			D	A
B	D		c	E	
C	A	E	B	F	D
E	F	D	C	A	B

462. THE TEN BARRELS

Arrange the barrels in one of the following two ways, and the sides will add up to 13 in every case—the smallest number possible:

```
        0                      0
      8   6                  7   8
    4   9   5              5   9   3
  1   7   3   2          1   6   4   2
```

By changing the positions of the side numbers (without altering the numbers contained in any side) we get eight solutions in each case, not counting mere reversals and reflections as different.

463. LAMP SIGNALLING

With 3 red, white, or green lamps we can make 15 variations each (45). With 1 red and 2 white we can make the same, 15, and each way will admit of 3 variations of color order, 45 in all. The same with 1 red and 2 green, 1 white and 2 red, 1 white and 2 green, 1 green and 2 white, 1 green and 2 red (270). With 1 red, 1 white, and 1 green we can get 6 by 15 variations (90). With 2 red or 2 white or 2 green we can get 7 patterns (21). With 1 red and 1 white, or 1 red and 1 green, or 1 white and 1 green, we can get 14 variations each (42). With 1 lamp only we can get only 1 signal each (3). Add together the numbers in parentheses (45, 270, 90, 21, 42, and 3), and we get the answer, 471 ways.

464. THE HANDCUFFED PRISONERS

The following is a solution. Every prisoner will be found to have been hand-cuffed to every other prisoner once, and only once.

1–2–3 2–6–8 6–1–7 1–4–8 7–2–9 4–3–1 4–5–6 5–9–1 9–4–2 2–5–7 3–6–4
5–8–2 7–8–9 3–7–4 8–3–5 6–9–3 8–1–5 9–7–6

If the reader wants a hard puzzle to keep him engrossed during the winter months, let him try to arrange twenty-one prisoners so that they can all walk out, similarly handcuffed in triplets, on fifteen days without any two men being handcuffed together more than once.

In case he should come to the opinion that the task is impossible, we will add that we have written out a perfect solution. But it is a hard nut!

465. SEATING THE PARTY

The number of different ways in which the six occupants of the car can be seated under the conditions is 144.

466. QUEER GOLF

The two best distances are 100 yards (called "the approach"), and 125 yards ("the drive"). Hole 1 can be reached in three approaches, hole 2 in two drives, hole 3 in two approaches, hole 4 in two approaches and one drive, hole 5 in three drives and one backward approach, hole 6 in two drives and one approach, hole 7 in one drive and one approach, hole 8 in three drives, and hole 9 in four approaches—26 strokes in all.

467. THE ARCHERY MATCH

Mrs. Finch scored 100 with four 17's and two 16's; Reggie Watson scored 110 with two 23's and four 16's; Miss Dora Talbot scored 120 with one 40 and five 16's. Her score can be made up in various ways, except for the fact that the bull's-eye has to be got in somewhere, and this is the only place where it can occur.

468. TARGET PRACTICE

The total score was 213, so each man scored 71, and this could be done in the following manner: One man scored 50, 10, 5, 3, 2, and 1; another scored 25, 20, 20, 3, 2, and 1; and the third man 25, 20, 10, 10, 5, and 1.

469. TOM TIDDLER'S GROUND

The large majority of competitors who tried to solve "Tom Tiddler's Ground," when it first appeared in London's *Daily News,* succeeded in securing bags containing only $45.00.

The correct answer is $47.00 contained in ten bags, all deposited on outside plots, thus: 4, 5, 6 in the first row, 5 in the second, 4 in the third, 3 in the fourth, 5 in the fifth, and 5, 6, 4 in the bottom row. If you include five bags containing $6.00 each, you can secure only nine bags, and a value of $46.00.

470. THE SEVEN CHILDREN

There are 5,040 ways of arranging the children, and 720 different ways of placing a girl at each end. Therefore, the chances are 720 in 5,040, or 1 in 7. Or, which is the same thing, the chances are 1 to 6 in favor, or 6 to 1 against, there being a girl at both ends.

471. TIC TAC TOE

Number the board, as in Figure A. Mr. Nought (the first player) can open in one of three ways: he can play to the center, 5, or to a corner, 1, 3, 7, or 9, or to a side, 2, 4, 6, 8. Let us take these openings in turn. If he leads with a center, then Mr. Cross has the option of a corner or a side. If he takes a side, such as 2 in Figure A, then Nought plays 1 and 4 successively (or 1 and 7), and wins. Cross must take a corner, as in Figure B, and then Nought cannot do better than draw. If Nought leads with a corner, say 1, Cross has five different replies, as in Figures C, D, E, F, and G (for 4 here is the same as 2, 7 the same as 3, and 8 the same as 6). If he plays as in Figure C, Nought wins with 5 and 4; if he plays as in D, Nought wins with 7 and 3; if as in E, Nought wins with 9 and 7; if as in F, Nought wins with 5 and 3. Cross is compelled to take the center, as in Figure G, to save the game, for this will result in a draw. If Nought opens with a side, say 2, as in Figures H, J, K, L, and M, and Cross plays as in H, Nought wins with 5 and 1; and if he plays as in J, Nought wins with 1 and 5. Cross must play as in K, L, or M to secure a draw.

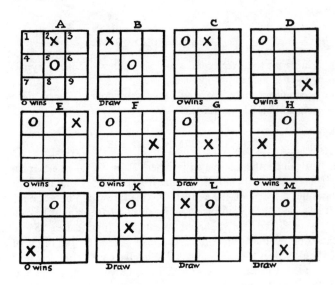

I have thus shown the play for Nought to win in seven cases where Cross makes a bad first move, but I have not space to prove the draws in the remaining five positions B, G, K, L, and M. But the reader can easily try each of these cases for himself and be convinced that neither player can win without the bad play of his opponent. Of course, either player can throw away the game. For example, if in Figure L Nought stupidly plays 3 on his second move, Cross can play 7 and 9 and win. Or if Nought plays 8, Cross can play 5 and 7 and win.

Now, if I were playing with an equally expert player I should know that the best I could possibly do (barring my opponent's blunders) would be to secure a draw. As first player, Nought, I should know that I could safely lead with any square on the board. As second player, Cross, I should take a corner if Nought led with a center and take the center if he led with anything else. This would avoid many complexities and should always draw. The fact remains that it is a capital little game for children, and even for adults who have never analyzed it, but two experts would be merely wasting their time in playing it. To them it is not a game, but a mere puzzle that they have completely solved.

472. THE HORSESHOE GAME

Just as in tic tac toe, every game should be a draw. Neither player can win except by the bad play of his opponent.

[For a complete analysis of the game, see Édouard Lucas, *Récréations Mathématiques,* Vol. III, pp. 128–131.—M. G.]

473. TURNING THE DIE

The best call for the first player is either "2" or "3," as in either case only one particular throw should defeat him. If he called "1," the throw of either 3 or 6 should defeat him. If he called "2," the throw of 5 only should defeat him. If he called "3," the throw of 4 only should defeat him. If he called "4," the throw of either 3 or 4 should defeat him. If he called "5," a throw of either 2 or 3 should defeat him. And if he called "6," the throw of either 1 or 5 should defeat him. It is impossible to give here a complete analysis of the play, but I will just state that if at any time you score either 5, 6, 9, 10, 14, 15, 18, 19, or 23, with the die any side up, you ought to lose. If you score 7 or 16 with any side up you should win. The chance of winning with the other scores depends on the lie of the die.

474. THE THREE DICE

Mason's chance of winning was one in six. If Jackson had selected the numbers 8 and 14 his chances would have been exactly the same.

475. THE 37 PUZZLE GAME

The first player (A) can always win, but he must lead with 4. The winning scores to secure during the play are 4, 11, 17, 24, 30, 37. In the first game below the second player (B) puts off defeat as long as possible. In the second game he prevents A scoring 17 or 30, but has to give him 24 and 37. In the third game he prevents A scoring 11 or 24, but has to give him 17, 30, and 37. Notice the important play of the 3 and the 5.

A	B		A	B		A	B
4	1 (*a*)		4	1		4	1
3	1 (*b*)		3	1		3	4
(11) 2	1		(11) 2	3 (*d*)		(17) 5	1
(17) 5	1 (*c*)		5	1		3	4
3	2		(24) 4	3 (*e*)		(30) 5 (*f*)	1
(24) 1	2		5	1		3	1
(30) 4	1		(37) 4			(37) 2	
3	2						
(37) 1							

(*a*) Or A will score 11 next move. (*b*) B could not prevent A scoring 11 or 17 next move. (*c*) Again, to prevent A immediately scoring 24. (*d*) Preventing A scoring 17, but giving him 24. (*e*) Preventing A scoring 30, but giving him the 37. (*f*) Thus A can always score 24 (as in the last game) or 30 (as in this), either of which commands the winning 37.

476. THE 22 GAME

Apart from the exhaustion of cards, the winning series is 7, 12, 17, 22. If you can score 17 and leave at least one 5-pair of both kinds (4–1, 3–2), you must win. If you can score 12 and leave two 5-pairs of both kinds, you must win. If you can score 7 and leave three 5-pairs of both kinds, you must win. Thus, if the first player plays a 3 or 4, you play a 4 or 3, as the case may be, and score 7. Nothing can now prevent the second player from scoring 12, 17, and 22. The lead of 2 can also always be defeated if you reply with a 3 or a 2. Thus, 2–3, 2–3, 2–3, 2–3 (20), and, as there is no remaining 2, second player wins. Again, 2–3, 1–3, 3–2, 3–2 (19), and second player wins. Again, 2–3, 3–4 (12), or 2–3, 4–3 (12), also win for second player. The intricacies of the defence 2–2 I leave to the reader. The best second play of first player is a 1.

The first player can always win if he plays 1, and in no other way. Here are specimen games: 1–1, 4–1, 4–1, 4 (16) wins. 1–3, 1–2, 4–1, 4–1, 4 (21) wins. 1–4, 2 (7) wins. 1–2, 4 (7) wins.

477. THE NINE SQUARES GAME

I should play MN. My opponent may play HL, and I play CD. (If he had played CD, I should have replied HL, leaving the same position.) The best he can now do is DH (scoring one), but, as he has to play again, I win the remaining eight squares.

478. THE TEN CARDS

The first player can always win. He must turn down the third card from one of the ends, leaving them thus: 00.0000000. Now, whatever the second player does, the first can always leave either 000.000 or 00.00.0.0 or 0.00.000 (order of groups does not matter). In the first case, whatever the second player does in one triplet the other repeats in the other triplet, until he gets the last card. In the second case, the first player similarly repeats the play of his opponent, and wins. In the third case, whatever the second player does, the first can always leave either 0.0, or 0.0.0.0, or 00.00, and again get an obvious win.

[Victor Meally points out that the first player can also win by first turning the second card from either end, or the fourth card from either end.—M. G.]

479. THE DOMINO SWASTIKA

It will be seen that by placing the four extra dominoes in the positions shown a perfect swastika is formed within the frame.

480. DOMINO FRACTIONS

The illustration shows how to arrange the dominoes so that each of the three rows of five sum to 10. Give every fraction the denominator 60. Then the numerators of the fractions used must sum to 1,800, or 600 in each row, to produce the sum 10. The selection and adjustment require a little thought and cunning.

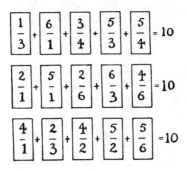

481. A NEW DOMINO PUZZLE

These four dominoes fulfill the conditions. It will be found that, taking contiguous pips, we can make them sum to any number from 1 to 23 inclusive.

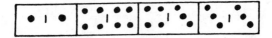

[Victor Meally has improved Dudeney's solution. The following chain of four dominoes, 1–3, 6–6, 6–2, 3–2, gives sums from 1 through 29. Meally also points out that three dominoes, 1–1, 4–4, 4–3, have sums from 1 through 17. —M. G.]

482. A DOMINO SQUARE

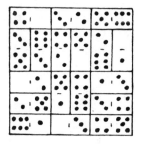

The illustration explains itself. The eighteen dominoes are arranged so as to form the required square, and it will be found that in no column or row is a number repeated. There are, of course, many other ways of doing it.

483. A DOMINO STAR

The illustration shows a correct solution. The dominoes are placed together according to the ordinary rule, the pips in every ray sum to 21, and the central numbers are 1, 2, 3, 4, 5, 6, and two blanks.

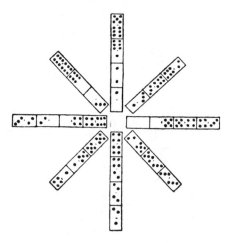

484. DOMINO GROUPS

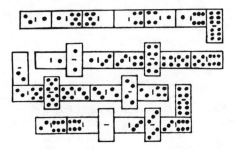

The illustration shows one way in which the dominoes may be laid out so that, when the line is broken in four lengths of seven dominoes each, every length shall contain forty-two pips.

485. LES QUADRILLES

The illustration shows a correct solution, the two blank squares being on the inside. If in the example shown before all the numbers had not happened to be found somewhere on the edge, it would have been an easy matter, for we

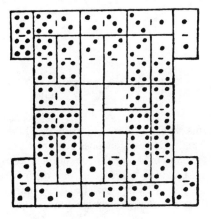

should have had merely to exchange that missing number with a blank wherever found. There would thus have been no puzzle. But in the circumstances it is impossible to avail oneself of such a simple maneuver.

[For more domino problems of this type, known as quadrilles, see Édouard Lucas, *Récréations Mathématiques,* Vol. 2, pp. 52–63, and Wade E. Philpott, "Quadrilles," in *Recreational Mathematics Magazine,* No. 14, January–February 1964, pp. 5–11.—M. G.]

486. DOMINO FRAMES

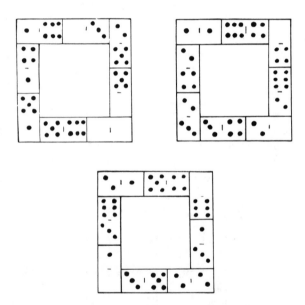

The three diagrams show a solution. The sum of all the pips is 132. One-third of this is 44. First divide the dominoes into any three groups of 44 pips each. Then, if we decide to try 12 for the sum of the sides, 4 times 12 being 4 more than 44, we must arrange in every case that the four corners in a frame shall sum to 4. The rest is done by trial and exchanges from one group to another of dominoes containing an equal number of pips.

487. DOMINO HOLLOW SQUARES

It is shown in the illustration how the 28 dominoes may be arranged in the form of 7 hollow squares, so that the pips in the four sides of every square add up alike. It is well to remember this little rule when forming your squares. If the pips on your dominoes sum, say, to 7 (as in the first example), and you wish the sides to add up 3, then 4 × 3 — 7 gives us 5 as the sum of the four corners. This is absolutely necessary. Thus, in the last example, 4 × 16 = 64 — 43 tells us that the four corners must sum to 21, as it will be found they do.

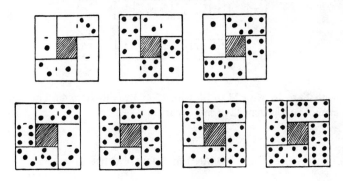

488. DOMINO SEQUENCES

If we draw from the set the four dominoes 7-6, 5-4, 3-2, 1-0, the remaining dominoes may be put together in proper sequence. Any other combinations of these particular numbers would do equally well; thus we might withdraw 7-0, 6-1, 5-2, and 4-3. Generally, for any set of dominoes ending in a double odd number, those withdrawn must contain together every number once from blank up to two less than the highest number in the set.

489. TWO DOMINO SQUARES

The illustration on page 400 shows how the twenty-eight dominoes may be laid out so as to form the two required squares with the pips in each of the eight sides summing to 22. With 22 as the constant sum, the corners must sum

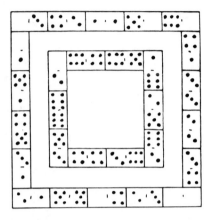

to 8, with 23 to 16, with 24 to 24, with 25 to 32, with 26 to 40. The constant sum cannot be less than 22 or more than 26.

490. DOMINO MULTIPLICATION

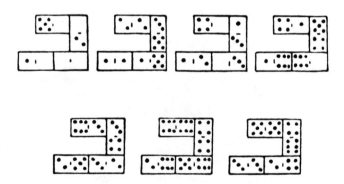

Here all the twenty-eight dominoes are used, and they form seven multiplication sums as required.

491. DOMINO RECTANGLE

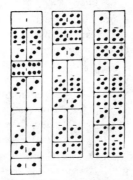

The illustration shows how the twenty-eight dominoes may be arranged so that the columns add up to 24 and the rows to 21.

492. THE DOMINO COLUMN

Place the second column under the first, and the third under the second (the column is broken merely for convenience in printing), and the conditions will be found to be fulfilled.

493. ARRANGING THE DOMINOES

There are just 126,720 different ways of playing those 15 dominoes, counting the two directions as different.

494. A NEW MATCH PUZZLE

The smallest possible number is 36 matches. We can form triangle and square with 12 and 24 respectively, triangle and pentagon with 6 and 30, triangle and hexagon with 6 and 30, square and pentagon with 16 and 20, square and hexagon with 12 and 24, and pentagon and hexagon with 30 and 6. The pairs of numbers may be varied in all cases except the fourth and last. There cannot be fewer than 36. The triangle and hexagon require a number divisible by 3: the square and hexagon require an even number. Therefore the number must be divisible by 6, such as 12, 18, 24, 30, 36, but this condition cannot be fulfilled for a pentagon and hexagon with fewer than 36 matches.

495. HURDLES AND SHEEP

If the enclosure is to be rectangular, the nearer the rectangle approaches to the form of a square the greater will be the area. But the greatest area of all will always be when the hurdles are arranged in the form of a regular polygon, inscribed in a circle, and if this can be done in more than one way the greatest area will be when there are as many sides as hurdles. Thus, the hexagon given earlier had a greater area than the triangle. The twelve-sided figure or regular dodecagon therefore encloses the largest possible area for twelve hurdles—room for about eleven sheep and one-fifth. Eleven hurdles would only accommodate a maximum of about nine and nine-twenty-fifths, so that twelve hurdles are necessary for ten sheep. If

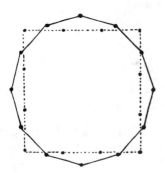

you arrange the hurdles in the form of a square, as shown by the dotted lines, you only get room for nine sheep.

496. THE TWENTY MATCHES

The illustration shows how two enclosures may be formed with 13 and 7 matches respectively, so that one area shall be exactly three times as large as

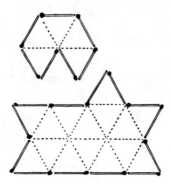

the other, for one contains five of those little equilateral triangles, and the other fifteen.

There are other solutions.

497. A MATCH PUZZLE

The illustration shows one of the four distinctive ways of solving this puzzle, with eleven, an *odd* number of matches. If you first enclose an outside row, as A, then you can enclose the square, B, in any position, and complete the solution with eleven matches in all.

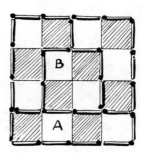

498. AN INGENIOUS MATCH PUZZLE

It will be seen that the second I in VII has been moved, so as to form the sign of square root. The square root of 1 is, of course, 1, so that the fractional expression itself represents 1.

499. FIFTY-SEVEN TO NOTHING

Remove the two cigarettes forming the letter L in the original arrangement, and replace them in the way shown in our illustration. We have the square root

of 1 minus 1 (that is 1 less 1), which clearly is 0. In the second case we can remove the same two cigarettes and, by placing one against the V and the other against the second I, form the word NIL, or nothing.

500. THE FIVE SQUARES

Place the twelve matches as in the diagram and five squares are enclosed. It is true that the one in the center (indicated by the arrow) is very small, but no conditions were imposed as to dimensions.

501. A MATCH TRICK

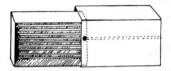

You must secrete the match inside in the manner shown by the dotted lines in the illustration, so that the head is just over the edge of the tray of the box. In closing the box you press this extra match forward with the thumbnail (which, if done carefully, will not be noticed), and it falls into its place. Of course, one of the matches first shown does not turn round, as that would be an impossibility, but nobody ever counts the matches.

502. THREE TIMES THE SIZE

The illustration shows how two enclosures may be formed with 13 and 7 matches respectively, so that one area shall be exactly three times as large as the other. The dotted lines will show that one figure contains two squares and an equilateral triangle, and the other six squares and three such triangles. The 12 horizontal and vertical matches have not been moved.

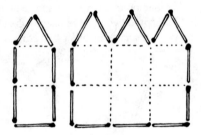

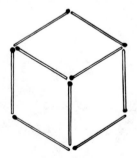

503. A SIX-SIDED FIGURE

The illustration shows the simple answer. We did not ask for a *plane* figure, nor for the figure to be *formed* with the 9 matches. We show (in perspective) a *cube* (a regular six-sided figure).

504. TWENTY-SIX MATCHES

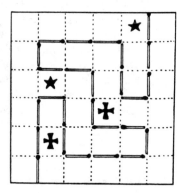

The illustration shows how the 26 matches may be placed so that the square is divided into two parts of exactly the same size and shape, one part containing two stars, and the other two crosses.

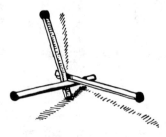

505. THE THREE MATCHES

Arrange the three matches as shown in the illustration, and stand the box on end in the center.

506. EQUILATERAL TRIANGLES

Remove the four matches indicated by the dotted lines, and the remainder form four equal triangles.

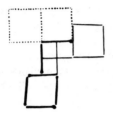

507. SQUARES WITH MATCHES

In the illustration the dotted lines indicate the six matches that have been removed. The thin lines show where they are replaced, and the thick lines indicate the six that have not been moved.

508. HEXAGON TO DIAMONDS

The illustration will show by the dotted lines the original position of the two matches that have been moved.

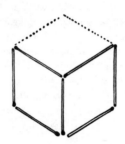

509. QUEER ARITHMETIC

Arrange 10 matches thus—FIVE. Then take away the 7 matches forming FE (seven-tenths of the whole), and you leave IV, or four.

510. COUNTING THE MATCHES

There were 36 matches in the box with which he could form a triangle 17, 10, 9, the area of which was 36 sq. in. After 6 had been used, the remaining 30 formed a triangle 13, 12, 5, with an area of 30 sq. in.; and after using another 6, the 24 remaining would form a triangle 10, 8, 6, with an area of 24 sq. in.

511. A PUZZLE WITH CARDS

Arrange the pack in the following order face downwards with 9 of Clubs at the top and 5 of Spades at bottom: 9 C., Jack D., 5 C., ace D., King H., King S., 7 H., 2 D., 6 S., Queen D., 10 S., ace S., 3 C., 3 D., 8 C., King D., 8 H., 7 C.,

4 D., 2 S., ace H., ace C., 7 S., 5 D., 9 H., 2 H., Jack S., 6 D., Queen C., 6 C., 10 H., 3 S., 3 H., 7 D., 4 C., 2 C., 8 S., Jack H., 4 H., 8 D., Jack C., 4 S., Queen S., King C., 9 D., 5 H., 10 C., Queen H., 10 D., 9 S., 6 H., 5 S.

[All such arrangements for spelling cards can be solved quickly by starting with the last card to be spelled, then performing all the required operations in reverse order, finishing with the full pack, or packet, of cards.—M. G.]

512. CARD SHUFFLING

To shuffle fourteen cards in the manner described, so that the cards shall return to their original order, requires fourteen shuffles, though with sixteen cards we require only 5. We cannot go into the law of the thing, but the reader will find it an interesting investigation.

[For the mathematical theory of this shuffle, see W. W. Rouse Ball, *Mathematical Recreations and Essays,* revised eleventh edition, edited by H. S. M. Coxeter (Macmillan, 1960), pp. 310–311. The shuffle is sometimes called "Monge's shuffle" after Gaspard Monge, a famous eighteenth century French mathematician who was the first to investigate it.—M. G.]

513. A CHAIN PUZZLE

To open a link and join it again will cost 3¢. By opening one link at the end of each of the thirteen pieces the cost will be 39¢, so it would be cheaper than that to buy a new chain. If there happened to be a piece of twelve links, all these twelve could be opened to join the remaining twelve pieces at a cost also of 36¢. If there had happened to be two pieces together, containing eleven links, all these could be opened to join the remaining eleven pieces at a cost of 33¢.

The best that can be done is to open three pieces containing together ten links to join the remaining ten pieces at a cost of 30¢. This is possible if we break up the piece of four links and two pieces of three links. Thus, if we include the piece of three links that was shown in the middle row as one of the three link pieces, we shall get altogether five large links and five small ones.

If we had been able to find four pieces containing together nine links we should save another 3¢, but this is not possible, nor can we find five pieces containing together eight links, and so on, therefore the correct answer is as stated, 30¢.

514. A SQUARE WITH FOUR PENNIES

The illustration indicates how we may show a square with four pennies. The sides of the square are the lines beneath Britannia.

515. SIMPLE ADDITION

Add IV turned upside down below VI and you get XI.

516. A CALENDAR PUZZLE

Every year divisible by 4 without remainder is bissextile (leap year), *except* that every year divisible by 100 without remainder is *not* leap year, unless it be also divisible by 400 without remainder, when it *is* leap year. This is not generally understood. Thus 1800 was not leap year, nor was 1900; but 2000, 2400, 2800, etc., will all be leap years. The first day of the present century, January 1, 1901, was *Tuesday*.

The present century will contain 25 leap years, because 2000 is leap year, and therefore 36,525 (365 × 100 + 25) days, or 5217 weeks and 6 days; so that January 1, 2001, will be 6 days later than Tuesday—that is Monday. The century beginning January 1, 2001, will contain only 24 leap years, because 2100 is not leap year, and January 1, 2101, will be 5 days later than Monday, last mentioned, that is Saturday, because there are 5217 weeks and only 5 days. It will now be convenient to put the results into tabular form:

January 1, 1901—Tuesday.
January 1, 2001—Monday.   6 days later (2000, leap year)
January 1, 2101—Saturday.   5 days later
January 1, 2201—Thursday.   5 days later
January 1, 2301—Tuesday.   5 days later
January 1, 2401—Monday.   6 days later (2400, leap year)

It will thus be seen that the first days of successive centuries will be Tuesday, Monday, Saturday, and Thursday—perpetually recurring—so that the first day of a century can never occur on a Sunday, Wednesday, or a Friday, as I have stated.

517. THE FLY'S TOUR

Before you join the ends give one end of the ribbon a half-turn, so that there is a twist in the ring. Then the fly can walk over all the squares without going over the edge, for we have the curious paradox of a piece of paper with only one side and one edge!

[Dudeney has described what is now well known as the Moebius strip, one of the great curiosities of topology.—M. G.]

518. A MUSICAL ENIGMA

The undoubtedly correct solution to this enigma is BACH. If you turn the cross round, you get successively B flat (treble clef), A (tenor clef), C (alto clef), and B natural (treble clef). In German B flat is called "B" and B natural "H," making it read BACH.

It reminds me of an organ fugue by

C. P. Emanuel Bach, based on the family name and beginning as in the illustration.

519. SURPRISING RELATIONSHIP

If there were two men, each of whom marries the mother of the other, and there is a son of each marriage, then each of such sons will at once be uncle and nephew to the other. This is the simplest answer.

[Victor Meally supplies two more answers: (1) Each of two women marries the father of the other, (2) A man marries the mother of a woman, and the woman marries the father of the man.—M. G.]

520. AN EPITAPH (A.D. 1538)

If two widows had each a son, and each widow married the son of the other and had a daughter by the marriage, all the relationships will be found to result.

521. THE ENGINEER'S NAME

It is clear that the guard cannot be Smith, for Mr. Smith is certainly the engineer's nearest neighbor, and his income is, therefore, exactly divisible by 3, which $10,000.00 is not. Also the stoker cannot be Smith, because Smith beats him at billiards. Therefore the engineer must be Smith, and as we are concerned with him only, it is immaterial whether the guard is Jones and the stoker Robinson, or vice versa.

[This is one of Dudeney's most popular puzzles. It became the prototype of scores of later logic problems, sometimes called Smith-Jones-Robinson puzzles, in honor of Dudeney's original problem. James Joyce refers to the problem ("Smith-Jones-Orbison") in the mathematics section of *Finnegans Wake* (p. 302), and Dudeney himself is mentioned in footnote 1 on page 284. —M. G.]

522. STEPPING STONES

Number the stepping stones 1 to 8 in regular order. Then proceed as follows: 1 (bank), 1, 2, 3, (2), 3, 4, 5, (4), 5, 6, 7, (6), 7, 8, bank, (8), bank. The steps in parentheses are taken in a backward direction. It will thus be seen that by returning to the bank after the first step, and then always going three steps forward for one step backward, we perform the required feat in nineteen steps.

523. AN AWKWARD TIME

The Colonel's friend said that 12:50 is clearly an awkward time for a train to start, because it is ten to one (10 to 1) if you catch it.

524. CRYPTIC ADDITION

If you turn the page upside down you will find that one, nine, one, and eight added together correctly make nineteen.

525. THE TWO SNAKES

We cannot say how much of each snake must be swallowed before a vital organ is sufficiently affected to cause death. But we can say what will *not* happen—that the snakes will go on swallowing one another until both disappear altogether! But where it will really end it is impossible to say.

526. TWO PARADOXES

If W and E were stationary points, and W, as at present, on your left when advancing towards N, then, after passing the Pole and turning round, W would be on your right, as stated. But W and E are not fixed points, but *directions* round the globe; so wherever you stand facing N, you will have the W direction on your left and the E direction on the right.

In the reflection in a mirror you are not "turned round," for what appears to be your right hand is your left, and what appears to be your left side is the right. The reflection sends back, so to speak, exactly what is opposite to it at every point.

[If the reader does not understand Dudeney's brief explanation of the mirror paradox, he should consult the first chapter of my *Ambidextrous Universe* (Basic Books, 1965), where it is considered at greater length.—M. G.]

527. COIN AND HOLE

Strange though it may at first appear, a half-dollar may be passed through that small hole (made by tracing around a penny) without tearing the paper. This is the largest coin that can be used. First fold the paper across the center of the hole and drop the coin into the fold. Then, holding the paper at A and B, bring the hands

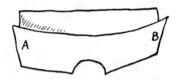

together upwards, and the coin may be squeezed through the hole.

528. A LEAP YEAR PUZZLE

Since the new style was adopted in England in 1752, the first year with five Wednesdays in February was 1764. Then 1792 and 1804. By adding 28, we then get 1832, 1860, 1888. Then we make the jump to 1928, 1956, 1984, and 2012. The answer is, therefore, 1888 and 1956. Normally it occurs every twenty-eighth year, except that 1800 and 1900 (which were not leap years) come in between, when the rule breaks down. As 2000 will be a leap year, twenty-eight years from 1984 is correctly 2012.

529. BLOWING OUT THE CANDLE·

The trick is to lower the funnel until the dotted line, CA, on the top in the puzzle illustration, is in line with the flame of the candle. Any attempt to blow the candle out with the flame opposite the center of the opening of the funnel is hopeless.

530. RELEASING THE STICK

If you take the loop and pull through it as much of the coat above and below the buttonhole as is necessary, it will be possible to pass the lower end of the stick through the buttonhole and get it in the required position. To disentangle it you reverse the process, though it is rather more perplexing. If you put it on your friend's coat carefully while he is not looking, it will puzzle him to remove it without cutting the string.

531. THE KEYS AND RING

First cut out the keys and ring in one piece, as here shown. Now cut only half through the cardboard along the eight little dark lines, and similarly cut half through on the eight little dotted lines *on the other side of the cardboard.* Then insert a penknife and split the card below the four little squares formed by these lines, and the three pieces will come apart with the keys loose on the ring and no join.

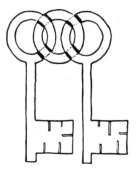

532. THE ENTANGLED SCISSORS

Slacken the string throughout so as to bring the scissors near the hand of the person holding the ends. Then work the loop, which is shown at the bottom of the figure, backwards along the double cord. You must be careful to make the loop follow the double cord on its course, in and out, until the loop is free of the scissors. Then pass the loop right round the points of the scissors and follow the double cord backwards. The string will then, if you have been very careful, detach itself from the scissors. But it is important to avoid twists and tangles, or you will get it in a hopeless muddle. But with a little practice it may be easily done.

533. INTELLIGENCE TESTS

What is wrong with the dream story is the obvious fact that, as the dreamer never awoke from his dream, it is impossible that anything could be known about it. The story must, therefore, be a pure invention.

The answer to the second question is: By immersing them in water and calculating from the rise of the water in the vessel.

534. AT THE MOUNTAIN TOP

The surface of water, or other liquid, is always spherical, and the greater any sphere is the less is its convexity. The spherical surface of the water must, therefore, be less above the brim of the vessel, and consequently it will hold less at the top of a mountain than at the bottom. This applies to any mountain whatever.

535. CUPID'S ARITHMETIC

All the young mathematician had to do was to reverse the paper and hold it up to the light, or hold it in front of a mirror, when he would immediately see that his betrothed's curious jumble of figures will read: "Kiss me, dearest."

Index

Index

About the Editor

Martin Gardner, like Henry Ernest Dudeney, has established a place for himself as a leading puzzlist. He is editor of the Mathematical Games Department of *Scientific American,* and his books on scientific subjects include *Mathematical Puzzles and Diversions* and *Fads and Fallacies.*